1971

8.40h EE

This book may be kept

FOURTEEN DAYS

A fine will be charged for each day the book is kept overtime.

GAYLORD 142			PRINTED IN U.S.A.

THE SUBCONSCIOUS IN GOGOL' AND DOSTOEVSKIJ, AND ITS ANTECEDENTS

SLAVISTIC PRINTINGS AND REPRINTINGS

edited by

C. H. VAN SCHOONEVELD

Indiana University

75

1969
MOUTON
THE HAGUE · PARIS

THE SUBCONSCIOUS IN GOGOL' AND DOSTOEVSKIJ, AND ITS ANTECEDENTS

by

LEONARD J. KENT

Quinnipiac College

1969

MOUTON

THE HAGUE · PARIS

LIBRARY OF CONGRESS CATALOG CARD NUMBER: 69-20327

Printed in The Netherlands by Mouton & Co., Printers, The Hague.

To Nils G. Sahlin

TABLE OF CONTENTS

PREFACE

I selected this topic primarily for two reasons: first, the need for a focused and sustained examination of the subject — related papers and books which contribute to the topic tend to touch it incidentally or too restrictively; second, my conviction that the sophisticated use of the subconscious by Gogol' and Dostoevskij is frequently undervalued by a considerable number of my contemporaries.

This book attempts to deal with some large questions: How important a role may earlier awareness and literary use of the subconscious — dreams, hallucinations, delirium, forgotten memories, premonitions, psychogenic illness, etc. — have played in the work of Gogol' and Dostoevskij? Granting that both authors make major contributions in this area, what are these contributions; how is their delineation and use of the subconscious different from that of earlier writers; and how, in this matter, do they differ from each other, if at all? If aspects of the subconscious may indeed be used as valid literary devices, are these devices effective, and if they are, of what does this effectiveness consist? Does the artistic depiction of subconscious forces serve to illuminate the author as well as his work? Is it perhaps possible that an examination of a writer's particular treatment of the subconscious in his fiction may supplement what we otherwise know of his view of life?

The artistic use of the subconscious was hardly original in nineteenth-century Russian literature; consequently, I felt it worthwhile to approach the longer parts of this work only after suggesting a literary and historical framework which might support my comments on the appearance and use of the subconscious.

The book is divided into five parts. In the Introduction I take a stand concerning the question of literary indebtedness, hoping to establish that Chapter I, which deals with possible antecedents, although more broad than deep, does not represent an oversimple view of the question, but is rather a reflection of my feeling that a broad perspective may there be usefully employed. Chapters II and III are more extensive than Chapter I because primarily they involve a reading of immediately relevant texts, and it is in the *fiction* of Gogol' and Dostoevskij that answers, if they are at all forthcoming, must be sought. Chapter IV presents my conclusions.

This book, in its first draft, was accepted as a doctoral dissertation by Yale University in 1965. It was written under the supervision of Professor René Wellek, for the Department of Comparative Literature. The debt of gratitude I owe to Professor Wellek cannot easily be expressed. Whatever may be of value in this book should reflect upon him. I also wish to thank Professors Lowry Nelson, Jr., Peter Demetz, R. W. B. Lewis, Cleanth Brooks, and Dean George Springer for being part of my happy experience at Yale.

Nils G. Sahlin, President of Quinnipiac College, is the gentleman most responsible for many of the good things that have happened to me these past six years. It is with enormous pleasure that I dedicate this book to him — with respect and great affection.

Quinnipiac College   *Leonard J. Kent*
Hamden, Connecticut
January, 1967

INTRODUCTION

The problem of literary indebtedness is complex, and its complexity should preclude stark conclusions. Extreme positions, even in rare cases of singular clarity, should be mitigated and reconciled to avoid debilitating what may otherwise be a meaningful contribution to scholarship. 'Source mongering' will not serve; neither will arguments for, nor implications of, total originality.[1] The problem of indebtedness never merely involves how

[1]   With apologies to Cleanth Brooks' "symbol mongering". Professor Charles Passage, for example, in a heavily documented discussion of more than seven pages dealing with Gogol''s *The Portrait* (*The Russian Hoffmannists*, The Hague, 1963, pp. 145-152), lists Tieck, Walpole, Hoffmann, Maturin, Odoevskij, Matthew Lewis, etc., as sources. I have made the statement that *The Portrait* "is a German romance which happens to be written in Russian and, in its final version, suggests that Gogol' is the author only because of the unmistakable didacticism infused in it" ("Introduction", *The Collected Tales and Plays of Nikolai Gogol*, New York, 1964, p. xxxi), but I go on to note that "in its final version (1842) its didacticism offers us insight into Gogol''s ever-increasing preoccupation with religion, morality, and the horrible wages of sin". Gogol', then, from my point of view, has left his signature behind, and it is *his* story. Even if Gogol' knew and used all of the texts cited by Passage — an almost inconceivable situation — his very selectivity tells us about his own creativity. Passage, an extreme example, can even comfortably go so far as to "define" the story: "Fundamentally, *The Portrait* may be defined as a reworking of the Franzesco-inset from *Die Elixiere des Teufels* with skillful overlay of additions from other works, most notably from *Melmoth the Wanderer*" (*op cit.*, p. 151). In an earlier volume, Passage, when discussing sources, employs a pseudo-scientific vocabulary, e.g., 'experimenting', 'combination', 'formula', 'transforming', 'alchemy', 'plus' — these are all taken from one paragraph (*Dostoevski the Adapter*, Chapel Hill, 1954, p. 3). At the other extreme stands Valer'yan Majkov, one of Dostoevskij's closest friends. He badly overstates a point of view, almost certainly reacting against the Dostoevskij-is-another-Gogol' sentiment propagated by Belinskij: "... the creative method ... [Dostoevskij's] is original in the highest degree, and he is the last one who may be called an imitator of Gogol'. If you were to apply this term to him you would be obliged to call Gogol' an imitator of Homer and Shakespeare ..." (quoted in Vladimir Seduro's *Dostoyevski in Russian Criticism*, New York, 1957, p. 11). Among many who are completely silent on the question of Dostoevskij's possible indebtedness to Gogol', or who handle it in a most perfunctory way, which implies that the question is trivial, are Charles Turner, *Studies in Russian Literature* (London, 1882); Maurice Baring, *Landmarks in Russian Literature* (London, 1910); Shakhnovski, *A Short History of Russian Literature* (London, 1921); Avrahm

much an author read or heard of other authors or of dominant thought, nor which volumes his library contained, nor the availability of texts in languages known to the author; nor does it ever merely involve being identified with a group or movement sharing a common heritage and direction; nor does literature merely reflect chronology, national identity and character, and that most elusive quality often described as the 'soul' of a people.[2] ABC relationships and conclusions are deleterious in that they subvert the very process they seek to exalt — creativity.[3]

It should be a commonplace that even the least sensitive and receptive are, in great measure, products of conditions and attitudes which are themselves born of a highly sophisticated process involving assimilation and filtration of the past and immediate.[4] Also, the creative man, surely no less than others, reflects in part what he has been taught and what he has learned he is expected to reflect. Fresh experience is always exposed to prior knowledge and present awareness. He reacts to his total heritage according to his unique make-up, more or less consciously, governed by exposure, capability, proclivity, and motivation. He functions within a frame of reference, and he cannot remove himself from the pressure of this reality. The creative process cannot remove him from himself. He must reflect; he is in everything he does.

'Indebtedness' is not synonymous with 'dependency', and irrefutable evidence of indebtedness must not imply a lack of original focus and contribution. Further, a multitude of fortuitous circumstances may have played their parts. What of intuition? Coincidence? Offered in another context, these words bespeak a point of view I accept:

... but I would be the first to admit that causal explanations and even historical antecedents do not accomplish much. We must leave something to chance, to

---

Yarmolinsky, who deals with the question in a few lines: "In dubbing Dostoevsky a second Gogol his contemporaries were referring to certain tricks of style ...." (*Dostoevsky*, New York, 1936, p. 100); Ivar Spector, *The Golden Age of Russian Literature* (Los Angeles, 1939); Richard Hare, *Russian Literature* (London, 1947). For comment on the question of Gogol's influence on Dostoevskij, see below, note 10.

[2]   Overemphasis here can result in very misleading conclusions, e.g., Gogol''s being discussed under "Cheerfulness of the Russian People" in Baring's book (*op. cit.*).

[3]   In a more general context, gross oversimplification approaches its zenith in a book such as Ivar Spector's (*op. cit.*). Spector offers us an all-explaining and all-inclusive diagram of "the development of a typical Russian novel ... for the benefit of the Western reader".

[4]   Which T. S. Eliot has argued, in his fine essay "Tradition and the Individual Talent", positively affects the writer; it accounts for the historical sense which "compels a man to write not merely with his own generation in his bones, but with a feeling that the whole of the literature of his own country has a simultaneous existence and composes a simultaneous order" (reprinted in *Literary Opinion in America*, ed. Morton Zabel, New York, 1951, p. 92).

genius, to a constellation of circumstances, possibly to that obscure force, national character.[5]

Availability of texts, dominant thought, common movements, national character, are valid areas for research. Chronology is, too, despite E. M. Forster's amusing attempt to exorcise the "demon".[6] Identifying labels are also useful, but only if we appreciate their limitations, consistently understand that, at best, they describe common tendencies and that they are not self-sufficient descriptive realities.[7]

In turning to examine the possible and probable sources of indebtedness, I am most especially interested in the influences relevant to the literary use of the subconscious in Gogol' and Dostoevskij. Perhaps Edward Carr supplies a general framework for departure by pointing out, in what D. S. Mirsky considers "an eminently sensible book",[8] that

... the principal influences, native and foreign, which were moulding Russian fiction when Dostoevsky began to write, were three in number — the sentimental novel (mainly French), the fantastic novel (mainly German and English), and ... the "naturalistic" novel created by Gogol.[9]

But he is too restrictive for our purpose. "When Dostoevskij began to write" his indebtedness to Gogol' was so great that I even consider them as sharing at that point a common heritage.[10] By amending

[5] René Wellek, "German and English Romanticism: A Confrontation", *Studies in Romanticism*, IV, 1 (1964), p. 56. See his review of Passage's *Dostoevski the Adapter* in *The Journal of English and German Philology*, LV, 1 (1956), pp. 173-177.

[6] In *Aspects of the Novel* (New York, 1954). Helen Muchnic's answer in *Introduction to Russian Literature* (New York, 1964, p. 12): "... there is no denying that an author's pitch is given by his generation no matter how familiarly the tone of his voice may sound in ages other than his own".

[7] I think it is valid and helpful, for example, to speak of 'Monk' Lewis and Hoffmann and Gogol' as 'romantics', Flaubert and Fontane and Tolstoj as 'realists', Zola and Hauptman and Dreiser as 'naturalists', even though we understand that uniqueness militates against restrictiveness. These labels are not, after all, really arbitrary, and they do suggest certain tendencies and common denominators. They cease being useful only when they lose a certain degree of flexibility.

[8] In an eminently sensible introduction to Carr's book. See below, n. 9.

[9] *Dostoevsky* (London, 1931), p. 39.

[10] The question of Dostoevskij's indebtedness to Gogol' receives some attention in de Vogue, *The Russian Novelists* (Boston, 1887), a very important book because it did so much to introduce Dostoevskij to the West; Mirsky, *A History of Russian Literature* (New York, 1926; Carr, *op. cit.*; Lavrin, *Dostoevsky* (New York, 1947); Simmons, *Dostoevsky: The Making of a Novelist* (New York, 1962); Muchnic, *op. cit.* There are much fuller discussions on the Gogol'-Dostoevskij relationship in Yu. Tynyanov, *Dostoevskij i Gogol'* (Moskow, 1921); and Dietrich Gerhardt, *Gogol und Dostoievskij in ihrem künstlerischen Verhältnis* (Leipzig, 1941). The Gogol' influence on the early Dostoevskij was very considerable. It is especially evident in style, choice of protagonists, and theme. There is mutual attention to *Kleinmalerei*, the intrusion of the

"mainly French" to "English and French", adding "eighteenth-century Mesmerism and its sources in folklore and literature and science", I arrive at a more comprehensive body of possible source material: the English and French sentimental novel, the German and English fantastic (Romantic, Gothic) novel, mesmerism and its sources. Each of these — and I restrict myself — very probably ultimately contributed something to the use and treatment of the subconscious as we find it in Gogol' and, especially, the early Dostoevskij. I reserve specific comment on other possible influences on the later Dostoevskij until the final pages of his chapter because chronology afforded him exposure to later works and traditions as well. Obviously, the 'topics', even if distinct, are hardly separable; overlapping and 'cross-fertilization' are taken for granted. It is not my purpose to squeeze and dismember possible source material until it yields 'unmistakable evidence' that it affected the authors I write about; rather, by dealing more or less historically with distinct entities, it is hoped that, cumulatively, the first chapter will present a meaningful whole suggesting something about the quality, scope, and richness of the broad background to which Gogol' and Dostoevskij were heirs.

---

tongue-in-cheek first-person author in third-person narratives. The similarities between Gogol''s Akakij Akakievič and Dostoevskij's Devuškin or Goljadkin, for example, are manifest. The use of the grotesque is frequently similar, and so on. Much of the early Dostoevskij reads like Gogol':

"I [Devuškin] offered him some tea. He refused from politeness, refused for a long time, but at last he took a glass. He would have drunk it without sugar, began apologizing again, when I tried to persuade him that he must have sugar; he argued for a long time, kept refusing, but at last put the very smallest lump of sugar in his glass, and began declaring that his tea was extremely sweet" (*Poor People*, C. Garnett, trans., *Three Short Novels by Dostoevsky*, New York, 1960, p. 247). And this: "... but don't ask about the backstairs: winding like a screw, damp, dirty, with steps broken and the walls so greasy that your hand sticks when you lean against them. On every landing there are boxes, broken chairs and cupboards, rags hung out, windows broken, tubs stand about full of all sorts of dirt and litter, eggshells and the refuse of fish; there is a horrid smell ... in fact it is not nice" (above, p. 152). Would Petrovič the tailor have been lost in such a setting? Gogol''s touch is everywhere: "He came to in the Nevsky Prospect, and then only by virtue of a head-on collision with someone that made him see stars." (*The Double*, George Bird, trans., Bloomington, 1958, p.143). Even Goljadkin's cry of "Drive on!", the use of the carriage to break a mood and remove our hero from a highly emotional situation, the symbolization of the speeding carriage as a vehicle of hope, freedom, seem very similar to the function of Čičikov's carriage in *Dead Souls*. But the differences, of course, are no less striking, even when dealing with the early Dostoevskij. I need here only mention that Dostoevskij provokes sympathy, Gogol', generally, sardonic chuckles; Dostoevskij's characters have depth, Gogol''s do not; the total Dostoevskij canvas, even in his first work, is somehow larger, less precise, murkier, less self-conscious, less highly polished, and, in a sense, less artificial.

I

TOWARDS THE LITERARY "DISCOVERY"
OF THE SUBCONSCIOUS

The acceptance of the mind as a psychobiological reality, of psychogenesis, of the role of the subconscious, and all that these imply, is relatively recent. But groping, somehow sensing that there is a 'soul' beneath the tissues, the very dim awareness that there are in humans forces potent albeit invisible is not;[1] nor is the basic insight which underlies what Jean Paul much later was to describe as the *Doppeltgänger* ("So heissen Leute, die sich selber sehen").[2]

Antiquity sensed what it could not know, and demons were exorcised by torturing the body.[3] The Greeks and Romans, eminently more sophisticated, groped too, searching out the 'soul' by reaching out to touch the afflicted who would not otherwise respond. Very early in history, the laying on of hands supplemented the giving of drugs. Significantly, Olympus-enshrined Heracles, the protector of health-giving springs, was also called *Dactylus*; and the Romans called the same cure-gifted finger *Medicus*.[4] This emphasis on curative touch, on the laying

---

[1] Folklore and mythology and studies of primitive societies supply very full evidence of this awareness. Among the more informative books of value in this area are *The World's Great Folk Tales*, ed. J. R. Foster (New York, 1953): "... dreams ... optical and auditory illusions and other psychological phenomena were very much a part of ancient life"; Frazer's prodigious study ,*The Golden Bough* (London, 1911), especially II, "Taboo and the Perils of the Soul"; his *Folk-lore in the Old Testament* (London, 1918); Lucien Lévy-Bruhl's The *"Soul" of the Primitive*, trans. L. A. Clare (London, 1928). See also E. L. Margetts, "Concept of the Unconscious in the History of Medical Psychology", *Psychiatric Quarterly*, 27 (1953), in which Margetts supports this premise: "Almost since the dawn of civilization man has had an inkling of understanding that mind activity outside of our waking consciousness does exist."

[2] And he apparently inverted the term which was to prove so useful to other German Romantics. It appears in *Siebenkäs* ("Da die Doppeltgänger vor eine Säule kamen ..."), *Werke*, II (München, 1959), p. 66. Hoffmann and others often used his spelling.

[3] It seems that much of the violence associated with primitivism stems from exorcism rites. According to Lévy-Bruhl (*op. cit.*), the wandering soul-double, which invades foreign bodies, could be put to rest only when its source, its original body, was discovered and destroyed. Corpses, therefore, were often mutilated in a ritualistic orgy.

[4] See H. J. Rose's *A Handbook of Mythology* (New York, 1959), pp. 167, 274.

on of hands, was Hebrew too: the most conspicuous anatomical part of the anthropomorphic Yahweh stalking through the Old Testament is his hands.[5] Christ, drawing perhaps from both Hebrews and Greeks, often reached beyond the body to treat the 'soul' which crippled it:

... In my name shall they cast out devils. ... and if they drink any deadly thing, it shall not hurt them; they shall lay hands on the sick, and they shall recover.
[So then after the Lord had spoken unto them, he was received up into heaven, and sat on the right hand of God.][6]

Perhaps Christ's 'devils' were pagandom's 'souls', Yahweh's 'evil spirits', 'lying spirits', and 'unclean spirits', and Greece's 'demons'. Faith, of course, healed because suggestion was therapeutically sound, because, by any name, 'soul' represented the various strata of subconsciousness. But the sainted or saintly had no monopoly on such cures — despite a very long list of such illustrious healers as St. Patrick, St. Bernard, St. Peter of Amiens, the Venerable Bede — and the wedding of church and state during the Middle Ages seemingly endowed temporal authorities with like powers: the 'regal touch' became merely another of the inherent gifts implicit in the divine right of kings.[7]

The Dark Ages, concerned primarily with supernaturalism, motivated by patriotic fervor, surely added no light to the Greco-Roman and Hebraic-Christian intuitive insight into 'soul'. As late as 1597 an English physician, representing the stage of contemporary enlightenment, wrote a book in which he conclusively proved that the regal touch was exclusively a Saxon endowment.[8] Not to be outdone, the Chancellor of

---

[5]   The number of references to hand in the Old Testament is considerable, partially because the ancient Hebrews used hands as symbolic indicators of psychical properties, i.e., positioning of hands revealed moods and desires, etc. But the hand (yadh ‏י ד‎) is usually so closely associated with power that it becomes almost a perfect synonym for it in certain passages. The laying on of hands symbolizes this power. "And Israel stretched out his right hand, and laid it upon Ephraim's head ... and his left hand upon Manasseh's head, guiding his hands wittingly; for Manasseh was the firstborn" (Genesis 48:14); and so closely does it represent God's power that it can be an exact equivalent for the personal pronoun: "I have made the earth, and created man upon it: I, even my hands, have stretched out the heavens ..." (Isaiah 45:12).

[6]   St. Mark 16:17-19.

[7]   And, as Boswell so dutifully and amusingly records in his Life of Johnson (London, 1960, p. 32), Johnson himself was 'touched' by Queen Anne, because of a "supposition that he was almost blind .... His mother, yielding to the superstitious notion, which, it is wonderful to think, prevailed so long in this country, as to the virtue of the regal touch; a notion which our kings encouraged .... This touch, however, was without any effect." See also extensive note in World's Great Folktales, op. cit., p. 330, n. 6.

[8]   Dr. William Tooker, Charisma, seu donum sanitas, sive explicatios quaestionis in dono sanandi strumas concesso regibus Angliae.

the University of Montpellier, no fool, wrote a heated denial, establishing that only French kings possessed such heaven-sent and purely-Gallican gifts. [9]

But there were men — occultists, to be sure — who as early as the sixteenth and seventeenth centuries probably could have understood something about Ivan Karamazov's headaches, men who took up the candle and began an accelerating march towards an awareness that forces other than those God-inspired and -directed played a role in man's well-being, that symptoms were not diseases but indications of disease, and that "The spirit is the master, the imagination the tool, and the body the plastic material"[10] — all things considered, a very anachronistic point of view.

Later in the seventeenth century, Deists such as John Toland (who had the ignominious distinction of having his *Christianity not Mysterious* burned by a hangman in Ireland) and Thomas Woolston (who was indicted for blasphemy and sent to die in prison for insisting that Bible miracles were merely allegorical) sought but never found rationalistic answers for apparently mystical phenomena.[11] Nicolas Malebranche, who combined psychological investigation and mystic idealism — "the vision of all things in God" — came closer than anyone before him to defining 'suggestion' and its powers in "La communication des imaginations fortes", a section of his *Recherche de la vérité*.[12]

Descartes, among others, by relentlessly emphasizing man as a thinking creature — even if one questions the validity of his basic proposition, *Cogito ergo sum* — and by insisting upon a dualism between mind and body (which Malebranche would later more exactly formulate), cast a shadow of suspicion on the prevalent vague notions of a controlling

---

[9] Andreas Laurent, *De mirabili strumas sanandi vi solis Galliae regibus concessa.*
[10] Attributed to Paracelus (Philippus Aureolus Theophrastus von Hohenheim), a fervent believer, but perhaps the first significantly to approach 'miracle cures' rationalistically. He and his followers (e.g., Johann Baptist von Helmont, a very early investigator of body fluids and chemistry) were important to Mesmer, hence, to nineteenth-century psychology. (Browning honored him with a long poem, "Paracelus": "What fairer seal / Shall I require to my authentic mission / Than this fierce energy? — this instinct striving / Because its nature is to strive?")
[11] Toland and Woolston, particularly undermined the cult of mysticism which precluded any enlightened discussion of the nature of 'miracles'. By threatening the rigid church-inspired and -enforced status quo, they widened a crack which had already appeared in the wall of silence used by the church to prevent 'blasphemous excursions into the marvelous', set an irreversible tone conducive to accelerating scientific inquiry.
[12] 6th ed., 1712. For Malebranche, a theology student until Descartes' ideas converted him to philosophical studies, the chasm which he felt separated the human soul from its body was so great that only God could bridge it.

soul.[13] Later, Locke, in his *Essay Concerning Human Understanding*, by assuming that man must be conscious of his thinking, postulated that if the soul could possibly operate independently while the host body was asleep and not conscious of the soul, the soul being distinct from its host. This being the case, the sleeping soul and the waking man would be different identities, and Socrates awake would be a different person from Socrates asleep.[14] Locke rejected his hypothesis, but the Mesmerists were later to accept it and extend it, agreeing that there is indeed a sleeping soul and that it thinks independently. Both states being on the level of consciousness, dualism of consciousness made dualism of identity possible within the personality of a single man.[15]

But the seventeenth and eighteenth centuries bowed low to the cult of the faith healers, the 'touchers': Valentine Greatrakes stroked his way to fame, and a hundred years later exorcists like Johann Gassner continued to work their tainted wonders.[16] Late in the eighteenth century, in 1778, Franz Anton Mesmer created a sensation in Paris, and Mesmerism was added to the science and vocabulary of all the West. From his obscure theories germinated much of the insight that ultimately led to the discovery of the subconscious mind so critical to psychological studies in general, and to the literature of the German Romantics and the nineteenth-century Russian authors in particular. But Mesmer and German psychopathological studies in Mesmerism need wait while I return to examine the origin, force, direction, and early literary development of that most sophisticated concept, the double, and of the dream, itself a manifestation of the subconscious.

[13]   For Descartes, the dualism between mind and body and their properties are mutually exclusive. Only the intervention of God can unite them. Malebranche later explained processes in the nerves and brain as merely the *occasion* of God's producing a corresponding mental result, *occasionalism*. Leibniz, working it out differently, postulated the 'pre-established harmony' between the mental and physical worlds, etc. See *Selected Writings of Descartes*, ed. N. Kemp Smith (New York, 1952), and an attack upon Cartesianism, G. Ryle's *The Concept of Mind* (New York, 1949), which also discusses Descartes' precursors and followers. But perhaps it was the 'tone' of his search that was most crucial: aiming for certainty, by insisting that everything must be submitted to reason, he threatened all things vague and ineffable, 'soul' among them.
[14]   (New York, 1959), Book II, Chapter 1.
[15]   See Ralph Tymms' *Doubles in Literary Psychology* (Oxford, 1949), p. 22. Tymms' first chapter, "The Origins and Development of the Double", is most informative.
[16]   Greatrakes (also Greatorex, 1629-83), specialized in king's evil, i.e., afflictions of the throat. His fame throughout Ireland was very great, even after he failed in an attempt to cure before the king. Gassner (1727-79), a German Catholic priest, provoked a bitter feud between believers and scoffers. His exorcism rites were complex and elaborate.

Ralph Tymm's valuable book[17] traces the genesis and development of the double. His comments, buttressed by the studies done by A. E. Crawley, Otto Rank, Lucien Lévy-Bruhl, and Sir J. G. Frazer, are as fascinating as they are revealing.

Crawley, dealing with the double as it appeared in primitive religious beliefs, notes a distinction between doubles duplication-born and doubles division-born, distinct but not separate psycho-approaches.[18] The division-born double, despite splitting off from a material host, may itself not be material and may be spiritual.[19] Otto Rank[20] supports the view that both duplication and division of personality stem from primitive man's sight (or imagined sight) of himself away from himself, i.e., shadows, reflections, dreams, and hallucinatory experiences in which a "self" existed away from self. The reaction of primitives to such a self-double must have been laden with anxiety, partly because taboos associated with such reflected selves were seemingly intrinsic in primordial cultures, being rooted in ideas that these spiritual doubles were parts of self, and that injury would be transferable.[21] The soul-double was peripatetic; it roamed independently of sleeping, sick, or dead bodies. It followed, then, that if a wandering soul haunted a body other than its source, it could be exorcised when its source was detected, attacked, and destroyed.[22]

Most important, the cult of the wandering soul-double served as root for a plethora of folktales, myths, superstitions, and stories which were very pervasive. Werewolves and vampires and *revenants*, for example, were offshoots, as, on the other hand, were guardian angels.[23] Folklorists have uncovered papyri dating from 1250 B.C. containing tales of wandering souls that must have been much older.[24] A huge body of

[17] *Op. cit.*, n. 15.

[18] See discussion in "Doubles", *Encyclopaedia of Religion and Ethics* (London, 1908).

[19] *Loc. cit.*

[20] *Der Doppelgänger* (Leipzig, 1925), pp. 68-94.

[21] I.e., a shadow was carefully guarded, lest an "injury" to it result in a corresponding injury to the body casting the shadow. It is interesting to observe how extremely long-lived most superstitions are. In much of the Western world, for example, many people persist in insisting that others avoid stepping on their shadows, desist in shattering their reflections in water. See "Taboo and the Perils of the Soul", in Sir J. G. Frazer's *The New Golden Bough*, ed. T. H. Gaster (New York, 1959), esp. pp. 148-160.

[22] See above, n. 16. Also Frazer, *op. cit.*, "The Riddance of Evil", pp. 432-470. Exorcism is fully detailed in both Old and New Testament too. See 1 Samuel 16:16; Acts 19:13; Matthew 12:27; Luke 11:19.

[23] The other side of the coin. Seemingly also a manifestation of what Crawley calls the 'separate soul' (*op. cit.*).

[24] E.g., "The Egyptian Brothers", which is "connected with the Osiris myth, which is

material dealing with such things as otherworld and transformed lovers, fairies and ogres, devils and ghosts and witches — all transfigurations or emanations of the soul-double — exists; and it is apparent that the cult of the errant soul, the "bi-present corpse", the double, found literary representation centuries before the Germans found it so fascinating and, by making it a literary device *par excellence*, made the subconscious itself the apotheosis of nineteenth-century literary sophistication.

In different forms, and serving diverse functions, doubles appear with some consistency from the dawn of writing. Influentially, the most important early appearance is in Plautus.[25] Most often the stress seems to have been on comic application, but, in singular fashion, yet another version of the double served in Gothic novels too, and in the book that must bear some responsibility for our contemporary mania for science fiction, *Frankenstein*, Mary Shelley's almost-mad scientist consciously creates a monsterself, complete with human appetites and sensitivity — an evil golem.[26]

Molière's use of the double as a thematic device in *Amphitryon* (itself influenced by Plautus) is very germane. It seems clearly to anticipate a vital part of Hoffmann's treatment of the *Doppelgänger*: Jupiter, even while impersonating the hero, tries to convince Alcmene that he is really two Amphitryons at once, one self a torpid husband, one a passionate lover, and that both selves are within him[27] — a graphic presentation of

---

related in turn to that of Attis, the Phrygian Adonis" ("Adventures of the Soul", *Great Folktales*, *op. cit.*, p. 318; see same source, pp. 44-50, for "The Egyptian Brothers").

[25] In *Menaechmi*, from which Shakespeare's *Comedy of Errors* was adapted. Enormously popular in its own day (about 220 B.C.), it was no less popular during the Renaissance. A comedy in which twins make alternate appearances, and, until the fact that there are indeed twins is explained to the other characters in the play, a 'double' functions. The twin theme is, of course, also exploited in *Twelfth Night*, but in more sophisticated fashion because, the twins being of different sex, disguise is also necessary.

[26] Since the appearance of *Frankenstein*, the monster has even been given the name of his creator, has appeared, as Frankenstein, in innumerable films and, having come full circle, now appears on television as a beneficent and misunderstood monstrosity in a comedy series, "The Munsters". The golem is apparently a Hebrew creation born of desperation. In the form of a man., created of clay, he is given life by prayer, bearing on his forehead the Hebrew word for truth, *aemet* (אמת). He can be destroyed only by erasing the first letter on his forehead, which shortens the word to *met* (מת), 'death'. There are numerous versions of the story. Professor Foster calls his "The Golem of Prague" (*Great Folktales*, *op. cit.*, pp. 267-275). The name survives in Yiddish and Hebrew. A dunce, in the vernacular, is a 'golem'.

[27]   Sosie: Je ne l'ai pas cru, moi, sans une peine extrême:
        Je me suis d'être deux senti l'esprit blessé,
        Et longtemps d'imposteur j'ai traité ce moi-même

internal duality, "linked up with the presence of two identical people: division and duplication are interacting forces in creating this conception."[28]

Mesmer's 'le magnetisme animal' and contemporary psychopathological studies drew heavily from occultist doctrines, formulated but never rationally understood, which, in turn, had fed on the mystique of the double in all its forms. The development of the double in German romantic literature seems to have stemmed in considerable measure from psychology, from Mesmer and his theory of the magnetic union of souls. Romantic to the core, *Phantasieromantiker* were eager to exploit imagination, and in Mesmerism and 'doubleness' they found material at once extravagant and — because it had attracted so much scientific comment — 'real'; that is, the very appeal of Mesmerism lay in part in its own duality: its darkness and light.

Mesmer himself came upon 'magnetism' slowly. Steeped in the work of the occultists, the thesis he did for his medical degree, *De Planetarum Influxu*, was based on ancient theories involving fluid-body relationships. His first significant step was his theory that the stars were not the sole influence on fluids (the *fluidum*). Intuitively — and intuition was almost always his best "scientific" weapon — he came to the conclusion that the body itself might harbor a magnetic, curative fluid. Contact between human bodies, then, might cause healing by forcing interaction of fluids. Later he concluded that the *fluidum* might, after all, be connected with electricity (magnets, which had been recommended by Paracelsus, were readily available in artificial form, and the science of electricity was accelerating). Magnets were soon supplemented by passes of the hand over the patient's body.[29] Evolutionally, he arrived at a *rapport* theory, i.e., a hundred years before Liébault and Bernheim were to inform the world finally about therapeutic suggestion, Mesmer took a

---

       Mais à me reconnaître enfin il m'a forcé:
       J'ai vu que c'était moi, sans aucun stratagème;
       Des pieds jusqu'à la tête, il est comme moi fait,
       Beau, l'air noble, bien pris, les manières charmantes;
          Enfin deux gouttes de lait
          Ne sont pas plus ressemblantes;
       Et n'était que ses mains sont un peu trop pesantes,
          J'en serais for satisfait. (II, 1)

[28] *Doubles in Literary Psychology*, p. 21.
[29] For detailed comment on Mesmer's evolution as a 'therapist' and his techniques, see Margaret Goldsmith's *Franz Anton Mesmer: A History of Mesmerism* (New York, 1934), esp. chapts. 5, 6. See also *Memoire de F. A. Mesmer*, trans. J. Eden (New York, 1957), and Toni Rothmund's *Mesmer, Genie oder Scharlatan* (Berlin, 1940).

long first step by theorizing that there was perhaps a correlation between the minds of patient and physician. His animal magnetism created a sensation in Paris in 1778, partly because it was "new", partly because it often achieved cures, partly because of the spectacular show it afforded, partly because quacks — and they were everywhere, for, as one of them commented, "Je ne fais rien, mais je guéris" — and the generally negative attitude of respectable scientists[30] had made it a topic of wink-encouraging conversation. Two births followed: hypnotism was born of 'magnetic seances', which, in turn, fathered the most indispensable observation of all: there were two 'bodies' in the body. While hypnotized, traits of character not before seen came to the surface. Perhaps it was merely a merging of souls between patient and doctor. But then how could one account for the patient's knowledge of things unknown to the doctor? And what of the patient's responding to influences beyond the hypnotist's? And what of the hypnotic state itself? Psychotherapy — treatment based upon treating overt and covert anxieties by not merely recognizing their presence but by discovering sources[31] — stems from Mesmer's unconscious uncovering of hidden personality and all its implications, e.g., the inner self might be wholly different from the impression created by the surface self (beneath rational consciousness there was a 'night side'). Mesmer, who stumbled all the way to freeing the subconscious (and he was concerned with cosmic mysteries, not the mind) added irrevocably to the frame of reference of literary consciousness.

The dream, too, has a most ancient history. It appears with consistency in all literatures.[32] A common experience uncontrollable by conscious will, inexplicable to reason, dreams were early regarded as objectively real experiences. Later, concomitant with an awareness of the 'unreality' of dream events — and we can trace 'dream' through the Anglo Saxon to *Traum*, itself related to the German verb *trügen* — the dream state was

---

[30] Despite the fact that such figures of the *Rationalisme* as Voltaire and Diderot were still alive when Mesmer reached Paris in 1778, scholars were particularly hostile to unorthodoxy in science. Heterodoxy was reserved for matters of religion. They were too rational to host the unproven. But not so with the masses. They could hardly wait to conjure up symptoms so that they could be treated.

[31] For a good discussion of psychotherapy and its meaning and techniques, see S. R. Slavson's "Dynamics of Psychotherapy", *Child Psychotherapy* (New York, 1952), pp. 160-195.

[32] See *Die Verwendung des Traummotivs in der englischen Dichtung bis auf Chaucer* by A. M. Baake (Halle, 1906); E. L. Ehlich's *Der Traum im Alten Testament* (Berlin, 1953); Jackson Lincoln's *The Dream in Primitive Cultures* (London, 1935); A. J. J. Ratcliff's *A History of Dreams* (Boston, 1923), especially "Dreams in Literature", pp. 193-240.

often desired, elaborately prepared for,[33] primarily because, representing the visit of a god or spirit, it made the dreamer a medium of divine energy. The dream could also be a bearer of evil omens. The search for their meaning was as incessant as it was intriguing, and professional dream interpreters and dream manuals — still available to those who have no use for Freud or Jung — antedate the Old Testament.[34]

In the Old Testament the attitude toward dreams is ambiguous — communication from God, a highly inferior means of revelation, and so on.[35] But dreams seem, generally, to have threatened the Hebrew hierarchy, perhaps because dreamers and God-inspired prophets of revelation seemed too much to merge, and the "dreamer of dreams" was often most harshly dealt with.[36] As a metaphor, 'dream' is consistently employed, often with stunning poetic effect: "And the multitude of all the nations that fight against Ariel ... shall be as a dream of a night vision."[37] No less effective is its use as a simile, often in immediately bordering verses, e.g.: "It shall even be as when an hungry man dreameth, and, behold, he eateth; but he awaketh, and his soul is empty."[38]

Most dreams, for both Hebrews and Greeks, were very highly symbolic.[39] So, too, the dream almost always involved intercourse with

---

[33]   Dream incubation is an ancient practice. The Egyptians had temples particularly suited for this purpose, and, after fasting and prayer, the suppliant probably waited for his god to answer him in his sleep. In Greece, too, incubation existed, was part of the religious code. Asklepios was a god especially helpful in providing therapeutic dreams. See *A Handbook of Greek Mythology, op. cit.*, pp. 139-141.

[34]   See "Dreams and Sleep", *Encyclopaedia of Religion and Ethnics, op. cit.* In Syria, Babylonia and Egypt, dream interpreters, 'Masters of the Secret Thing', were often court officers. They considered dreams to be real, not symbolic. Dream-interpreting books seem to have been especially popular in 19th century Russia. In America, *Napoleon's Book of Fate* and *Raphael's Dream Book* (and the mystical names are a promotional device) are still available.

[35]   As a communication from God, see Job 4:13. Numbers 12:6 treats dreams as inferior technique of revelation; in Jeremiah 23:25, 27:9, 29:8, we read that habitual dreaming is not a definite sign of divine inspiration; and in Genesis 40:8 and in Daniel 2:26ff. it is clear that the interpretation of dreams belongs only to God.

[36]   In Deuteronomy 13:1, for example, we read: "If there arise among you a prophet, or a dreamer of dreams, and giveth thee a sign of wonder ... saying, Let us go after other gods ... that prophet, or that dreamer of dreams, shall be put to death ...."

[37]   Isiah 29:7.

[38]   *Ibid.*, verse 8.

[39]   E.g., Prometheus' words:

Hearken the rest,
And marvel further, what more arts and means
I did invent — this, greatest: if a man
Fell sick, there was no cure, nor esculent

. . . .

supernatural powers. The appearance of dreams in Greek literature, however, seems much less didactically revelatory, and, of course, is often a very sophisticated literary device.[40] The Roman view of dreams, more tinged with skepticism perhaps,[41] seems to have been essentially Greek. The Middle Ages, infused with demons and demonolaters, which anticipate the Gothic novel, must have played shuddering host to the "night side of the mind", and nightmares were probably much the stuff of which dreams consisted.

I cannot here trace the enormous number of appearances dreams make in literature — and how few works are devoid of dreams! — but I note that before the German Romantics brilliantly exploited the substrata of consciousness (of which the dream is a striking manifestation) in their works, the dream, generally, served literature as an effective and highly stylized device of one of several kinds: an introductory, launching device;[42] an escape-from-reality technique (which, if we trust Chaucer's words in

---

    Men pined and wasted, till I showed them all
    . . . .
    I fixed the various rules of mantic art,
    Discerned the vision from the common dream,
    Instructed them in vocal auguries
    Hard to interpret ....
        (Aeschylus' *Prometheus Bound*, trans. Elizabeth B. Browning)
The Greeks made a distinction between whether a dream was seen or heard, i.e., whether it was 'vision' or 'oracle'. If the dream was highly symbolic (i.e., "shrouded in symbols") great oracles, like the oracle at Dodona, might be called in to interpret the symbols (See "Divination, Omens, Oracles" in G. L. Dickenson's *The Greek View of Life* (University of Michigan, 1960) for the lengths to which the Greeks were concerned with symbols, 'omens'). In the Old Testament, Joseph, of course, is the champion dream interpreter (Genesis 40); God-inspired, he has no difficulty with symbols in dreams. The story of Jacob's dream (Genesis 28), for example, is highly symbolic; the ladder, reaching up, obviously symbolizing preferment.

[40] E.g., Achilles' dream of Patroclus, after the funeral feast for his friend (*The Iliad*); and Jocasta's famous lines, so meaningful to Freud:
    Why should man fear since chance is all in all for
    him, and he can clearly foreknow nothing?
    . . . .
    As to your mother's marriage bed, — don't fear it.
    Before this, in dreams too, as well as oracles, many
    a man has lain with his own mother.
    (*Oedipus Rex*, trans. David Greene)
[41] Pliny, for example, attributed some dreams after heavy meals to normal activity; Cicero viewed all dreams as natural, nondivine.
[42] A technique which seems to have come into English by way of Macrobius, who commented on Cicero, and became perhaps the most popular technique employing dreams. See C. S. Lewis' *The Discarded Image* (Cambridge, 1964), pp. 63-67, for Macrobius' species of dreams.

House of Fame, was a delightful solution to enervating monotony);[43] one admirably suited for allegory;[44] love and dream visions;[45] prefiguring (suspense-creating) device.[46]

Perhaps Shakespeare and his contemporaries and near contemporaries were the first to utilize dreams as a psychologically organic part of their works. Revelatory, natural to all men, the dream in drama, it could be argued, supplemented the soliloquy as a device for exploring or throwing bare the inner man. Indeed, the dream serves Shakespeare in multiple ways, and the "strange dream! that gives a man leave to think", the "troublous dream", do, in fact, tell us not only of inexorable supernatural forces, but of obscure inner forces as well.[47]

[43] Early in the poem, we read:
> But why the cause is [of dreams], noght wot I.
> Wel worthe, of this thyng, grete clerkys.
> That trete of this and other werkes;
> For I of noon opinion
> Nyl as now make mensyon.
> But oonly that the holy roode
> Turne us every drem to goode!
> . . . .
> Ne no man elles be beforn,
> . . . .
> So wonderful a drem as I
> . . . .
> The which, as I kan now remembre,
> I wol yow tellen everydel.
> (lines 52-65)

The technique is beautifully employed in *Don Quixote*, Part II, Chapter XXIII, where the 'valiant knight', having fallen asleep, dreams "of the amazing things... in the Cave of Montesinos, an adventure the grandeur and impossible nature of which have caused it to be regarded as apocryphal" (trans. Samuel Putnam, New York, 1958, p. 656).

[44] In Chaucer, of course; and in *Piers Plowman*, Spenser's *Daphnaida*, Bunyan's *Pilgrim's Progress*, etc.

[45] E.g., the most successful and profound use of it, *The Divine Comedy*. *The Roman de la Rose* had turned the dream from religion to love; Chaucer was one of very many who frequently used it as a love vision.

[46] Surely a staple of the Gothic novel, the device is ancient, very widely used, appears in such disparate authors as Shakespeare, Richardson, and Poe. Plato, of course, "dreamed" his *Republic; The Fairy Queen* is a fragment of a series of dreams; the English Romantics are thrilled by the word (Shelley, for example uses it, as noun and verb, in all its grammatical forms, more than 200 times) and the act, De Quincey and Coleridge aiding incubation with drugs; Lamb was disturbed because of "the poverty of my dreams" compared to Coleridge's, etc. The longest dream in literature seems to be Joyce's *Finnegan's Wake*: from the first word to the last.

[47] E.g., Cleopatra's dream of Antony as "His legs bestrid the ocean" (*Antony and Cleopatra*); Romeo's "strange dream!" (*Romeo and Juliet*); Gloucester's "troublous dream" (*King Lear*); Calpurnia's dream (*Julius Ceasar*); Clarence's dream (*Richard III*), etc. In *Hamlet, King Lear*, and *Macbeth* — and it is perhaps significant that

But intuitive utilization leads often to only haphazard or superficial employment and effectivness, and I am not convinced that any author prior to the German Romantics understood or consistently and fully explored the dream device and its implications as an organic and inseparable part of a literary work; surely, no one exploited it with as much sophistication as the Germans — especially Hoffmann, in whom the symbolic dream seems to have reached its full-blown potential — Gogol', and, most of all, Dostoevskij.

they are late works — it could be argued that the subconscious plays a major role. But the problem is fraught with difficulties. Both Lear and Macbeth, for example, see hallucinations, but are these not the result of conscious guilt? Then, again, when Macbeth sees the ghost of Banquo he may be wholly aware of its meaning and it need not be considered a sub-surface projection, yet his conscious will cannot suppress it, despite the fact that his own reaction to the ghost very negatively affects his kingship because he is being watched by so many officers and members of the court. Does he perhaps want to punish himself? Is he helpless to control his situation? Lady Macbeth, at first, seemingly, too powerful to be guilt-ridden, the driving force behind the murder of Duncan, disappears from the play later to reappear sleepwalking. Surely the dagger and the spot that will not be erased must be considered manifestations of guilt, but are they unconscious manifestations? Is there not textual evidence that she was, despite her covert determination, aware of her baleful influence? "Naught's had, all's spent, / Where our desire is got without content. / "Tis safer to be that which we destroy / Than by destruction dwell in doubtful yoy" (III, ii, 4-7). In *Hamlet*, the ghost is seen by others, especially Horatio, and we cannot doubt its "existence" in its first appearance. What of its reappearance in Gertrude's bedroom, when Hamlet alone sees it? Is it his subconscious reminding him to cease his procrastination, to get on with the job of revenge, does it supplement his conscious knowledge of his guilt? Or, to further complicate matters, is the appearance of the ghost in the bedroom fully comprehensible if one holds that at least a large part of Hamlet's procrastination may be traced to his oedipal involvement, that such involvement would naturally be most pronounced in the bedroom — and how concerned Hamlet is with the "seamy sheets"? Brutus too sees a ghost, but has not he always been aware that he could never plan and participate in Caesar's murder without guilt? It is not clear how conscious Shakespeare himself was of the implication inherent in these dream and ghost scenes (and that the Elizabethans loved such scenes is here irrelevant). Surely they serve him well as a dramatist, serve to illuminate character or, at least, reinforce what we already know, but his works certainly reflect the acceleration towards the awareness of the subconscious. In *Macbeth* these lines draw attention to themselves. Macbeth:

Canst thou not minister to a mind diseas'd;
Pluck from the memory of a rooted sorrow;
Raze out the written troubles of the brain
And with some sweet oblivious antidote
Cleanse the stuff'd bosom of that perilous stuff
Which weighs upon the heart?

The doctor's answer:

Therein the patient
Must minister to himself.
                (V, iii, 40)

See also *A Midsummer Night's Dream*, IV, i, 221 and V, i, 2; *Troilus and Cressida*, III, iii, 311; *The Merchant of Venice*, I, i, 1, etc.

But there are other blocks building a path to the *Phantasieromantiker*, each indispensable: the sentimental novel and the earlier Gothic novel.

It would not be difficult to trace the sentimental novel back at least as far as the romance, the tale of courtly love, to the proliferous *Amadís de Gaula* and its multitude of literary children, but that would not serve.[48] We are interested in the *sentiment intérieur* which Rousseau and others held to be an irreproachable guide to behavior; for the sentimental novel itself, the non-German romantic novel, with a bow in the direction of the romances, was essentially, in philosophy, Rousseauistic.

Sensibility seems to have been in part a result of what Fairchild describes as "protestant decay",[49] i.e., seventeenth-century Protestanism was an enormous liberating force which unshackled, encouraged (made fit subject for literary respectability) those parts of the "inner man" which were to lead to sensibility and all its implications. Although not exclusively an offshoot of Protestanism — Toland, for example, was an Irish Catholic, and even French Catholicism could not preclude the spread of deistic sentiment — Deism, that so nebulous and ineffable quality under which humanitarianism and liberalism and sensibility thrived, itself in part a result of the enervation of religious orthodoxy, became host to the nonconformist.[50]

In literature, sensibility, emotionalism, sentimentality, demanded that the focus shift from the concentration on nobility to that of the ordinary, the bourgeois — the unashamedly "real". Indeed, one of the great contributions of the sentimental novel is, I feel, its redefinition of the hero image. When social position and knowledgeability were no longer considered adequate or indispensable requisites, the pathetic, introspective, self-lacerating hero who is to so dominate the nineteenth-century novel was germinating; and because the pathetic hero and situation demanded a recognizable, bourgeois setting, the sentimental novel evicted the *Luftmensch*, and, without a tenant, there was no longer any reason for *Schlösser in die Luft zu bauen*.

The sentimental approach, basically new, opened fresh vistas: by extending the realm of the novelist's perspective and by exploiting his sympathetic imagination, characterization, sophisticated psychological delineation, became first a possibility and then a reality. When the heart

---

[48] *Don Quixote*, of course, is its most illustrious 'child', and it is imbued with sentiment. Sentiment is apparently intrinsic within the courtly tradition.
[49] See his *Religious Trends in English Poetry* (New York, 1939); Fairchild holds that the core of sentimentalism rests in the concept that feeling must be good because man is.
[50] See James R. Foster's chapter "Sensibility and Deism" in his *History of the Pre-Romantic Novel in England* (New York, 1949).

became the *position centrale*, pleasure and pain, languor and delicious agony, what Yorick, in *Sentimental Journey*, calls "the soul within", were emancipated. It was no longer enough to know "what?"; now there was a "why?" too, and the psychological novel may have drawn its first breath.

As early as the last decades of the seventeenth century (influenced by *Princesse de Clèves*), a group of French women apotheosized the heart and paid copious attention to the emotions of their forever-fainting heroines.[51] And in England the genre flourished early too.[52] In fact, the production of sentimental novels was enormous on both sides of the Channel, not only because the lachrymose was in vogue, but, too, because writers like Prévost had elements of the fantastic and supernatural infused in their works[53] — the Gothic novelists could not but be affected by these — and these titillated and 'thrilled' many areas of response.

But no author approached the influence of Samuel Richardson, whose works were so badly (but delightfully) underestimated by Dr. Johnson: "Why, sir, if you were to read Richardson for the story, your patience would be so much fretted that you would hang yourself. But you must read him for the sentiment."[54]

Richardson, unctuously smug, self-righteous, sweet-smelling, precious Samuel Richardson, the master of "the principle of protracted rape", a man who "hunted with the hounds and ran with the fox", was yet a master of creating what Hazlitt was to so aptly call "artificial reality", and was to push the possibilities of the novel of feeling further than it had ever been pushed before. Everyone who wrote after him knew his novels, not least of all the German Romantics and the Russians.[55]

In Richardson's novels, seemingly superfluous and repetitive comments by his characters are, carefully observed, differently enough expressed so that what becomes critical is not the specific object of the comment, but the comment itself. We are able to analyze characters precisely to that degree in which they express themselves differently from others. Delineations of intricacies of character are thus inherent in Richardson's technique.[56]

[51] *Ibid.*, pp. 19-44.
[52] *Loc. cit.*
[53] *Ibid.*, p. 56.
[54] In Boswell's *Life of Johnson*, ed. G. B. Hill (London, 1887) II, p. 175.
[55] And often characters in their fiction enjoy reading him, e.g., Puškin's Tatjana, Dostoevskij's Devuškin.
[56] Leslie Stephen, echoing a considerable body of contemporary comment on Richardson, notes, in his introduction to *Pamela* (London, 1935, p. 35): "The virtuous characters give and receive an amount of eulogy enough to turn the strongest stomachs.

He has also been taken to task by critics (sounding like Tolstoj describing Dostoevskij[57]) who fail to appreciate the functionality of his "carelessness" and "profusion",[58] i.e., critics who seem not to be aware that Richardson, by choice, is dealing with the most human qualities of humanity. Ambiguity, confusion, repetition, ambivalence, are inexorable parts of human beings, and, as such, serve Richardson's art better than could the "cool" and detached prose of a writer like Flaubert.[59]

As for Richardson's prolixity, his "superfluous detail", it serves him even as it is to serve Tolstoj. We are not here interested in how it functions to lend an aura of reality (though it does), but in how it works to illuminate psychologies.

The luxury of prolixity allows Richardson to focus on and pause at every movement, every expression, every extended silence, every reason for thought (motive), every thought, every reaction to thought, every afterthought, the seen and, more importantly, the felt — all useful to add psychological dimensions.

Richardson wrote the novel seeded but ungrown by his time. The sentimental epistolary novel, so admirably suited for self-examination and for external scrutinization, in Richardson's hands achieved a unique intimacy and intensity of character and situation.[60] What Wilbur Cross calls Richardson's "dramatic manner",[61] was highly conducive to psychological study; and what many consider the shoddy and cheaply-won suspense created by the 'will-she-or-won't-she-and-if-she-will-why-does-

---

How aimable is A.! says B.; how virtuous is C., and how marvelously witty is D.! And then A., C., and D. go through the same performance, adding a proper compliment to B. in place of the exclamation appropriate to themselves."

Among others who seem to underestimate Richardson's works: L. Cazamian, "Richardson", *The Cambridge History of English Literature*, X (London, 1952); Oliver Elton, "Pamela", *A Survey of English Literature: 1730-1780*, I (London, 1928); Martin Battestin, "Introduction", *Joseph Andrews and Shamela* (New York, 1961).

[57] Reported in Maksim Gorkij's *Literary Portraits* (Moscow, 1959), p. 77: "He [Dostoevskij] wrote abominably, he made his style ugly on purpose ...."

[58] See, for example, Edmund Gosse, "Richardson", *English Literature* (New York, 1935), III, p. 306.

[59] A degree of "carelessness" may even add a sense of massiveness, a sense of texture, body. Bigness itself tends to suggest that the stuff of life is contained within. It often tends to lessen the awareness of the artificiality inherent in all art. There is a very thin line between art and artifice. When, for example, Hemingway succeeds, the well wrought prose is unobtrusive, form and content merge; when he fails, the very measured quality of his lines seem a parody of themselves, and the reader may become uncomfortably conscious of Hemingway's self-consciousness.

[60] How many famous stories there are about the women who begged Richardson not to let Clarissa die! Rarely have so many confused art for life.

[61] *History of Henry Fielding*, II (New York, 1918), p. 158.

she?' plot must not obscure the fact that Richardson very probably was, in considerable measure, responsible for introducing into fiction the analysis of emotion and motive, what might be called, in its fullest sense, introspection.

It might be argued that there is no one in all of Gogol' or Dostoevskij who is very similar to anyone in the sentimental novel in any but a most superficial way, and I would agree; yet, I cannot see how the heroes and "anti-heroes" of the Russians could have been created without it. The broken and the humbled and his setting, the insulted and the injured, the self-lacerating misfit, the introspective pariah, the author's internalized perspective — all drew nourishment from Richardson, the most brilliant representative of sentimentality.

Richardson's age bespoke conditions and attitudes which made it possible for Akakij Akakievič to be important enough to be a hero, for Raskol'nikov's emotional and intellectual distress to be the focus of a large and great book, for Anna Karenina's suicide to be perfectly comprehensible if we but appreciate that, despite external evidence to the contrary, her sense of values is indistinguishable from bourgeois morality. The Gothic novel, the shivering child of the sighing father, served too.

The oppressive rationalism of the eighteenth century found more than a modicum of relief in the headlong pursuit of the irrational, the inexplicable, the shameless indulgence in sensations, in what Johnson called "the hunger of the imagination which preys incessantly on life",[62] just as it had been assuaged by the self-righteous attention to suffering, to moral dilemmas, to all the niceties intrinsic in sensibility as it found expression in the novel of sentiment.

The translations of the *Arabian Nights* very early in the century had a most diverse appeal and a most pervasive influence, from the "dejected reasonableness" of Johnson's *Rasselas* on one hand, to that symphony of sadism, Beckford's *Vathek: An Arabian Tale* on the other. Between these extremes there was a proliferation of Gothic expression — all more or less withered branches of a single tree — which might be represented by the almost ludicrous mumbo jumbo realism of Walpole, or by the more artistically successful *The Monk*, Lewis's lively and extravagant account of Ambrosio, a man of the cloth who has too much libido to be at peace beneath his cassock (and here can be seen an incipient effort at psychological characterization, as the monk stands between religion and passion, *zerrissen*[63]).

---

[62]   Quoted in Walter Allen's *The English Novel* (New York, 1954), p. 88.
[63]   Only twenty when he wrote it, part of the compelling quality of *The Monk*, its

The pursuit of the exotic and its literary expression uncovered a trembling new world, a multi-faceted world which I have elsewhere described as a world in which

The irrational ... that lurks behind visible activity was lighted up. The spiritual and mystical became prominent. The dark corner became more important than the sun-drenched field. The shadows grew more central than the subjects who cast them. This view of life, focusing on the small, cramped, closed, struggling section of humanity, discovered man inextricably bound in a tightly constructed and airless room. Melancholia bathed the setting and its people, a melancholia intimately interwoven with sentimentality, yet expressing the "brooding" rather than the "aching" heart.[64]

Of all the English Gothic novelists — and, viewed from a twentieth-century perspective their pervasiveness seems astounding, even if it is wholly comprehensible in chronological context — Ann Radcliffe seems the best; but even she ('the Shakespeare of Romance writers', according to a contemporary estimate) seems mediocre beside the great German efforts in the *Schauerroman*. An 'arch-Gothicizer', her works are of interest on many levels. Of especial interest are her attempts to explain rationally the supernatural occurrences in her novels, and its implications as to the frame of expectancy of her readers. But, for my ends, it is her presentation of the psychic and even morbid psychological states in man that singles her out.[65]

Very much a scenic writer, consciously dramatic — before her, Walpole's preface to the first edition of *The Castle of Otranto* contains the line "The rules of the drama are almost observed throughout this [his] piece" — she is a very conscious and effective creator and manipulator of suspense as an artistic device. Limited by her inability to create individualized characters, she yet contributed what one critic has aptly called "the spirit of curiosity and awe before the mystery of things".[66] But she contributed much more, and her contributions are vital because Gogol' and Dostoevskij, bespeaking the Russian attitude toward the

---

insight into motivation, almost certainly stems from the fact that, as a whole, the novel may be viewed as the concrete expression of erotic fantasies.

[64] "Introduction", *The Collected Tales and Plays of Nikolai Gogol*, p. xvii.
[65] See Alice M. Killen, *Le Roman Terrifiant ou Roman "Noir"* (Paris, 1920); Jacob Bräuchli, *Der Englische Schauerroman um* 1800 (Weida i. Thür, 1928); Montague Summers, *The Gothic Quest* (London, 1938); C. F. McIntyre, *Ann Radcliffe in Relation to Her Time* (New Haven, 1920).
    Schedoni, arch villain in *The Italian*, grotesquely evil, is probably the most "rounded" character in all of Radcliffe. Schedoni's paroxysms of passion serve to uncover what Hawthorne would have called his "secret heart".
[66] *Ann Radcliffe in Relation to Her Time*, p. 90.

Gothic, reveled in them, and we need only look at *A Terrible Vengeance* or *The Landlady* to realize how profound an effect she may have had on Gogol' and Dostoevskij. It is not just the melodramatic, the horrible, the fantastic. They could have read these in other examples of the Gothic novel. There was another dimension in *The Mysteries of Udolpho* and in *The Italian*, a dimension Gogol' and Dostoevskij (and Hoffmann before them) were aware of. Lionel Stevenson puts it well:

In departing from realism Mrs. Radcliffe stumbled upon the whole realm of the unconscious. The standard situations ... are those which recur in everyone's nightmares .... No matter how crudely Mrs. Radcliffe described these things, she had the knack of stimulating the reader's own dream-making function, which then took over and supplied the private horrors of each individual imagination. Probably, too, her central theme — a pure, pale maiden persecuted by a vicious but dominating sadist — became a powerful sex symbol .... Unuttered risks of incest sometimes hover around the heroine through the uncertainty of her parentage. Even the heroine's excessive refinement, preventing the slightest mention of crime or of any strong emotion, helps to strengthen the morbid suggestiveness.[67]

And "stumbled" seems to be an appropriate word; it describes a condition precluded by later, singularly conscious efforts in "the whole realm of the unconscious".

The nightmarish tone of the Gothic novel in general, its *Bangigkeit*, its oppressiveness, its luxuriating in hyperbolic emotions, its often prosaic characters shuddering before the unknown, were important. Under such conditions, man cannot just be, just act. He is, rather, forced to react, forced to be aware of his own reactions. The pressures of environment and of dissatisfied and threatened self militate for a search; and if the external world yields only disinterested silence, when there is no longer any place to look, any place to go, internalization becomes a necessity. But if some of the characters of Mrs. Radcliffe and 'Monk' Lewis were to some extent internally at war, or at least forced by heightened emotions and extravagant settings to project subconscious fears, they could not yet approach the atmosphere of total personal holocaust because there were still easy answers: the setting was patently fantastic and the fantastic has little relation to life. Nothing supernatural happened at all, imagination was indulging itself; the just, in any case, survived intact and were supposedly strengthened, even as those who were wicked at heart suffered and died. The non-German Gothic novel still owed heavy allegiance to sentimentality, and to its father, Rousseau. Regardless of the bleakness of the setting, rose-colored glasses were before the faces of those who wrote.

[67] *The English Novel: A Panorama* (New York, 1960), p. 131.

I think that two critical steps remained to be taken by literature before the subconscious could become a sophisticated and integral part of the novel: the setting was to become either grossly fantastic or, with castles turned to hovels, nonfantastic; and the rose-colored glasses were to be fitted with black lenses.

It was the Germans who tossed the coin of man's existence into the sultry air and, by looking at its nether side — indeed, by insisting that both sides were "nether sides" — rediscovered the other part of man, a part infinitely more comprehensive. Phantasmagoria would never be the same again. It was no longer to be only a struggle between a chaste girl and a sneering prince, between a libido that insists and a church that desists. Man had much more serious problems now. The stakes were very high indeed. He was to struggle for his identity, for the very meaning of existence itself. If he lost he might disappear; much worse, he might discover that he never existed at all.

It seems fair to suggest that, viewed from a broad perspective, the best things produced by German romanticism became a possibility only when orthodox religion became incapable of meeting what so often seems to be one of man's needs: belief in the existence and authority of an immaterial and intangible power. The *Aufklärung* eroded the foundations of orthodoxy, but it left thirsting souls, and these sought elsewhere for the supernatural. Swedenborg pointed the way. Convinced by dreams that he had found the key to unlock the secrets of the spiritual world, he added to and helped solidify the mysticism in the air. Somehow, occultism, mesmerism, psychic phenomena, and spiritualism blended — they were never really separate in the late eighteenth and early nineteenth-century context — and became indistinct but puissant elements which joined forces in the search for God. In Germany, the erosion of orthodoxy was irreversible. Restrictions in concerns social and political strangulated activity in these areas. It was rather to aesthetics and philosophy that men turned, for in these freedom could not be denied.[68] God and His promise to reward in afterlife those who realized that their years on earth were but a preparation for the paradise that awaited them could no longer arrest the minds of men no longer disposed in their restlessness to accept miracles and their rewards in an orthodox sense. A pessimism

[68] I, of course, oversimplify a very complex and intricate period. See Ralph Tymms, "The Social Background", *German Romantic Literature* (London, 1955), pp. 35-51; also A. J. P. Taylor, *The Course of German History* (London, 1946). For a concise discussion of the philosophic, religious, and political background of German Romanticism see Harvey W. Hewett-Thayer, *Hoffmann: Author of the Tales* (Princeton, 1948), pp. 114-139.

which was to find its most powerful voice in Schopenhauer — and who else would name his poodle *Atma*? — pervaded Germany. Life took on new meaning: no meaning. Reality itself, first questioned and then doubted, began to lose its defining edge and flowed effortlessly into and absorbed the diaphanous world of dreams, becoming itself absorbed. The world of cause and effect, so familiar and comforting and reassuring because it reduced complexity to comprehensible terms, began to dim. If evidence of the existence of powers beyond man were to be found at all (and it needed finding), it would be found in the far corners of the imagination and the imaginative. It would be found in myths, in fairy tales; it would be found in compulsive artists and lunatics and the unseen forces that drove them; it would be found in dreams, so unintelligible and cryptic; it would be found in manifestations of the subconscious, in the double, in the monster beneath the normal exterior, in the hypnotic trance (in which the subject himself, unable later to recall his own behavior, functioned as a grisly automaton even as he drew from invisible wells things long beyond conscious recall). In a sentence, evidence of the existence of powers beyond man would have to be found in the world beyond man and what he had understood to be the nature of reality. It would have to be found in the fantastic, the romantic, and Gothic.

But German literature of the period is different from the romantic works of England and France. Her best works stretched and reshaped the Gothic genre even as they worked within it. Castles and moats and twilight were incidental to the design and needs of the German authors. The hyperbolic tone and setting, so essential to other Gothicizers, would be relaxed, would gain in horror because the loudest shriek in a world of shrieks cannot match the numbing impression of a single scream shattering an everyday world. Italian villains and their pasteboard and frenetic literary existence would reappear again in America, especially in Hawthorne and Poe,[69] but the Germans found evil beneath the mask of normality. Their attitude, and the quality of their horror at the realization that 'the power of blackness' lurks and can be seen everywhere, is in their

---

[69]   See, for example, Hawthorne's *Rappaccini's Daughter*. Almost all of Poe's villains strike me as 'Italian'. Hawthorne knew Hoffmann well, and his obsession with the ancestral curse (pervasive in his works, but in its fullest form in *The House of the Seven Gables*) may stem, in part, from Hoffmann's *Das Majorat*. Americans knew something of Hoffmann at least as early as 1824, when copies of *Blackwood's*, in which he appeared in English, came to our shores by boat. Mesmerism was known too, and in a story by Poe called *Mesmeric Revelation*, we read of what Poe called "the *rationale* of mesmerism" (*The Collected Tales and Poems of E. A. Poe*, New York, 1938, p. 88). The story describes an experiment in which a patient, after a "few passes", is thrown into "the mesmeric sleep".

works. Unlike American Puritanism and the literature it inspired, the Germans could not merely withdraw from this blackness like Bartleby the scrivener by simply noting "I would prefer not [to become involved]". Understanding the irony of life, they could not join Hawthorne's minister in his self-imposed asceticism. The American romantics were believers. If they winced at this 'power of blackness', they yet accepted it as partial payment for their share of Original Sin. The Germans, of course, saw it before the Americans, but they had the advantage of detachment; besides, who owed anything to an impotent God? The world was, after all, an evil place not because God willed it to be, but simply because it was. There was no need to rationalize it. Evil was the most consistent reality of all. Perhaps Hawthorne's Goodman Brown saw it too, but then, 'sin' was the touchstone to understanding — sin and the inexorable commandments from heaven. One need only read the Germans to understand how different their fictional world is. Here is a deceptively calm section from Hoffmann's wonderful tale, *Das Fräulein von Scuderi*, and it is very much to the point that the reputation of the man being described is impeccable:

Réne Cardillac war damals der geschickteste Goldarbeiter in Paris, einer der kunstreichsten und zugleich sonderbarsten Menschen seiner Zeit. Eher klein als gross, aber breitschultrig und von starkem, muskulösem Körperbau, hatte Cardillac, hoch in die fünfziger Jahre vorgerückt, noch die Kraft, die Beweglichkeit des Jünglings. Von dieser Kraft, die ungewöhnlich zu nennen, zeugte auch das dicke, krause, rötliche Haupthaar und das gedrungene, gleissende Antlitz. Wäre Cardillac nicht in ganz Paris als der rechtlichste Ehrenmann, uneigennützig, offen, ohne Hinterhalt, stets zu helfen bereit, bekannt gewesen, sein ganz besonderer Blick aus kleinen, tiefliegenden, grün funkelnden Augen hätten ihn in den Verdacht heimlicher Tücke und Bosheit bringen können.[70]

And we discover, of course, that Cardillac carefully plans and commits multiple murder, each time plunging a dagger into the heart of a victim for whom he had made jewelry. Why need he commit such crimes? Because of the "angeborne Trieb, so lange niedergedrückt ...." The "inborn drive" may be repressed, but there is always the implication that it broods and waits for its chance to emerge. Evil itself is restricted and controlled from without. When Cardillac is finally undone it is only because he is a puppet and must always kill exactly the same way. He is a double, too, a sane gifted craftsman by day, a mad murderer by night.

And which child grows up not knowing of Mr. Sandman? We even sing songs to hurry him along. But it is not Hoffmann's *Sandmann*.

---

[70] *Poetische Werke*, IV (Berlin, 1958), p. 195.

Morbidity converts the common and the pleasurable to horror, even as a child asks an old woman (Every Oldwoman), who looks after his youngest sister, about the *Sandmann* and is told:

"Ei Thanelchen", erwiderte diese, "weisst du das noch nicht? Das ist ein böser Mann, der kommt zu den Kindern, wenn sie nicht zu Bett gehen wollen, und wirft ihnen Hände voll Sand in die Augen, dass sie blutig zum Kopf heraus-springen, die wirft er dann in den Sack und trägt sie in den Halbmond zur Ätzung für seine Kinderchen; die sitzen dort im Nest und haben krumme Schnäbel, wie die Eulen, damit picken sie der unartigen Menschenkindlein Augen auf."[71]

Horror in the normal. The Gothic more threatening because it lives in light. Perversion in the respectable. Tension in the commonplace. A promise of nightmares. Confused and frightened man in a world in which he functions like a puppet because he obeys impulses he cannot control and because there is no face behind the manipulator of strings forcing him to dance his macabre way through a meaningless life.[72] But this is hardly a foreign world. Gogol''s madman and Dostoevskij's underground man would recognize it. This is what they react against, in flight or vitriol. This is the world of man even estranged from himself, of doubles and double doubles; the world where the deepest recesses of man must be searched and exposed. External man is superficial, hence trivial. Within him, however, lay the whole murky subconscious, the "sidereal" self.

The subconscious, "freed" by Mesmer and his followers, accessible through dreams and hypnotic states, constantly projecting its needs and demands, defended and promulgated in such influential books as *Die Symbolik des Traumes*,[73] became, then, an inevitable part of the general

---

[71] *Der Sandmann, Werke*, II, p. 373.

[72] See René Wellek, "German and English Romanticism", *op. cit.*, p. 47, for additional comment. For a very good discussion of the grotesque and its implications see Wolfgang Kayser's *Das Groteske, seine Gestaltung in Malerei und Dichtung* (Olden-burg, 1957).

[73] G. H. Schubert (Leipzig, 1940). According to Tymms (*Doubles in Literary Psychology*, p. 42), Schubert was "one of Hoffmann's principal sources of psycho-logical information". Schubert defends Mesmer's theories in a most elaborate way, describing physiological rather than psychological reasons for the unconscious per-sonality. "Conscience" is here the voice telling us to think and do what is incom-patible with our nature. Schubert discusses what he calls *doppelte Persönlichkeit*, draws a distinction between these and "magnetized subjects". The former are totally divided personalities, cannot recall anything that happened during the emergence of the second self; the latter, recall the most obscure events when they are hypnotized. See also *Hoffmann: Author of the Tales*, esp. pp. 119, 120. For technical discussions of mesmerism and related fields, Hoffmann, according to Hewett-Thayer, used as sources Kluge's *Versuch einer Darstellung des animalischen Magnetismus als ,Teil-*

climate that was to become so influential in nineteenth-century Russia.

The literature concerning possible direct influences on Gogol' and Dostoevskij is extensive. The debate itself is sometimes exasperating, often enlightening. Perusal of the literature does, however, create a general impression of additional crosscurrents to which Gogol' and Dostoevskij may have been exposed. Surely there is no reason not to believe that they both knew a good deal of Western romantic literature, that they were as immersed in its traditional motifs and modes of expression as their contemporaries.

In an informative essay written early in his career, "Gogol' and English Literature", Professor Ernest Simmons minimizes the existence and role of all foreign influences on Gogol': "though writing at a time when Russian literature was still under the strong influence of Western European letters, Gogol ... was himself scarcely touched by this influence".[74] Simmons, however, does point out the probable influence of Tieck, and, in a footnote, writes that "several of the more eerie tales in *Dikan'ka* and in *Arabesques* smack of the fantasies of Hoffmann".[75] Simmons can find only one instance of a "direct influence of an English work on Gogol ...."[76] He argues that De Quincey's *Confessions*

---

mittel (Berlin, 1811); Reil's *Rhapsodien über die Anwendung der psychologischen Curmethode auf Geisteszerrüttungen* (Halle, 1803); Bartels' *Grundzüge einer Physiologie und Physic des animalischen Magnetismus* (Frankfurt am Main, 1813); and Hufeland's *Über Sympathie* (Weimar, 1811).

For a detailed study of the appearance of the unconscious in literature and its development in science, see L. L. Whyte's highly informative *The Unconscious before Freud* (New York, 1960); also Alexander Gode von Aesch, *Natural Science in German Romanticism* (Columbia, 1941), esp. "Science and Literature", pp. 14-31.

Dostoevskij seems to have relied rather heavily on Carl Gustav Carus' *Psyche, zur Entwicklungsgeschichte der Seele*. It is mentioned in the recollections of Baron Alexander Wrangel, in *Letters of Fyodor Dostoevsky*, trans. E. C. Mayne (New York, 1964), p. 298, as one of the books Dostoevskij was thinking of translating. Carus' book itself owes much to Schubert, to mesmerism. Carus claimed nothing less than to have uncovered the nature of the unconscious mind. The opening sentence of the volume bespeaks the author's point of view: "The key to the understanding of the character of the conscious life lies in the region of the unconscious". Carus concerns himself with the relationship between consciousness, unconsciousness, and with the stages within these extremes, with the emergence of the former from the latter. Tymms (*Doubles in Literary Psychology*, p. 98) writes: "It may well be supposed that this conclusion guided Dostoevsky towards the theme he so often represents: the emergence of half-formed emotional reactions into the conscious mind." Tymms draws from Smith and Isotoff, "The Abnormal from Within: Dostoevsky", *Psychological Review*, XXII, 4, pp. 61-72.

[74] *Modern Language Review*, XXII (1931), p. 445.

[75] *Loc. cit.*, n. 2.

[76] *Ibid.*, p. 446. Gogol' could only have known in it the French translation of Alfred de Musset, 1823, and Musset, Simmons writes, was in several instances "obliv-

of an English Opium-Eater was probably known to Gogol' and may have influenced *Nevskij Prospekt*,[77] but concludes that "it is not to be denied that all these analogies may be the result of pure literary coincidence ...."[78] In any event, Gogol', according to Simmons, seems not to be directly indebted to English sources in large measure.[79]

Gogol''s possible indebtedness to American authors has not, so far as I know, been treated in detail. Almost an exact contemporary of Poe, there is no convincing evidence that he knew his work.[80] Hawthorne's *Twice-Told Tales* did not appear in print until 1837, by which time all of Gogol''s major fiction, with the exception of *Dead Souls*, had been published. It has been suggested that a Russian translation of Washington Irving may have influenced Gogol''s *The Portrait*.[81] The argument for the German influence as the major influence is very much stronger than it is in Dostoevskij's case, and, from my bias, more significant.

The popularity and the breadth of the appeal of the German Romantic movement may be appreciated if we realize that Ludwig Tieck, for example, was sought out by such writers as H. C. Robinson, Coleridge, and Carlyle; Ticknor, Irving, and Cooper; Ampère, Marmier, and Montalembert. V. A. Žukovskij ("forerunner of Puškin ... profoundly interested in German literature") was apparently one of the earliest of the important

---

ious of how false he had been to the spirit of his English author". Simmons also mentions the possible influence of Scott on *Taras Bul'ba*, and is unconvincing when he writes that "only in the complete subordination of the love element ... does Gogol seem to have learned something directly from the great romancer". Gogol' hardly needed Scott to subordinate the love element.

[77] It appeared in Russian in 1834, only a year before *Nevskij Prospekt* was published, but there was an 1828 French version upon which the Russian translation was based.

[78] "Gogol and English Literature", *op. cit.*, p. 450.

[79] I think Professor Simmons underestimates the influence of the English Gothic novel. At the least, Gogol' was influenced by it through Hoffmann. Simmons probably underestimates the German influence as well.

[80] Gogol', much poorer at languages than Dostoevskij, seems to have known only Italian and French to any extent. Poe was not available in Russian translation much before the 60's, when Dostoevskij himself wrote an introduction for the second set of tales to be offered to the Russian public (see below, n. 101).

[81] In *The Russian Hoffmannists*, p. 147, Passage notes the comment by Čudakov that Irving's *The Adventure of the Mysterious Picture* (which had appeared in Russian translation in 1829) may have influenced Gogol''s work, adds, "at least it formed part of the literary atmosphere in which Gogol wrote". But there is also evidence that Irving may have been influenced by the Germans. See H. A. Pochmann, "Irving's German Tour and its Influence on his Tales", *PMLA*, XLV (1930), pp. 7150-7187; also his "Irving's German Sources in the Sketch Book", *Studies in Philology*, XXVII (1930), pp. 477-507. See also E. H. Zeydel, "Washington Irving and Ludwig Tieck", *PMLA*, XXVIII (1931), pp. 946, 947.

connecting links between Germany and Russia. Žukovskij called Tieck "the father of German romanticism in Russia, and the poetic uncle of the German and English devils and witches".[82]

Stender-Petersen, in "Gogol und die deutsche Romantik",[83] Matenko, in "Tieck's Russian Friends",[84] Gorlin, in *Gogol und E. Th. A. Hoffmann*,[85] Hewett-Thayer, in *Hoffmann: Author of the Tales*,[86] Tymms, in *Doubles in Literary Psychology*,[87] Passage, in *Dostoevski the Adapter* and *The Russian Hoffmannists*,[88] are among those who argue for the more or less pervasive influence of German romanticism in nineteenth-century Russia.

Stender-Petersen is convincing as he argues that Tieck's *Karl von Berneck* and *Pietro von Albano* probably supplied the plot of *A Terrible Vengeance*, that Hoffmann's *Aus dem Leben dreier Freunde* may have been the source of *The Portrait*, that Piskarev (in *Nevskij Prospekt*) is like Hoffmann's Anselmus in *Der goldene Topf* — and Gorlin supports this view. He convinces me that the influence of the Germans was all-pervasive. Matenko is no less convincing in describing the esteem in which Tieck was held, the international following he commanded. Gorlin maintains that Hoffmann's influence on Russian letters was greater than that of anyone else, and that by 1830 (a year before *Dikan'ka* was published) Hoffmann was nothing less than a cult. Hewett-Thayer supports Gorlin's position: "The emergence of Russia in the nineteenth century as the producer of a major literature counted Hoffmann among the directive forces".[89] Tymms makes very clear Dostoevskij's "predilection for Hoffmann's works".[90] Passage, though extreme and rigid, supplies information that supports, the view of those who argue for the German influence in Russia. There is adequate evidence that Gogol' and Dostoevskij were at least exposed to German romanticism. An elaborate list of "parallel" plots, themes, devices could be compiled, at considerable risk, and has been,[91] but I prefer to present the German influence in more general terms.

---

[82]   Percy Matenko, "Tieck's Russian Friends", *PMLA*, LV, 4 (1940), p. 1138. This essay supplied much of the information in this paragraph.
[83]   *Euphorion*, XXIV, 3 (1922), pp. 628-653.
[84]   *Op. cit.*
[85]   (Leipzig, 1935).
[86]   *Op. cit.*
[87]   *Op. cit.*
[88]   *Op. cit.*
[89]   *Op. cit.*, p. 388.
[90]   *Op. cit.*, p. 98.
[91]   See *Dostoevski the Adapter*, esp. pp. 201-203, and *The Russian Hoffmannists*, esp. pp. 253-261.

More outgoing and cosmopolitan than Gogol', heir, of course, to the same heritage as Gogol', Dostoevskij leaves no doubt as to whom he considered to be the most important foreign author he knew. No author is more strongly endorsed in his letters, and, with the exception of Puškin and Gogol', mentioned so often in his works as Hoffmann.

A letter dated 9 August 1838, contains this comment: "[I read] the whole of Hoffmann in Russian and German (that is, "Kater Murr", which hasn't yet been translated), and nearly all Balzac [Balzac is great!]."[92] On 1 January 1840, he wrote: "We [he and Šidlovskij, a friend]... talked much of Homer, Shakespeare, Schiller, and Hoffmann — particularly Hoffmann".[93] Among other places in Dostoevskij's works, Hoffmann is mentioned in *White Nights, The Insulted and the Injured,* and *The Possessed.*[94]

In *Time,* January of 1861, there appeared Dostoevskij's editor's foreword to a translation of three of Poe's short stories, *The Black Cat, The Tell-tale Heart,* and *The Devil in the Belfry.* Dostoevskij praised Poe highly, but felt him to be inferior to Hoffmann. He calls Poe "a particularly strange writer ... though with great talent". Goes on to write:

Edgar Poe may be called a writer who is more capricious than fantastic. Almost always, he takes the most singular actuality, puts his hero into the most exceptional external or psychological position, and with what power of perspicacity, with what striking verity does he tell the state of man's soul! Besides this ... [there] is the vigor of his imagination. ... the power of specific detail. ...[95]

But Dostoevskij has reservations:

Poe permits only of the external possibility of a non-natural event (giving proofs, moreover, for its possibility ... usually cleverly), and once having permitted of this, is in all other respects wholly true to actuality. Such is not the fantasy, for example, of Hoffmann. [He] personifies the forces of nature in forms: he introduces into his stories sorceresses, spirits, and sometimes even seeks his

---

[92]   *Letters of Fyodor Dostoevsky, op. cit.,* p. 4.
[93]   *Ibid.,* p. 11. On p. 262, same text, D. V. Grigorovič is quoted to the effect that the first Russian books he knew he got from Dostoevskij, *Kater Murr* and *The Confessions of an English Opium-Eater.* On p. 268, Grigorovič cites what Belinskij wrote in a letter: "[Dostoevskij's] 'Mistress of the Inn' [i.e., *The Landlady*] is terrible stuff! He has attempted a combination of Marlinsky and Hoffmann, with a dash of Gogol."
[94]   In *White Nights and Other Stories,* trans. C. Garnett (London, 1957), p. 20; *The Insulted and the Injured,* trans. C. Garnett (London, 1957), p. 3 ("The old man and the dog" [it occurred to the narrator, seemed as if they] had somehow stepped out of some page of Hoffmann ...."); *The Possessed,* trans. C. Garnett (London, 1957), p. 481, respectively.
[95]   *Dostoevski the Adapter,* p. 191. Passage reprints the full text, from which these quotations were taken.

ideal beyond the earth, in some extraordinary world, accepting this world as a higher thing, as if he himself believed in the actual existence of this secret, enchanted world.

People call him the equal of Hoffmann. ... this is not true. Moreover, Hoffmann is immeasurably greater ... as a poet. With Hoffmann there is an ideal, indeed, not always explicit, but in this ideal there is purity, there is real beauty, genuine, peculiar to man.

Dostoevskij also mentions three of Hoffmann's works: *Meister Martin* (in which there is "purity, real beauty"), *Signor Formica* ("that most graceful and most charming tale"), and, once again, *Kater Murr* ("his best production").

Dostoevskij's interest in Poe, his admiration — albeit qualified — for his works is hardly surprising, especially in view of the almost indubitable fact that Poe was, at least in some measure, influenced by Hoffmann too.[96] Besides, both Poe and Dostoevskij shared a strong proclivity for the Gothic, for the hyperbolic, for madmen, for the psychological. There is about many of the works of both a denseness, a heaviness, an aura of foreboding, an unavoidable suggestion of doom, of the utter hopelessness of survival on the level of reality. For Poe, much more romantic than mystic, the imagination, sensuous fantasies amidst the musty remains of decaying civilizations, make existence possible — barely possible. For him, like Gogol', the bottomless grave yawns black, awaits.[97] The agony of reality is no less acute in Dostoevskij, but there is an implicit optimism not found in Poe. Dostoevskij believed in the healing power of faith: mankind will somehow — it is never really explained — be regenerated, perhaps through a miracle. The members of the ant colony will cry out their individuality, crawl separately toward salvation, a crushing load on their backs. Besides, for Dostoevskij suffering is different from what it is in Poe. It has a special meaning, is

[96]   There is considerable literature on the subject. Palmer Cobb, in *The Influence of E. T. A. Hoffmann on the Tales of Edgar Allan Poe* (Chapel Hill, 1908, convinces himself and the reader of Poe's debt; see also Gustav Gruener, "Notes on the influence of E. T. A. Hoffmann upon Edgar Allan Poe", *PMLA*, XIX (1904), pp. 1-25.

[97]   The similarities between the works and life of each man is sometimes striking. For both, to use Edmund Wilson's appropriate title to a piece on Gogol', there was a "demon in the overgrown garden". Both were neurotic, used their literature to objectify neuroses, wrote hyperbolically, almost restricted themselves to short works, utilized the grotesque, were highly skilled craftsmen, etc. Poe sometimes approaches Gogol''s lyric beauty (as in *Ligeia*, which I consider good Poe); Gogol' sometimes seems like melodramatic Poe. Gogol', from my point of view, is superior, but the similarities between the two refute E. M. Forster's amusing attempt to minimize the role of chronology. Writing at exactly the same time, Gogol' and Poe reflect early nineteenth-century currents. For a detailed comparison of the two, see A. Kaun, "Poe and Gogol: A Comparison", *Slavonic Review*, XV (1937), pp. 389-399.

charged with its own positivism because it bespeaks freedom; and freedom, hard-bought through suffering, is man's highest attainment.[98]

There is nothing in any of the three Poe stories Dostoevskij mentioned that seems to have been influential in any direct way. Poe, like Radcliffe before him, "gives only of the external possibility of a non-natural event". Even the supernatural is relegated to the demands of reality. Poe deals with psychological states, but, again, almost inevitably, in a conventional, romanticized way; he details what Lewis and Radcliffe only suggest. His rich imagination is yet restricted. It is more hyperbolic than it is deep. Poe's vision is so subjectively oriented that he rarely ventures to convert the personal into the universal, the immediate into a wide implication of the forces, seen and unseen, which control man, their victim. Intense, measured, lush, brooding, his prose serves its function well, but it may be too consistently morbid to achieve the horror which the cosmic and grotesque make so effective in the German Romantics, which understatement makes so effective in an author like Hawthorne.

Poe usually describes his personal nightmares and fantasies. His failure to express a meaningful, depersonalized, mature vision or point of view, may account, in part, for his limitation. Besides, there is little in Poe that Dostoevskij could not have found in more profound and 'poetic' form in the Germans, or in the English Gothic novel, or Le roman terrifiant, or, indeed, have arrived at himself. As early as 1846, with the appearance of The Double, Dostoevskij's sophisticated treatment of the subconscious and the pathological was well established — much to the consternation and disgust of Belinskij. William Wilson, very good Poe, and in many ways his most Dostoevskijan tale,[99] was written in 1839. Of course, Gogol' had already made use of doubles.

Everything points to German romanticism as being important to Gogol' and Dostoevskij, a point on which I cannot find a dissenting comment. I need describe what it was that so attracted nineteenth-century Russia in general, what there was in it that may have affected the treatment of the subconscious as it appears in Gogol' and Dostoevskij in particular.

[98]   Dostoevskij's consistent point of view, most clearly seen in "The Grand Inquisitor" section of The Brothers Karamazov.
[99]   It is one of the very few pieces by Poe to which Dostoevskij's stricture concerning Poe's concern for the "external possibility of a non-natural event" cannot be applied. Wilson's double is visible to others as well as to Wilson; Wilson kills himself by plunging his sword into his double, thereby murdering himself. Poe is content to leave the matter unexplained. It is clear that the Doppelgänger is Wilson's moral self, but its reality to the world at large is left unsolved, as it is in Hoffmann, Gogol', and Dostoevskij.

The river of the subconscious flowing toward Hoffmann was fed by many literary streams: Novalis, Brentano, Arnim, Kleist, Fouqué, Chamisso, Eichendorff, and Kerner, among others; and there were two major tributaries: Jean Paul and Tieck.

Jean Paul's forte is the fantastic and the grotesque, realism turned inside out — inverisimilitude.[100] His heroes seem to me to be epitomized representatives of romanticism: sensuous and sensitive, all-feeling, ceaselessly-dreaming, almost non-acting men. His are little heroes, and their problems are, viewed from without, little problems, but they turn to their incredibly rich imaginations to remove themselves to the lush world of fantasy. Even as they live in two worlds, Jean Paul is fascinated by the idea of doubles and duality, may have been most responsible for having made the theme of the *Doppelgänger* so popular in early nineteenth-century Germany. Béguin, the historian of dreams in German romanticism, writes:

Poursuivi par l'idée de 'double' et la hantise de son dualisme, Jean-Paul y échappe entièrement à l'instant du rêve, et ce dualisme meme n'est jamais chez luice qu'il sera chez tous ses successeurs: la perpétuelle coexistence d'un moi qui vit et rêve, et d'un autre moi, qui assiste en spectateur critique à la vie comme au rêve.[101]

There is an intrinsic duality in Jean Paul, an 'I' which participates in life, an 'I' which observes, both in a state of perpetual coexistence. The mythological characters which so enriched much of Goethe and Schiller are no more; instead there are almost-statureless figures[102]

---

[100]   But he stradles two centuries, belongs to the old one as well as the new. If Jean Paul's works are romantic, they are yet moralizing; if they are sentimental, they are yet ideal; if they are fantastic, they have about them a serenity, an idyllic charm. So very different from anything in Richardson, the common tie of sentimentality bound his romances to the very same audience that only a generation before was delighting in *Clarissa Harlowe*. And there is everywhere the sublime image, as in the nightmare opposing atheism, a "Blumenstück" in *Siebenkäs:* "Christus fuhr fort: 'Ich ging durch die Welten, ich stieg in die Sonnen und flog mit den Milchstrassen durch die Wüsten des Himmels; aber er ist kein Gott. Ich stieg herab, so weit das Sein seine Schatten wirft, und schauete in den Abgrund und rief: 'Vater, wo bist du?' aber ich höre nur den ewigen Sturm, den niemand regirt, und der schlummernde Regenbogen aus Western stand ohne eine Sonne, die ihn schuf, über dem Abgrunde und tropfte hinunter. Und als ich aufblickte zur unermesslichen Welt nach dem göttlichen Auge, starrte sie mich mit einer leeren, bodenlosen Augenhöhle an; und die Ewigkeit lag auf dem Chaos und zernagte es und widerkäuete sich — Schreiet fort, Misstöne, zerschreiet die Schatten; denn Er ist nicht!'"

[101]   A. Béguin, *L'âme romantique et le rêve* (Paris, 1946), p. 190.

[102]   E.g., Gottwalt Harnisch, in *Flegeljahre*, who is goodhearted, utterly retiring, and self-effacing (until forced to attempt to become a man of the world — an effort in which he is predestined to fail).

often meeting duplications of their own selves. Also, Jean Paul was "le premier, il a aperçu entre sa connaissance du rêve et son expérience esthétique des affinités profondes."[103]

His imaginative exuberance offended Schiller (perhaps 'frustrated' is a better word: "if [Jean Paul] had made as much good use of his riches as other men made of their poverty ..."), and Schiller's attitude is comprehensible in view of Jean Paul's capriciousness, "blurring", more than occasional incoherence, but it is a very limited point of view. Jean Paul is not truly concerned with reality; he is, rather, concerned with that which is behind and beyond reality, with the invisible abstractions which reality merely serves to symbolize. As such, his reality is only comprehensible in his terms, the disjointed, abruptly-shifting reality of the kind created by the romantic irony of someone like Laurence Sterne.[104]

His *Doppelgänger* are imbued with implications. Mostly, they consist of friends serving as ego and alter ego, but the complexity inherent in his doubles goes beyond a mere split of a single identity into two parts, a neat dichotomy. He wrote:

Einige Menschen werden verbunden geboren, ihr erstes Finden ist nur ein zweites, und sie bringen sich dann als zu lange getrennte nicht nur eine Zukunft zu, sondern auch eine Vergangenheit ....[105]

These are friends who have somehow been born together yet have existed separately, only to meet and supply not only a future but fill in a half-empty past, a past only half real because it was only half lived. Bound together by a single soul, two bodies function independently, yet both are mutually complementary. And in Jean Paul's world of doubles, there are other kinds: the actual doubles — sometimes as many as five pairs[106] — functioning within the covers of a single book, within the limitations of a single fictional world, or (in what Tymms calls "this delirium of doubleness"[107]) a *Doppelgänger* serving in one novel may step

---

[103]   *L'âme romantique et le rêve*, p. 190.
[104]   Whose *Tristram Shandy* was, apparently, no less popular in Germany than in Russia. Sterne's audacious manipulation of the separate parts composing the story (e.g., a marbled page), his determined (and, I think, sophisticated and effective) efforts to shatter the illusion of reality at almost any cost, found kindred souls among the romantics. Hoffmann, for example, most admired Sterne and Jean Paul.
[105]   *Titan, Werke*, II, p. 165.
[106]   In *Siebenkäs*, Leibgeber and his double stand before a mirror, and there are four doubles. Leibgeber then rubs his eye so that he will see double, and there are then five doubles.
[107]   *Doubles in Literary Psychology*, p. 32.

completely beyond his fictional boundary and end up in the pages of another.[108]

Jean Paul's penchant for *Nebeneinanderstellung*, his concentration on the problem of dual identity, double personality, internal duality, on a world which somehow hovers between appearance and reality, wakefulness and dream, the rational and the absurd, the disjointed and the whole, the lyric and the grotesque — all, if not necessarily original in him,[109] took shape in his works in so appealing and sublime a manner that the German romantics who followed capitalized on the implications latent in his works.

He exploited the potential of the dream, moved it beyond the traditional and made it a fully integrated part of his work, a major part of its total meaning. The dream — the hyperbolic fantasies of under-functioning characters — itself became an aesthetic experience, characterizing the idealist, setting him apart from his self-foil, the realist. He developed the concept of separate (sometimes contradictory, but nevertheless interdependent and inextricably enmeshed) parts of a single personality, described a personality which had somehow managed to shake itself free of its host body, confront it, threaten its own concept of self, its own comprehension of reality. And we note the implication that there is a part of man which is repressed, a part of personality that cannot forever be confined and stilled, one that is eruptive and capricious, the subconscious that threatens to convert reality to fantasy, fantasy to reality.

Jean Paul's world, whatever his intentions might have been, begins to make concrete man's loss of identity, his inability to live within the restrictions of reality. German philosophy and science had combined to create a doubt as to what man was, even whether he was. Reflecting and shaping that which was already in the air, Jean Paul further complicated the issue of man's existence, and in so he doing helped establish a genre and a tone which was to survive German romanticism, even as it was to help sustain it.

There seems to be no valid reason to contradict the assertion that "Jean Paul is the main German romantic novelist, the *magnus parens* of German fiction".[110] He may well also be the father, several times removed, of

---

[108] Schoppe, Albano's tutor in *Flegeljahre*, is unmasked as Leibgeber, the sardonic double in *Siebenkäs*.

[109] E.g., I have mentioned the ancient history of the double. In Germany it made one of its appearances in Goethe's *Wilhelm Meisters Lehrjahre*. Hewett-Thayer comments that many of Jean Paul's motifs "were to be found in the German novel before Jean Paul" (*op. cit.*, p. 142).

[110] "German and English Romanticism", p. 43.

much of the focus and the treatment and quality of the subconscious as we find it in Gogol' and Dostoevskij, and he even helps us appreciate the soil from which even a twentieth-century figure like Kafka must have drawn much of his literary nourishment.

I named Tieck as one of the major tributaries leading to Hoffmann. Béguin notes that he was "en précurseur de la psychanalyse, il écrit que 'la volupté est le grand secret de notre être, la sensualité, le rouage le plus important de la machine humaine'".[111] After all, Tieck had written that

Poesie, Kunst, und selbst die Andacht [ist] nur verkleidete, verhüllte Wollust ... Sinnlichkeit und Wollust sind der Geist der Musik, der Malerei und aller Künste ... Schönheitssinn und Kunstgefühl sind nur andere Dialekta und Aussprachen, sie bezeichnen nichts weiter, als den Trieb des Menschen zur Wollust.[112]

Béguin states the case for Tieck succintly and well:

Après lui, chez Arnim comme chez Hoffmann et chez Brentano, on retrouve des éléments tieckiens. Mais, s'il a mis à la mode, plus encore qui Novalis et Jean-Paul, la poésie du rêve, il lui manqué cet héroisme et ce désir viril du triomphe qui inspirèrent à chacun de ses cadets d'audacieuses confrontations avec le rêve.[113]

Tieck's world is often kaleidoscopic, bewildering, unfathomable; nevertheless, despite (or perhaps because of) his willful obscurity, the worlds of dream and reality intermingle, all but lose their separate identities. It is different from Jean Paul's; there is little compassion, little which can be characterized as gentle. It is a hyperbolic, terror-filled world of the bizarre situation in which peculiarities of personality become manifest simply because they are forced to react to the unintelligible forces which engulf them. The *Märchen* describe an escapist world, but only ironically, for it is a world of horror, of irrational foreboding, of the swift and merciless execution of the mandates of an inexorable fate. The horrible serves Tieck well, for he is concerned with its effect on personality, and he even supplies psychological motivation for the reactions and behavior of his characters.

Aware of mesmerism, Tieck seems to have scoffed at it,[114] but there is a

---

[111] *L'âme romantique et le rêve*, p. 225.

[112] *Schriften*, VI, p. 213.

[113] *L'âme romantique et le rêve*, p. 238.

[114] See Ralph Tymms, *German Romantic Literature* (London, 1955), esp. p. 72, where he quotes Tieck from *Zerbino*: "... man glaubt manchmal, man hat eine ganz simple Narrheit am Leibe, aber da gehört in unsern Zeiten mehr zu, da hängt alles so kunterbunt zusammen, das dient alles, eine Wissenschaft, die Psychologie (ich möchte fast den Hut abnehmen, wenn ich das Wort nur nenne) zu befördern ...."

passage in one of his works, *Genoveva*, where the implication of the subconscious part of man and its role are clearly suggested:

> Allein die Macht der Zauberei ist gross,
> Die hat sie in ein andres Weib verwandelt,
> Die innre Bosheit arg herausgekehrt,
> Wie man im Traume oft die eignen Wünsche
> Zum innigsten Entsetzen kennen lernt.[115]

But above all it is Tieck's presentation of dreams, his concept of their
significance, which most interest me. There are many dreams in his
works. On a simple level, they function traditionally, that is, as an escape
mechanism from oppressive reality; but they have a much more ominous
implication as well, for in Tieck there is firmly implanted the chilling idea
that life itself may be but a dream. In a letter, Tieck wrote

> Nun ist es freilich sonderbar, dass ich einige ängstigende Verluste gewohnt bin,
> alles wie einen Traum zu empfinden und nicht daran zu glauben, so dass mir
> seit langem schon das wirkliche Leben mit allen seinen Ereignissen nur ein
> Traum vorschwebt ....[116]

The line between what is and what is merely imagined to be is sometimes
totally erased as a self-analyzing manic-depressive character who knows
what little he knows of life only vicariously, from reading, finally pro-
claims "Die Wesen sind, weil wir sie dachten".[117] It is Fichtian: the
world had been created by us, it exists only in our vision of it. A branch
that man had clung to was cut through, dropped to the ground. There
was no longer a subjective world *and* an objective world; objectivity
ceased to exist as a separate entity, becoming nothing more than a subjective creation; and the world of reality, created from the inside out,
merely reflects the fantasies of its inhabitants. As such, its potential is
limitless, but its concreteness is doubtful. The dream state becomes itself
no less real than wakefulness and reality because it creates them both;
separate existences merge and totally coalesce. Life becomes absurd, a
stupendous and numbing joke: the self-created paradise in which man,
a puppet, finds comfort and security because he confuses it for reality,
brings about his doom precisely because he must continue in this world
which so well meets his psychological and physical needs. But it is a
world in which he really cannot continue to live because it is, after all,

---

[115]   Quoted in *Doubles in Literary Psychology*, p. 36.
[116]   To A. W. Schlegel, on the occasion of the death of Schlegel's stepdaughter in
1800.
[117]   *Schriften*, VI, p. 178.

despite its apparent reality, only a figment of his overwrought imagination.

Tymms is hostile towards Tieck for several reasons,[118] especially because he finds him too romantic:

his success with the *Märchen*-genre depends on the more or less successful translation of the dream into literary form, without any necessary reference to real life. And this cult of the dream justifies the wildest and craziest extravagances of caprice, for everything is possible in the dream .... This is the reverse conception to Hoffmann's, according to which the dream revealed a higher reality — reality as we know it, but projected in wondrous dimensions and colouring, so as to transcend present reality, but not to negate it.[119]

But he grudgingly admits that there are "isolated and (as it seems) almost absent-minded flashes of psychological intuition which may penetrate, though they do not light up, the darkest corners of the subconscious mind".[120]

Tymms, it seems to me, banks too heavily on "reality". Surely the tone in Tieck — the tension between the actual and the imagined, the press of unseen forces, man-puppet reacting to what 'he cannot understand — creates a reality of its own which is translatable into "reality as we know it", or at least into reality as we might dread it to be. Tieck's malicious playfulness, his "infernal tinkering", seem to me to serve his ends very well indeed: his is a mad world peopled by pathological puppets, and the excesses of his style further underline the absurdity and uncertainty of man's existence. Tieck's fantasies may be no less fathomable than much of life itself.

Hoffmann seems to owe to Tieck something of his fascination for the puppetman controlled by a capricious or spiteful fate. If Jean Paul straddled two centuries, Hoffmann too has a divided allegiance: on the one hand, a true romantic, he exults in the pursuit of the unknown, prefers the enigma to the solution, the unintelligible to the rational,[121]

---

[118] E.g., he quotes with relish Friedrich Schlegel's letter to August Wilhelm, in which the former wrote, in October of 1797: "Er [Tieck] ist jetzt recht oft bei mir und interessiert mich sehr, ungeachtet er immer aussieht, als ob er fröhe und an Geist und Leib gleich mager ist." (See *German Romantic Literature*, p. 56, n. 1.) Tymms vocabulary is disparaging: "creaking device" (p. 73), "products of uninhibited selfpity" (p. 57), etc.

[119] *German Romantic Literature*, p. 76.

[120] *Ibid.*, p. 120

[121] The romantics, of course, were antirationalistic. Science failed them because even the brilliantly intellectual was too restricted. They sought to convert the unknown and unseen into the most profound meaning, to extract from the most prosaic the most exotic. The potential of the mystical was limitless, and they would not be limited.

but, on the other, there is textual evidence that the *Aufklärung* had not left him unaffected, for the miraculous is sometimes explained — much to the chagrin of a character who, expressing Hoffmann's own proclivity, prefers to be left in the dark.[122] The occult attracted Hoffmann the romantic; it sated him emotionally. Pushing his imagination to extremes, the detestable world of philistines (and their attachment to the sane, safe, controlled, complacent) was exorcised. For Hoffmann, the occult meant nothing less than emancipation from mediocrity, from what he called "zu viel Wirklichkeit". There is reality in Hoffmann, but it is a reality born of the implications of nonreality, a reality of singular meaning because it transcends the prosaic existence which, in the context of the mundane, has no meaning at all.

Hoffmann's fictional world is also divided, sometimes maddeningly. As in Jean Paul, the prosaic and the fantastic coexist, but in Hoffmann the very closely detailed fantastic becomes more real than the real itself. So too is it with the extrinsic and intrinsic; they reach beyond their normal confines, flow, silently and unobserved, one into the other; hence, doubles become a normal symptom of abnormal conditions. In such stories as Hoffmann's chilling *Die Doppeltgänger* we see what the intimate coexistence of the disparate accomplishes — and we gain insight into the Hoffmann technique: layers of the unintelligible build into a nightmare; the setting, seemingly prosaic, is imbued with the fantastic; there is a heavy concentration on words which recur with great frequency in Hoffmann, words which create and complement his tone — "geheimnisvolle", "wunderbares [Ereignis]", "dunkle", "unheimliche [Macht]", "[nur wie ein] Traum", etc. And there is the ironic, the laugh at the expense of self ("Muss denn in unserm, dem Himmel sei Dank! — aufgeklärten Zeitalter solch ein verderblicher Aberglaube"), and the grotesque ("Während der goldene Bock, das silberne Lamm fest einklammernd und über dasselbe weggebeugt, häufige Schmerzestropfen ins Gras fallen liess, schluchzte dieses vor herber Wehmut leise an der Brust des versöhnten Gegners. Es was ein erhabener Moment!"[123]).

Even more to my point, a hero (or, more properly, half a hero) such as Deodatus, sent away under mysterious circumstances to somehow see a creature he had created in his dreams, no sooner walks into an inn than he is confused for someone else, and he "konnte sich eines innern

---

[122] In *Kater Murr*, for example, Abraham explains to the frightened Kreisler that the double he had seen was merely the reflection of a mirror. Kreisler, bespeaking Hoffmann's point of view, is less grateful than peeved at this explanation of what he had thought was supernatural.

[123] *Werke*, VI, p. 505.

Schauers nicht erwehren, indem es ihm plötzlich vorkam, als sei er mit seiner Gestalt und seinem Wesen der unheimliche Spuk jenes ihm unbekannten Haberlands".[124] "Blass und verstört", he defends his appearance: "... da ich soeben mit meinem Ich in einen andern Menschen gefahren ...."[125]

In Hoffmann we read of chronic illness, of letters not written by one, yet in his handwriting. Strangers suddenly appear; there are rustling sounds and incantations, croaking ravens — it is a world of madness which helps explain why the hero feels his sanity slip away. It is a terrifying solipsistic world created out of dreams. How is it possible, for example, for two men identical in appearance to be in love with the same girl, though one of them has never seen her? It is not; that is, it is not unless one accepts the occult or the psychological as explanations. Perhaps we are witnessing nothing less than the total disintegration of personality, schizophrenic multiplicity. The subversion of a single self, in turn, subverts the whole concept of reality.

Cardillac, we have seen, was schizophrenic. So too is the Danish Major in *Der Magnetiseur*, a torn demon of wildly alternating moods, withdrawn one moment, charming and gregarious the next.

Schizophrenia in Hoffmann may be attributed to the occult extrinsic forces, to the disparate elements of personality, to subconscious guilt, or to a traumatic experience. The erosion of sanity makes the projection of self on to another figure comprehensible.[126] Hoffmann's insight into the causes and manifestations of clinical madness are, even within the context of the frenetic scientific and pseudo-scientific activity of his age, remarkable.

The dream and the dream world are crucial features in Hoffmann. The reader is often invited to define the distinction between the world of dreams and that of reality.[127] In *Die Bergwerke zu Falun*, there is a strange anticipatory dream — and in Hoffmann even traditional devices become unique — which not only foreshadows but directs; that is,

---

[124] *Ibid.*, p. 493.
[125] *Loc. cit.*
[126] See, for example, the effect of the elixir on Medardus, in *Die Elixiere des Teufels*. The disintegration of his former piety effects an escape from seclusion to involvement, but the escape is merely ironic for he is trapped by occult forces, becomes uncertain whether he is Medardus or, indeed, Viktorin, whom he thinks he has killed ("Ich bin das, was ich scheine, und scheine das nicht, was ich bin ...."). Medardus, both saint and devil, projects internal disintegration into the extrinsic world. He is even punished for the crimes he has committed, as his double (his nether self), having confessed, goes to his execution.
[127] See *Hoffmann: Author of the Tales*, *op. cit.*, esp. pp. 180, 181.

extrinsically formed by some occult power, it appears to Elis Fröbom and dictates his actions which ultimately lead to his doom.[128] Another puppet, Fröbom is destroyed by fate in the surreptitious guise of a dream.

Dreams may be telepathic: in *Das Gelübde* the exact moment of death is described in a dream; in *Das Majorat*, the old justiciar dreams of the simultaneous experiences of his nephew. Medardus, in *Die Elixiere des Teufels*,[129] dreams psychologically comprehensible dreams, is haunted by his guilt, by a past inconsistent with his present psychological and moral condition.

In *Kater Murr*, Hoffmann's mad world reaches its brilliant peak in inventiveness, satire, romantic irony, the disintegration of reality, with an erudite cat devouring the contents of his master's library, learning to write — despite the restriction of paws — becoming an illustrious author of such classics as *Concerning Mousetraps and Their Influence on the Views and Energy of Cathood* (of course, a political work). The cat is a Don Juan of the feline world, and we read in wonder of his love adventures, follow his growth from kittenhood to cathood. It is so fantastic that it goes beyond anything in Jean Paul. Confusing even when relatively coherent, it juxtaposes sense and nonsense, for the pretentious cat has written his memoirs on the proofs of Kreisler's biography, and the sheets are bound together. Unfinished, there yet emerges from this novel a marvelous hero, *Kapellmeister* Kreisler, on whom Hoffmann lavishes his sympathy because he is Hoffmann.[130] If Kreisler is mad because he cannot come to terms with the philistine world, his madness is only ironic. His is the world of sanity, the exalted world of sensitivity and acute imagination. Hoffmann again has turned reality inside out, has forced the reader to reorient his concepts. It is typical that we do not even really know, for example, who Kreisler is, for his memories are often Hoffmann's, cannot be correlated to the text. The novel is "a mystery wrapped in an enigma", but there is about it the quiet panic of desperation, the aura of the absurdity of reality, the delineation of the

---

[128] Julia and Hedwiga, in *Kater Murr*, also dream anticipatory dreams which are comprehensible only if one accepts the fact that they originated in the occult, not the psychological.

[129] His resemblance to 'Monk' Lewis' mad monk has not gone unnoticed, and other parallels have been suggested. See, for example, H. Koziol, "E. T. A. Hoffmann's 'Elixiere des Teufels' und M. G. Lewis' 'The Monk'", *Germanisch-Romanische Monatsschrift*, XXVI (1938), pp. 167-170. The Lewis influence, however, seems perfunctory.

[130] The Kreisler-Hoffmann relationship is securely established; Hewett-Thayer (in *Hoffmann: Author of the Tales*) calls his chapter on *Kater Murr* "Kreisler-Hoffmann".

glory of madness. It is a world that never existed, and one whose exuberant glory casts a pallor over the one that does.

Hoffmann, fascinated by the abnormal and the occult, was possessed of a fecund imagination that made its recreation possible. He is not an early clinical psychologist; abnormality and the subconscious and supernatural appeal to him esthetically, not scientifically. The real world, too confining, is squeezed dry and, as pulp, left behind, but the fantasies are significant because their implications reflect on reality: there is an absurdity about realness, a complexity about the seemingly simple, a meaningfulness about the apparently trivial; above all, there is man, controlled like a robot from without, a many-layered creature from within.

Hoffmann's world is the world of hyperbole, a world where anything is possible, a world between dream and reality, where reality and the subconscious create the dream and the dream creates the reality of divided man. It is a world of engulfing and identity-destroying reality, the descent into the endless darkness of life and the flight from it. Most significant of all, man's identity, crushed in the relentless machine of conformity and reality, is threatened; he becomes less than one self even as he becomes more than one self. He cannot be merely a physically functioning animal, nor can he be merely rational. The occult functions from without and the irrational, "sidereal" self, from within.

German romanticism exploited the full potential of imagination. In so doing, it apotheosized the subconscious. It was not lost on the Russians.

II

NIKOLAJ VASIL'EVIČ GOGOL'

It was in Gogol', Puškin notwithstanding, that the subconscious first became a sophisticated literary device in Russian literature. Part of this can be explained by chronology, part of it by the nature of the writer and the bent of his insight and talent.

Gogol' is not a psychological writer in the sense that Dostoevskij and Henry James are.[1] We know but little about the past of his characters; they are almost always "born" full-sized adults.[2] They are externally created, what Mirsky calls "exteriorized and objectivated symbols of his experience."[3] We know little about them unless we interpret them within a symbolic frame of reference, that is, unless facets of the externalization are taken to symbolize internal conditions. His works, in this sense, are different from Dostoevskij's. In Dostoevskij we often know very little about a character's external self, but the most initmate and intricate convolutions of personality are exposed. In *Crime and Punishment*, for example, plot itself is subjugated to the rich flow of mental states. It is difficult, therefore, not to know something of the internal forces motivating Raskol'nikov, for they are on display. In Gogol', on the other hand, plots are almost always clear;[4] we often know how fat or old characters

---

[1] Dostoevskij, sensitive to the established criteria of realism, considered himself more realistic than the realists precisely because he worked in depth, and, as such, was presenting universally significant types. James, of course, wrote novels in which almost all of the action is on a psychological plane, and, in a work like *Washington Square*, even the plot is psychological. Like many other critics, James exaggerated the apparent carelessness of Dostoevskij's prose, was appalled by its sweep and peculiar density. But James did recognize Dostoevskij's "rank" genius. For a good standard view of the psychological novel, see Leon Edel, *The Modern Psychological Novel* (New York, 1964), esp. pp. 11-65. Jung has some interesting and highly debatable things to say about the psychological novel in his *Modern Man in Search of a Soul*, esp. his chapter "Psychology and Literature", reprinted in English in *Criticism*, ed. Schorer, Miles, McKenzie (New York, 1958), pp. 116-121.

[2] I cannot recall a single child functioning as an important character in Gogol'.

[3] *A History of Russian Literature*, p. 158.

[4] Despite the fact that the line separating reality from fantasy is sometimes almost effaced, the basic plot line survives intact, is progressively developed.

are, what their complexions are like, what they keep in their bureau drawers, how much money they have or lack, even, at least by implication, what they aspire or do not aspire to become. It is, however, difficult to comprehend their inner selves, their conflicts and longings and motivation, unless we recreate it by conscientiously examining such evidence of the inner man as can be drawn from his subconscious projections: dreams, doubles, fantasies, a predilection for the escape offered by sleep, and so on. To read Gogol' without being aware of the potential for interpretation beneath the often brilliantly executed exterior is to mitigate the complexity and meaningfulness of his art. If, for example, Ivan Špon'ka dreams of goose faces *only* because it is funny, he is merely a one-dimensional buffoon. If, however, his dream reflects his needs, it adds depth to him and dimension to the story in which he appears.

There is abundant evidence that Gogol', because of his marked neuroses, projected his own needs into his works more consistently and clearly than most other authors;[5] but what the works tell us about Gogol' is secondary. To push too hard to convert literature into a total projection of self must lead ultimately to the type of literary criticism which seeks to make Dostoevskij guilty of all the crimes he depicts in his works.[6]

In some measure, Gogol''s projection of self must have been unconscious. He was, thus, able to write most bitter and sincere attacks on the "incredible" contemporary interpretation of *The Inspector General*, insisting that the arrival of the real Inspector General symbolized the call to the Last Judgment and was not the final irony of an anti-bureaucratic comedy.[7] But, on the other hand, there is also textual evidence that Gogol' was, on occasion at least, aware of the personal psychological implications of some of his works. To illustrate, it has often been pointed out that in *Vij*, an early story which is bizarre and fantastic, Gogol''s fears are manifest,[8] and it seems probable that Gogol' may have been

[5] The evidence for this point of view is too well documented to need further "proof". The best psychological study of Gogol', Janko Lavrin's *Gogol* (New York, 1926), makes this clear.
[6] Thomas Mann, for example, describes Dostoevskij as half saint, half sinner, a position possible only because he confused art with biography ("Dostoevsky — in Moderation", *The Short Novels of Dostoevsky*, New York, 1945).
[7] It is further irony that the critical storm caused by the play served to strengthen Gogol''s already powerful conviction that he must participate in the spiritual regeneration of his countrymen; he became more convinced than ever of art's potential for inculcating "moral truths". The "misinterpretation" of the play, however, disappointed him most bitterly, and he fled to Germany, unable to stand "the detestable faces in Russia".
[8] Revealingly, Gogol''s early pieces were all written under pseudonyms. This may, of course, have been partly due to his lack of confidence (wholly justified in the case

conscious that the strongly Gothic nature of the tale might well reflect its author, for he goes to some pains to convince the reader of his objectivity, writing, in a footnote:

Vij is a colossal creation of the popular imagination. It is the name among the Little Russians for the chief of the gnomes, whose eyelids droop down to earth. The whole story is folklore. I am unwilling to change it, and I tell it almost in the simple words in which I heard it.[9]

But Gogol' is not telling the truth. No one has ever uncovered this story in folklore. Some insist that it never existed, others that Gogol' considerably changed a tale he heard.[10] In any event, he has subjectified his material. Even in his most derivative tales there is, of course, the shaping process, the focus, the emphases which make them uniquely his own, as do the internal selectivity and the choice of one source rather than another.

Those pieces which critics often label "naturalistic" or "realistic" bespeak the fact that Gogol' must have determined that his experiences would serve to help create art, for they are the most subjectively oriented of all. They are introspective. Paradoxically, the romantic tales, based in part on folklore material, inhibited Gogol''s freedom to some extent and are the most objective.

With the exception of *Ivan Fëdorovič Špon'ka and His Aunt*, the stories which appeared in the two volumes of *Evenings on a Farm near Dikan'ka* are primarily based on Ukrainian folk sources — and we know how eagerly he gathered material about the Ukraine, "to the last ribbon".[11] *Vij*, which appeared in *Mirgorod*, may, with the reservations noted above, be added to this list. Of all the other works, *Taras Bul'ba*, "essentially an imaginative recreation of the tone and quality of an historical tradition",

---

of *Hanz* [sic] *Küchelgarten*), or, in the case of *The Eve of St. John the Baptist* (1830), to its resemblance to Tieck's *Liebeszauber*, which had very recently appeared in Russian translation, or, in other cases, to the incomplete nature of the pieces, and so on. It was apparently not before 1835 that Gogol' officially signed his work. His pseudonyms included, chronologically, 'V. Alov', 'OOOO', 'G. Yanov', 'Rudy Panko, Beekeeper'. His desire for anonymity has psychological implications as well.

[9]   *The Collected Tales and Plays*, p. 338.

[10]   Certain parts of the story more or less resemble several fairytales, and the description of the seminary is not unlike that which appears in Vasily Narežnyj's *Divinity Student*, but, in the main, it is original, intimately related to Gogol''s neuroses.

[11]   His mother supplied him with a good deal of material. If we believe that he needed Puškin's anecdote before he could write *The Inspector General* — and Nabokov (*Gogol*, New York, 1944, pp. 39, 40) quite correctly points out that the theme of mistaken identity need hardly have come from anyone in particular — it seems possible, in light of what we know of Gogol', that he needed at least a suggestion of plot before he could begin his creations.

stands apart, because its romanticism and nationalistic motivation preclude its appreciation as essentially a depiction of experience-recreated life. There are, then, nine stories, three plays, and one novel that deal, more or less, with "contemporary social reality". The earlier tales also offer material of interest and deserve some comment.

The early Gogol' is lighthearted, romantic, and unsophisticated fun, but even in his first story, the gay and fanciful *The Fair at Soročinsy*, Gogol' is not very far removed from shadow and gloom. The bright and vibrant and irreverent world of the fair — a world in which there are "a drunken Jew kneeing a woman on the rump. ... women hucksters quarreling with abusive words and gestures of contempt ... a Great Russian with one hand stroking his goat's beard, with the other ..." — is changed at the conclusion, the final lines making all that preceded deeply ironic, a common technique in Gogol':

Is it not thus that joy, lovely and fleeting guest, flies from us? In vain the last solitary note tries to express gaiety. In its own echo it hears melancholy and emptiness and listens to it, bewildered. Is it not thus that those who have been playful friends in free and stormy youth, one by one stray, lost, about the world and leave their old comrade lonely and forlorn at last? Sad is the lot of one left behind! Heavy and sorrowful is his heart, and nothing can help him![12]

It could be argued that folklore itself often stands on the verge of melancholy, and that the tone of these lines is consistent within the context of folk legend, but the frequency of the depressing conclusion, even in the more realistic stories which are otherwise overtly humorous (e.g. *The Tale of How Ivan Ivanovič Quarreled with Ivan Nikiforovič*), suggests another source, Gogol'. It is he who is "bewildered", "lost", "left behind". There is almost always a shadow spread over the gaiety. In this first story there is a passage which mingles two worlds in a way reminiscent of the German Romantics. The imagery recalls Tieck or Hoffmann:

A strange feeling, hard to put into words, would have overcome anyone watching how the whole crowd was transformed into a scene of unity and harmony, at one stroke of the bow of the fiddler .... Men whose sullen faces seemed to have known no gleam of a smile for years were tapping with their feet. ... everything was heaving, everything was dancing. But an even stranger and more disturbing feeling would have been stirred in the heart at the sight of old women, whose ancient faces breathed the indifference of the tomb, shoving their way between the young, laughing, living human beings. Caring for nothing, indifferent, long removed from the joys of childhood, wanting only drink, it was as if a puppeteer were tugging the strings that held his wooden puppets [freely translated from "как механик своего без безжизненного автомата"] making them

[12] *The Collected Tales and Plays*, pp. 32, 33.

do things that seemed human; yet they slowly wagged their drunken heads, dancing after the rejoicing crowd, not casting one glance at the young couple.[13]

Here there are common Gogol'ian themes: the unintelligibility of the world; emphemeral and superficial beauty; movement devoid of meaning; the ravages of age and the breath of the beckoning but indifferent tomb. For Gogol', childhood was no less an exalted stage than it was for Wordsworth or Rimbaud, but not because "trailing clouds of glory do we come / From God who is our home", nor because of childhood's "visionary gleam". For Gogol', childhood is a period of divorcement from the everyday, an escape from reality because it is not involved with it. It is a world of warm mothers and tales of long ago, especially comforting specifically because they are apocryphal. Shelley's "thorns of life" are, for Gogol', concomitant with maturity. Automatons jerk to music, move their heavy feet even as they drink to forget what they are, where they are, where they are soon to go. Their vision cannot penetrate happiness because it cannot comprehend it. Escape becomes a basic need. Reality is mitigated by encompassing it in the aura of a dream; the worlds of reality and fantasy so intermingle in many of Gogol''s stories that one wonders sometimes whether something happened or was merely imagined. Sleep is often sought, often left only with great reluctance. When Gogol' is most eloquent it is tranquility he is eulogizing: "How luxuriously warm the hours when midday glitters in stillness and sultry heat and the blue fathomless ocean ... seems to be slumbering, bathed in languor ...." Metaphors such as "sleeping rivers" are recurrent.[14]

Reality, within the framework of the early stories, is romanticized, but the response to the threats of reality is rooted in the subconscious wish to escape. Tsibulja, in *The Fair*, seeking relief from "the frightening pig's snout ... rolling its eyes as though asking', "What are you doing here, folks?'" creeps "shuddering under his wife's skirts". His position is exceptional. Sleep, usually accompanied by dreams, is much more common: "The fair began to hum with life [but] stretching and yawning, Čerevik lay drowsily under his friend Tsibulja's thatched barn ... and apparently he had no desire to part with his dreams". One hardly blames him; reality awaits him: "'Get up, get up!' his tender wife squeaked in his ear, tugging at his arm with all her might."[15]

---

[13] *Ibid.*, p. 32.
[14] Gogol''s attitude toward sleep is consistent. In *Dead Souls*, the last paragraph in chapter 6, its function is directly stated: "He [Petruška] slept deeply, wonderfully as only the fortunate can sleep, who know nothing about hemorrhoids, lice, or over-developed mental faculties".
[15] *Ibid.*, p. 26.

In *St. John's Eve* there is again the Gogol'ian mingling. The warm thoughts, typically, are reserved for the long ago, when, as a child, "on a long winter evening when frost crackled outside and sealed up the narrow window of our hut", Foma Grigor'evič was aware of his mother's "rocking the cradle with her foot, and singing a story which I can hear now". Even the tellers of tales were different then: Foma wishes his grandfather to eat "rolls made of fine wheat and poppy cakes ... in the other world", but now there are only gabblers "who drive you to pick up your cap". Side by side with Crimeans and Poles and Tartars and Jews (lining their pockets with Orthodox gold), are devils and witches. The supernatural forces are defeated, then enlisted to thwart the outside world. It is shut off. The Jews have been thwarted, the devil sobs plaintively in his hole. In the village "you would think everything was quiet nowadays". The escape has been accomplished.

Beneath the humor — and wonderfully rich it is! — highlighted by incipient evidence of the grotesque which in later works becomes pronounced, there is again the shadow cast by life. Foma Grigor'evič cannot completely take us in because he sustains himself with the past. His vision, moved ahead to his time, takes on, by implication, some of the pallor of the grave. His characters dance the *gopak*, but I am not certain that it is not their disengagement in time that prevents it from being converted into a *danse macabre*.

In *A May Night, or the Drowned Maiden*, there is again a mingling of the real (which, on occasion, is not quite real—"brooding evening dreamily embraced the dark blue sky, making everything seem vague and distant") and the fantasic. There is a dream which is yet not a dream, the first of several ghoulish women in Gogol', and, related, the typical Gogol' heroine, fleshless, chiseled from alabaster or marble.[16]

With the exception of Katerina (*A Terrible Vengeance*), and possibly Oksana (*Christmas Eve*), Gogol''s females are always one of four types: the vulgar and gross who actively pursue or invite sex; the ghoulish; the long-suffering, faceless mother figure; and, most frequently, the pink-cheeked, black-browed, asexual "divinity".

---

[16] There seems to be a connection between Gogol''s inability to create young women of flesh — with the exception of Katerina, in *A Terrible Vengeance*, and possibly Oksana, in *Christmas Eve*—and his ghoulish women, and his depiction of corpses. Probably not overtly homosexual — though his autobiographical piece in diary form, *Nights in a Villa*, in which he described his relationship with Wielgorgski, a friend, in very physical terms, might suggest as much — there is no reason to doubt his homosexual fantasies. In an essay called *Woman*, Gogol''s inability to appreciate females as less than "the language of the gods" is clear. Also, Gogol' constantly seems to equate sex with death.

It is no more necessary to have experienced love in order to write about it than it is essential to have been to war or to have committed murder before these can be described. The creative process, fed by imagination, can compensate for inexperience; indeed, can often overcompensate.[17] The often striking sexual suggestiveness of the text indicates the degree and quality of Gogol''s subconscious involvement.

It has been argued that Gogol''s attitude is chivalric and reflects the medieval attitude of the Cossacks toward sex and their "homosexual inclinations".[18] But such an answer is unsatisfactory because it seems to confuse effect for cause. It is not very convincing chronologically either.

The courtly tradition had long been dead, even before the barber helped burn romances in *Don Quixote*. It is not that the romance lost its basic appeal, but that taste was more sophisticated. Gogol''s audience had a different frame of expectancy, partly because Gogol' himself had made the vulgar and coarse respectable.[19] Gogol''s females are often shallow and limited not because prudishness dictated restraint — restraint evident in no other area in Gogol' — not because he lacked the luxury of prolixity, but, rather, because Gogol' lacked the detachment and perspective of normality.

It is not necessary to know about Gogol''s life to appreciate the implications diffused through the text. Many later stories often reveal more sophisticated manifestations of the subconscious, manifestations primarily of literary rather than analytical value, and these are, of course, my major concern, but, with consistency, the works contain implications of disillusioned romanticism, reflect an author who never matured emotionally, one who would sit with the gods because of the corrupting effects of flesh on earth, because neither emotionally nor spiritually is satisfaction to be gained from reality.[20] Satisfaction is primarily possible only in the world of fantasy, the lyrical world of the selfless and fleshless. In *A May Night* we see this escapist proclivity clearly.

The only kiss between the sweethearts, Levko and Galja, described in clichés, is immediately interrupted by Galja's much less physical concern: "'Stop! Enough, Levko! Tell me first, have you told your father [that we

---

[17] E.g., Hemingway knew war, but his depictions of it, especially in *A Farewell to Arms*, seem to me highly romanticized, far less effective than Crane's depiction of it in *The Red Badge of Courage*, though Crane's personal experience of war was very limited,
[18] See Isaac Bashevis Singer's review of *The Collected Tales and Plays*, "Book Week". New York, *Herald Tribune*, Aug. 23, 1964, esp. p. 15.
[19] In part, this is precisely what made the earliest stories so very popular.
[20] Gogol''s religiousness, instilled very early by his mother, seems to have been traumatic. His letters are full of references to this early inculcation, to the fires blazing in hell, which his mother "described so strikingly, in such a horrifying way".

want to be married]?'" The kiss is never resumed, despite the promise explicit in "tell me first". "'Told him what?' he said, as though waking from sleep". In Gogol''s world passion is but a dream; it is secret, private, often eroticism in disguise:

"Galja! Galja, are you asleep, or don't you want to come out to me? You are afraid ... that someone will see us, or perhaps you don't want to put your fair little face out into the cold? Don't be afraid: there is no one about, and the evening is warm. And if anyone should appear, I will cover you with my jacket, or hide you in my arms — and no one will see us. And if there is a breath of cold, I'll press you warmer to my heart, I'll warm you with my kisses, I'll put my cap over your little white feet. My heart, my little fish, my necklace! Look out for a minute. At least put your little white hand out of the window ..."[21]

Perhaps this is merely romantic, but it contains more than a hint of a general truth consistent throughout Gogol': relationships, on the surface at least, are puerile, sterile, 'white' — idealized. But in context, there is a subsurface reality which is richer and more complex.

"White-footed", "white-handed" Galja is told a story (which she vaguely recalls "as if it were a dream") about "a fair maiden, white as snow, as white as your little face". The maiden's mother having died, the father brought home a new wife, one "all pink and white", and young. With the coming of night, the father and his young bride go to their bedroom; immediately "the fair maiden [the daughter] shuts herself up in her little room. She felt sad at heart and began to weep". Ostensibly this is comprehensible because the daughter may have suspected the new wife to be a witch, or, more simply, because she was all alone. But witches have a special significance in Gogol'. They are almost always symbols of carnality. The symbol is converted at once into a terrifying black cat which steals up on the maiden, "sparks in its fur". Seizing her father's sword, the maiden cuts off one of its claws and it disappears. On the third day, the young wife emerges from her room, her arm bandaged, and the maiden guessed that her stepmother was a witch. On the fifth day, the father ordered his daughter from the house. "Only then did the maiden begin sobbing, hiding her white face in her hands .... 'The witch has ruined your sinful soul!'" she said, threw herself into the water and was seen no more.

Sandwiched between more realistic sections, the story of the drowned maiden reflects on what preceded and affects what follows. Analyzed, it adds dimension to the "bodiless" characters involved in the text. The

[21] *Collected Tales and Plays*, p. 50.

father's soul is "sinful" because sex is. The maiden's suicide is little different from Piskarev's (in *Nevskij Prospekt*); they are destroyed by carnality in others, subconsciously within themselves. On one level, a witch loved by a father leads to estrangement and death. On another, more profound, a daughter suffers a not uncommon agony of being introduced to a physical aspect of a father not before consciously realized, an aspect previously reserved for the sanctity of fantasies. The daughter, even physically, is very much like the witch, pink and white and young. She would be in the bedroom. To see her father enter it with someone else is no less painful than Hamlet's distress in Gertrude's bedroom.

Levko meets the drowned maiden in a dream. His vision, reflecting his author's, is of a "silvery mist [that] had fallen over everything around him". First he sees a white elbow; then that "she was white all over, like a sheet"; then she asks him to look at her "white feet". Reacting as Amadís de Gaula might have, Levko says, "I am ready to do anything for you, my fair lady!" "I am oppressed", the maiden says, "I am stifled ... find me my stepmother [disguised among the other maidens]." Levko looks on the bank, through a "delicate silvery mist"; maidens are "flitting, light as shadows, in smocks white. ... they were pale." Levko uncovers the witch — she had grown suddenly translucent, "something black could be seen in the inside" — "How", she asks, "am I to reward you, youth?" Normal men mouth an unvoiced answer, but Levko accepts a note that will force Galja's father to permit the marriage. "Overwhelmed with excitement", he awakes.

Moonlight shines on Galja as she sleeps, "a soft glow on her cheeks", murmuring his name. Levko comes to her window, wishes her well, "making the sign of the cross over her as he closed the window and gently moved away". God, peace, "and in a few minutes all the village was asleep".

The mayor can go on boasting of his having guided the Czarina; the distiller can go on belching forth huge clouds of smoke from his remarkable pipe; Kalenik can stagger along "slumbering streets" forever. Gogol''s surface world rests safe from reality, nestling under God's wing, sheltered from all but subconscious sensuality by the sleep-inducing warmth of cozy huts and a world of long ago.

In *Christmas Eve* there are more witches, more white-faced maidens and their self-effacing suitors. There is also the strongest suggestion in Gogol' that sensuousness and respectability are not inevitably incompatible. Oksana is disturbed by passion more clearly, more ostensibly, than any other girl in Gogol'. Her distress is graphically, if tersely, presented:

All night long the beauty turned over ... and could not fall asleep. Naked, she tossed sensuously in the darkness of her room. She reviled herself almost aloud; grew peaceful; made up her mind to think of nothing — and kept thinking all the time. She was in an absolute fever, and by the morning head over ears in love with the blacksmith.[22]

And when her sweetheart, the blacksmith, returns to her with the slippers she earlier demanded as the price for her love, she is no longer concerned about anything but him:

"No, no! I don't want the slippers!" she said, waving her arms and keeping her eyes fixed upon him. "I am ready without slippers ...." She blushed and could say no more.[23]

The relationship between Oksana and Vakula is exceptional in Gogol', but the rest of the story is not. The moon dominates the opening pages, and its light is cast over all that follows. Stolen by the devil, so hot it scorches his fingers, its symbolic effect is not unlike that of the moon in *The Diary of a Madman*:

Meanwhile the devil stole up to the moon and stretched his hand out to seize it, but drew it back quickly as though he were scorched, sucked his fingers and danced about, then ran up from the other side and again skipped away and drew his hand. But in spite of all his failures the sly devil did not give up his tricks. Running up, he suddenly seized the moon with both hands; grimacing and blowing, he kept flinging it from one hand to the other. ... at last, he hurriedly put it into his pocket and ran on as though nothing had happened.[24]

Its comic implications are clear, and it is perfectly in tune with the tone of the story: "So there is no moon, friend?" "No!" "It's strange, really! Let me have a pinch of snuff!" But is it merely comic, merely "folklorish"? Its function seems more sophisticated. With it in his pocket, the devil "was making love in earnest at Soloxa's". Vakula, soon to have it and free it, returns to a girl eagerly awaiting him.

I am suggesting that the symbols add depth to the text, complement it, supplement it. The energy expended in the pursuit and capture of the moon finds its realization in the more realistic section of the story. Poetically, symbols serve to make Oksana's "perfect fever" graphic as well as comprehensible. Suggestively, they heighten the readers' sense of ex-

[22]   *Ibid.*, p. 131.
[23]   *Ibid.*, p. 134.
[24]   *Ibid.*, pp. 93-94.

pectancy, project into the future and make it difficult to imagine that the first moments spent together by Oksana and Vakula will involve nothing but chivalric exchanges of mutual admiration. The moon, for example, understood in context to represent more than an appendage of a romantic setting, precludes such naïveté. It serves a literary function.

It is unlikely that Gogol' was conscious of the extent of the effectiveness of many of his symbols, or, indeed, consciously aware of their sexual connotation. But this is not relevant. The subconscious helped project the symbols which the conscious imagination and the creative impulse shaped into literary form. I do not agree that artists are necessarily neurotics, nor that art serves as therapy,[25] but it seems unsophisticated to insist that creation is wholly a conscious business. Man's complexity precludes such a point of view, even as does art's. In Gogol', a highly skilled and deliberate artist, the subconscious yet serves in ways other than the deliberate and artificial creation of dreams and doubles. Its involvement is more comprehensive, and the text is enhanced and the potential for appreciation is enlarged because it is. It is not a question of being a Freudian or not. Failure to establish a one-to-one relationship between the symbol and the concrete it allegedly represents immediately complicates the reader's conception of text. Gogol''s works insist upon a deeper reading than the apparent triviality of much of the subject matter might lead one to expect. Even so frail (and delightful) a story as *Christmas Eve* gains dimension by the conscious pursuit of projected symbolic language and situation. We must not predetermine what the symbols will mean; but we must not be uncomfortable because, *in context*, they point in a direction we would prefer to avoid.

This said, I must pause to comment on *A Terrible Vengeance*, *Vij*, and *Taras Bul'ba*, the first because it helps illustrate how a careful reading can discover complexities somehow unnoticed before, the second because of a fiendish female almost incomprehensible within the structure of the story, the third because it supports my previous contentions about much of Gogol''s works.

These stories are singularly Gogol'ian; that is, to know Gogol' is to be aware that these stories could only be his, despite their alleged debt to folk legends or German sources. The symbols are no different, the vision

---

[25] A standard Freudian view justifiably discredited. For Freud, the neurosis (and art, an expression of it) serves as a substitute for more direct gratification. In his essay on Leonardo da Vinci, for example, Freud thought he could explain the work of art directly from the personal experiences of the author, but he failed. See also Freud's unconvincing attempt to "explain" Dostoevskij, "Dostoevsky and Parricide", *Dostoevsky*, ed. René Wellek (Englewood Cliffs, N. J., 1962), pp. 98-111.

is now through "fine gray dust" instead of "delicate silvery mist", rivers are still slumbering, sleep is still exalted. *A Terrible Vengeance*, however, probably owing much to Tieck, is the most sophisticated of this genre. It is replete with dreams, nightmares, and a central situation that can most easily be described if we call it Oedipal.

Katerina suggests the sensuality Oksana voices; she is the only other truly feminine female in Gogol'. Physically closer to biblical heroines like Esther than any of her fictional sisters, she has black hair to complement the whiteness of her skin. There are two men in her life, her husband and her father. Both are patently masculine and aggressive. They loathe each other because the husband is a defender of "the Orthodox faith and [his] fatherland", while the father is a heathen "worse than the Uniats". There is also a more primitive source of tension described within the text: the father has never relinquished his lust for his daughter, despite her marriage, despite the son she carries in her arms.

As she begins to embroider, her "father came in, angry and frowning, with an outlandish pipe in his teeth ... asking what was the reason she had come home so late the night before". Comprehensibly, the husband is incensed. They challenge each other, Katerina throws herself on the bed as the men hack away at each other. When swords break, a shot is fired. Danilo is wounded, dashes for his gun. At Katerina's intervention, the struggle ceases; there is a hard-won peace beneath which emotions still blaze. Her father kisses her "with a strange glitter in his eyes", and she "shuddered faintly". That very night Katerina dreams:

"My dear husband, my precious husband, I had a strange dream, and as vivid as though it were real, that my father was that very monster whom we saw at the Captain's wedding. But I beg you, do not put faith in the dream: one dreams all manner of foolishness. I dreamed that I was standing before him [her father], was trembling and frightened, my whole body wracked with pain at every word he said. If only you had heard what he said ... [Gogol'"s ellipsis]."
    "What did he say, my darling Katerina?"
    "He said: 'Look at me, Katerina, how handsome I am! People are wrong in saying that I am ugly. I should make you a fine husband. See what a look there is in my eyes!' Then he turned his fiery eyes upon me. I cried out and woke up ...." [26]

"Yes, dreams tell many a true thing", her husband comments cryptically, but he immediately shifts to "but do you know that all is not quiet beyond the mountain ?"

Soon the father's tracks are followed to his mysterious castle, complete

[26]   *Collected Tales and Plays*, pp. 144, 145.

with bats and "mysterious symbols" on the wall. The moon shining into a room, Danilo, gripping a branch, stares through a window at his father-in-law, while "fingering his moustaches to make sure he was not dreaming." The old man, dressed like a high priest of carnality, in scarlet, approaches a table bedecked with a white cloth, and "at once the room was filled with transparent blue light". Even as Danilo watches, the old man becomes a Turk. "Your dream was true, Katerina!" Danilo thought.

A rosy light shines more brilliantly and something white like a cloud hovered in the middle of the room; and it seemed to Danilo that the cloud was not a cloud, but that a woman was standing there; but what was she made of? Surely not of air. Why did she stand without touching the floor ... why did the rosy light and the magic symbols on the wall show through her? ... her hair curled and fell over her shoulders like a pale gray mist .... Ah, it was Katerina!
     The sorcerer stood without moving. "Where have you been?" he asked, and the figure standing before him trembled.
     "Oh, why did you call me up?" she moaned softly. "I was so happy. I was in a place where I was born and lived for fifteen years. Ah, how good it was there! ... Oh, how my dear mother embraced me! ..." [27]

Suddenly: "Father! Why did you murder my mother?" The sorcerer bids her to be still. This remarkable scene continues, the father-Turk-sorcerer trying to seduce the spirit-Katerina, his voice soft with emotion: "You remember all I said to you yesterday?" "I remember, I remember! But what would I not give to forget them". Danilo: "Poor Katerina, there is much that she doesn't know that her soul knows!" This monster is asked to repent, but he has other things in mind: "I will have my way. I will make you do as I will. Katerina shall love me ... [Gogol''s ellipsis]."
     Simultaneously, Katerina is dreaming "a terrible dream" never truly revealed. When Danilo later unfolds what he had seen, Katerina replies, "No, I did not dream that my father murdered my mother; I did not dream of the dead". Then, "No, Danilo, you have not told the dream right. Oh, what a terrible man my father is!" Her husband answers, "... it is no wonder that you have not dreamed of that. You do not know a tenth part of what your soul knows."
     Drawn irresistibly to her father, Katerina frees him from the cell into which he is thrown, one from which he cannot escape because it was built by a holy hermit. Cossacks fight Poles, even in this fantastic world. Soon Katerina "sees" her father again, as he still "persisted in his godless design". His face disappears. Captain Gorobets tries to comfort

[27]   *Ibid.*, pp. 149, 150.

her, noting that dreams rarely come true. His young daughter-in-law offers to get a "wise woman". His son will protect her with his sword. But Katerina stares "gloomily and with dull eyes ...." " 'I will kill your child, Katerina', he shouted, 'if you do not marry me ... [Gogol' 's ellipsis.]' " Danilo is killed by the father. Growing more deeply distressed, Katerina, "her black tresses [floating] loose about her white neck", becomes incoherent. The father reappears once more, disguised as a friend of Danilo's, and he relates how Danilo once told him that "when it is God's will that I am gone, you take Katerina, take her for your wife ... [Gogol' 's ellipsis]". Recognizing her father, she tries to stab him, is herself killed. "The desperate sorcerer fled to the holy places in Kiev", but his accursed soul is damned; he is destroyed, chewed by other corpses who "fastened their teeth in the dead man's flesh".

The dream is used here basically as an anticipatory device, and, as such, functions to project horror into the future, create sympathy for the doomed; but it is a strange dream, and its position in the story — it takes place after the battle between father and husband — suggests another significance. The dream and the battle shed light upon each other, become truly comprehensible primarily when viewed together. It seems possible to suggest that Katerina suffers the horror of subconscious guilt, that the dream is so acutely distressing because it describes a condition she desires. It is even difficult to determine exactly whose life she feared for during the battle, for she uses only mutually applicable pronouns ("*his* white body", "my dear *one*"). The introductory situation, in which father and husband, both desiring her, stand as direct competitors, almost forcing her to choose between them, becomes especially significant in light of the dream. Katerina, further, seems aware of the implications: "If only you had heard what he said ...." But the ellipsis precludes certainty. She could not, however, be unaware of the look in his eyes. It is unlikely that it is of hate. Within the context of the story, jealousy and passion better explain it.

I have been suggesting that the eroticism of the story is manifest. Gogol' 's frequent use of ellipses serves not as a traditional suspense-creating device, but stops the action at the very point of revelation and suspends the possibility of final conclusion.

Even without very close analysis of the possibilities latent in the story, it seems clear that sex and sexual guilt here supply at least some of the motivation; that religion (salvation, holy hermits, the Antichrist, etc.) is the façade. The potential for an interpretation other than one based on a religious allegory is inherent in the story and in its profusion of provocative symbols and symbolic situations — in its dreams, theme, plot, even in the stated characteristics of those who function within it. It is difficult to separate what Katerina dreams from what she feels or knows, or what Danilo sees from what he thinks he sees or fears to be true. The worlds of nightmare and eroticism and desire and guilt and fear and reality are so enmeshed that it is impossible to make easy distinctions between them. And we need not. Viewed in its full potential, it is much more than a simple religious allegory (which, I suspect, would have been Gogol''s interpretation). It is, rather, a dark and seething and marvelously rich fictional world, one which gains in literary merit even as it becomes more and more clear that it is not at all clear.

I have noted that this is an exceptional work by Gogol', and it might be asked how it was possible at all if the interpretation I advance has any merit. It is not necessary to go into the biography of Gogol' to find a reasonable answer. Read on a surface level, its didacticism is typical: the members of the love triangle lie moldering in their graves; Danilo, a Christian and a Cossack, more sinned against than sinning, dies a heroic death, the blood of heathens on his sword, riding hard to free the world of the wretched Antichrist; Katerina has suffered grievously, grows incoherent from the pressure of her involvement, is murdered at the moment of recognition; the father, the greatest sinner of all, receives poetic justice in full and heaping measure, Gogol' embellishing the lengthy description of his agony as corpses which are never still pluck and chew his flesh.

Despite the possible influence of Tieck's *Karl von Berneck* and *Pietro von Albano*, it is Gogol'ian. The symbolic density and hyperbolic tone are strongly focused, the lines between dream and reality almost effaced. The conclusion is consistent: sexuality-heathenism has led to absolute chaos and destruction. For Gogol' there is no heaven on earth. Earth, at its best, merely suspends and sustains us. The pure voice from above directs us to heaven; the erotic voice which is within Everyman must be exorcised precisely because it demands to be heard.

Perhaps the erotic is implicit in the Gothic. Ann Radcliffe may have "stumbled" upon it, 'Monk' Lewis may have lived it, but the first villain in pursuit of the first maiden through the dense and symbolic world of the Gothic setting probably appealed to readers to a degree not necessarily commensurate with the quality of the writing or the intrinsic merit of the story being told. The diffculty of concretely explaining our predilection for such stories (and I doubt that the genre has ever died) must be partly due to our inability to verbalize our subconscious involvement. Our subjectivity complicates all reading; a text richer than the author knows becomes richer still. Gogol''s work is singularly effective partly because even common literary devices which consciously describe sub-conscious processes appear in an uncommon light, having been filtered through a mind especially rich in the material of fantasy.

[I do not think I am suggesting opening the floodgates of Cleanth Brooks' "symbol mongering". Symbols and the symbolic situation become meaningful for me only when they meet four criteria: frequency of appearance, relative consistency, position (focus), and intensity (ideali-zation) — all interrelated and inseparable. Each work is independent, yet I cannot cut away my awareness of story B if I know stories A and C as well. I cannot even cut away what I know of an author's biography; nor do I need to if I realize that such information may be helpful, interest-ing, corroborating. It must not, however, provide the base from which to interpret.]

Vij, published in *Mirgorod*,[28] belongs to the earlier Gogol' tradition. I have called it "basically a horror story infused with humorous elements, the prosaic, the realistic". Those sections which are not Gothic are generally consistent with the earlier pieces. It is the fantastic sections which most interest me.

The story — rather, the plot — is simple. Xoma, 'the philosopher', is hired to sit and pray over the body of a beautiful woman who, on her death bed, requested that only he pray "three nights for her sinful soul". Fortified with vodka, because "the stories and strange tales he had heard helped to work upon his imagination", Xoma goes to the church, looks at the face of the "brilliant beauty" and can hardly force himself

---

[28] In "Gogol''s Retreat from Love: Toward an Interpretation of *Mirgorod*" (*American Contributions to the Fourth International Congress of Slavicists*, The Hague, 1958, pp. 224-243), Hugh McLean notes that "The ordinary earthly love of live men and women was for Gogol' one of the least inviting and least successful of literary themes. ... how-ever, the theme of human sexual love, along with other manifestations of positive lyric feeling, is actually quite prominent in Gogol''s early stories; they have simply been overshadowed by the 'unromantic' — and superior — products of his later years ....
It is in *Mirgorod* that the crucial transition takes place between the early Gogol' who loves, or rather tries, yearns to love, and the late, mature Gogol', for whom the world is an absurd and dreary place peopled by puppets manipulated by the devil." I hold no basic quarrel with this; however, I have argued that Gogol's exaltation of sleep, his delight in treating the coarse, the puppets who already function in the very first story, etc., suggest that his pessimism is consistent. McLean is correct in stating that in Gogol''s "other post-Mirgorod works the love theme receded into insignificance". His hypothesis that Gogol''s works "do constitute a retrospective reenactment of the pathological emotional development in [Gogol''s] early life ..." supports my point of view. For McLean, "the four stories in *Mirgorod* mark four basic stages in this regres-sive [psychological regression] psychological process, which is a movement from a more advanced to a more primitive choice of libidinal objects."

to look away. He begins to read the prayers. "Dead stillness", "candles", "coffin", "church". The corpse gets out of the coffin, walks about the church, "moving her arms back and forth as though trying to catch someone". In complete terror, Xoma draws a circle around himself, pronounces the exorcisms "taught him by a monk". Almost at the very edge of the circle, trembling with anger and frustration, the corpse cannot reach him. "At last she stood still, holding up a menacing finger, and lay down again in her coffin."

It is the same the next night, but she is more horrible ("pronouncing terrible words with her dead lips; they gurgled hoarsely like the bubbling of boiling pitch ..."). Again he survives. The third night, the corpse shouts for Vij. All covered with black earth he comes, and, with his monsters, pounces on Xoma — who could not restrain himself from looking at him — and Xoma "fell expiring to the ground, and his soul fled from his body in terror".

Helen Muchnic, a senstitive and perceptive reader, has epitomized her concept of the meaningfulness of Vij:

The voluptuous ... witch's gallop and the ... vigil over the corpse have an op-pressive meaning that is Gogol's own. He used it [the folktale] as a symbol for his experience of powerlessness and guilt and of his fear that in the struggle between the good and bad in him the bad would triumph. It is for this reason one of the world's deep, poetic tales ....[29]

Basically, I agree. The peculiar effectiveness of the story does in some measure depend upon the suggestiveness of the situation. Striking a receptive chord in our subconsious, the story can no longer be appreciated on a single level, the Gothic becomes secondary to the psychological implications. The meaning it may have had for Gogol' seems not obscure, even without the support of the other works: an ambivalent attitude towards sex, a fear of being emasculated, death as the ultimate price for indulgence — and even the power of the mighty Orthodox church is helpless before the rush of sexual passion.

The story has been enriched and complicated by Gogol''s unique projection of subconscious fantasies and fears. It is precisely that which we cannot exactly explain which enables the story to take that enormous step that separates the particular from the general, a superficial motif from a universal theme, the fantastic and "unreal" from the meaningful. What destroyed Xoma is a question with as many answers as the range of imagination can supply. The most obvious answer, a ghoul, will not do because we could not then explain the effectiveness of the story beyond

[29] *An Introduction to Russian Literature*, pp. 86, 87.

the traditional context of "horror stories". It has about it the mystery and haunting quality of Poe's *Ligeia*.[30] A neurotic personality has verbalized his dreams; latent in the story, they come to life when exposed to the subconscious of the reader.

From my bias, there is nothing unusual about *Taras Bul'ba*. The only overt manifestation of the subconscious involves a single dream, and it is traditionally romantic and without revelatory function or effect. Despite what some consider its Homeric qualities, it is highly romantic. Only the older Cossacks and the mother have an aura of life about them, and even they are treated hyperbolically, Bulba as the epitome of purposefulness, the mother as the tender (and faceless) woman *par excellence*.

Poles and Jews perform their puppet duties, disappear. Sleep is described at its most exalted. The love affair between Andrei and the Polish girl is as contrived and unconvincing as anything I have ever read. It is a perfect example of Gogol''s allegiance to a chivalric code he could not let die. Because he was more or less recreating an historical period, there is a firmness, a control, that seems to have precluded the kind of subjectifying evident in so many of the other works. Here is an ABC world of absolute comprehensibility. It is rousing nonsense which finds its charm in our longings to remove ourselves from a world grown monstrous and complex, but it is sterile because it functions on a single level.

Ivan Fëdorovič Špon'ka (his story appeared in the second volume of *Dikan'ka*) is the first of a considerable number of grotesque anti-heroes. Like all of Gogol''s leading figures, Ivan Fëdorovič is a bachelor (Taras Bul'ba is married, but surely not in our sense of the word, unless it be to the Dnepr Cossacks), the first of those selfsatisfied mediocrities who function and create a world in which *pošlost'* thrives, a "real" world which is not real because of the intensity of its reality. He is merely a colossus of mediocrity until Gogol' begins the intensification and minute observation, the piling up of details that reduce him to absurdity, change him to a breathing vegetable. Špon'ka offended Gogol' because he is without spiritual nourishment; and Gogol''s anger is most manifest in his creation of grotesques. Ivan Fëdorovič has a dream that comes almost at the end of the story, and once more the effect of a concluding section is to alter the tone and substance of what preceded it, making it deeply ironic because it suggests things about Špon'ka not possible to appreciate

---

[30] Which seems to me one of Poe's most effective stories primarily because it is most intelligible only if we interpret the narrator to be neurotic, his leading character, Ligeia, to be a subconscious recreation of absolute perfection. See the highly amusing and elucidating comments of D. H. Lawrence, "Edgar Allan Poe", *The Shock of Recognition*, ed. Edmund Wilson (New York, 1955) esp. pp. 966-976.

before, because it changes a buffoon into the first of Gogol''s "little men". It makes possible the pathetic, the sympathetic. It converts an anti-hero into a figure who is heroic within the context of nineteenth-century realism. It even sheds light on Belinskij's judgment that Gogol' was "the first who looked boldly and directly at Russian reality".[31] The dream's importance to the story is crucial.

Špon'ka seems not to need a wife because he is perfectly contented as he is; he tells us as much. The worst his aunt can accuse him of is his *naïveté*. Ostensibly, his innocence is convincing: "a wife! No, Auntie, for goodness' sake ... you make me quite ashamed ... I've never had a wife ... I wouldn't know what to do with her!" But Špon'ka's aunt presses on with her demands that he marry. She has an answer for his *naïvité*: "You'll find out [what to do], Ivan Fëdorovič, you'll find out". Almost at once, now alone, the sweat beads on his face: "Living with a wife ...! Unthinkable! ... [we] would always have to be together ...!"

Ivan Fëdorovič went to bed, and "at last sleep, that universal comforter, came to him; but such sleep! He had never had such incoherent dreams". Everything whirls about him. He runs. Someone catches him by the ear: "It is I, your wife!" He wakes up (in the dream). He is married. A little house, a double bed. His wife is on a chair. He does not know how to approach her. She has the face of a goose. He turns, sees another wife with a goose face. Then another, and yet another. He runs away, takes off his hat — "it was hot" — but there is a wife in it. There is one in his pocket too, and sticking in his ear. He begins to hop on one leg; he must, says his aunt, "for [he] is a married man now". He goes toward her, but she is now a belfry, "and he felt that someone was dragging him by a rope up the belfry". "Who is pulling me?" he asks. The wife is, "because you are a bell". He insists that he is not. The "colonel of the P — infantry regiment" insists that he is. The wife becomes "a sort of woolen material". He takes her to a shopkeeper who tells him that a wife "is the most fashionable material! It wears well!" And the shop-keeper "measured and cut off his wife". He takes her to a Jewish tailor who complains that "that is poor material! No one has coats made of that now ...." Ivan Fëdorovič wakes up, in a sweat. He consults an

---

[31] V. G. Belinskij, *Selected Philosophical Works*, ed. M. T. Yëvčuck (Moscow, 1948), p. 182. Belinskij, writing from a strong bias, was most responsible for those interpretations which still exalt Gogol' as primarily a realist (though Belinskij's 'naturalism' had a more specialized meaning for him); Merežkovskij and the symbolists overreacted to Belinskij's extreme position, created one just as extreme. Belinskij's bias even precluded his appreciation for Dostoevskij's *The Double*, which he felt betrayed the natural school.

"abridged dream interpreter. But there was absolutely nothing in it that remotely resembled this incoherent dream".

Even on its most elemental level, the dream accomplishes a profound change in our views of Špon'ka. It indicates that he is less naïve than he is *afraid* of women and marriage; there is a soul beneath the gross, impenetrable exterior. Women will force him to do what he does not want to do; they will obligate him, make him hop on one leg. They will complicate his sweet existence, force him out of himself, make him expose himself. If, however, one insists that the dream is not revelatory, it functions to complement the grotesqueness of Špon'ka, being itself grotesque. But I am not arbitrarily restricted to these views. I think the Freudian insight is valuable here.[32]

The dream, Freud held, is close to conscious wish or fantasy; its intention to fulfill the dreamer's wishes. Later he concluded that some dreams symbolically reconstruct a traumatic situation so that it might be met and handled. For Freud, the analysis of dreams involved free association as well as retelling of the dream, a luxury denied us, but perhaps insights are nevertheless possible.

We know that Špon'ka does not want to marry. We know that his aunt wants him to. We know that he has very recently been in the com-

---

[32] Extreme Freudians, in their zeal to convert every mountain into a breast, have, most unfortunately, obscured much of the approach's basic value, created an aura of hostility which almost prevents dispassionate comment. Used with restraint, it can supplement other approaches we hold to be valid: the historical, biographical, Marxist, textual. I think one need not agree with Ernest Jones' comments on *Hamlet*, for example, to be profoundly impressed by the insights it offers and its sophistication, which I think is so much greater than that of so many more orthodox and conservative critics (e.g., E. E. Stoll, who takes refuge behind Pope's "A perfect judge will read each work of wit / With the same spirit that its author writ" — a naïve demand impossible of attainment). Freud held, in brief, that, unlike the conscious mind, which is involved with generalities and abstractions, the unconscious mind, struggling with it, deals with the concrete. The unconscious mind is, for Freud, "a wild beast caged in the heart of a city", hosts the libido, a sexualized *élan vital* that would have its way but cannot because of a censor (the superego) which is socially and culturally oriented and suppresses it. During sleep, however, the superego naps too, and the previously suppressed subconscious enjoys liberties without asking for permission. The libidinal matter is projected into dreams, in altered form, because it is still fearful of the superego. It is condensed; it flashes scenes and pictures; it is highly selective; it is symbolic. Dreaming, then, is close to conscious wish or fantasy; its intention is to fulfill the dreamer's wishes. Later, Freud concluded (after studying war veterans) that some dreams symbolically reconstructed a traumatic situation so that it might be met and handled. Freud realized the limitations inherent in just studying dreams, insisted upon free association as well before he could psychoanalyze. See Frederick Hoffmann, *Freudianism and the Literary Mind* (New York, 1959); Franz Alexander and Helen Ross, *The Impact of Freudian Psychiatry* (Chicago, 1961); F. L. Lucas, *Literature and Psychology* (Michigan, 1962).

pany of a young lady whom others (and, we infer, she too) consider marriageable. We know he is thinking deeply, that he falls asleep with difficulty, that he dreams the incoherent dream I have described. This we know. I think the dream suggests why Ivan Fëdorovič is afraid.

The women have goose faces. He does not see that his "wife" has a goose face until "he felt strange. ... did not know how to approach her", that is, he would approach her but cannot. Then the goose face. Geese are vicious fowl which often inflict severe injuries. Perhaps Špon'ka rationalizes: if I approach she will injure me, I will be emasculated; better to avoid her. The price of love is very high indeed, much too high. Flight. But it is hot even in the garden. Everywhere women wait. He is inexorably pulled closer. He is a bell who must respond to pressures. The wife is soft now, "a sort of woolen material". If only one could control the damage; if only she would leave him whole. The shopkeeper can do it; he can cut his wife to size. They will fit each other, the situation will be fully controllable. But no. No one, says the Jew, has that kind anymore. They all bite.

"It is quite true", Gogol' wrote in a letter to Aleksandra Smirnov, on the 24th (O.S.) of December, 1844, "that you will find in them [his early stories] little bits of my mental and psychical state in those days, but without my personal confession no one will ever notice or see them".[33] A fledgling science, psychoanalysis was at the time struggling merely to identify itself.

The dream reflects ironically on our initial concept of Špon'ka. It begins to answer the question "why?". We begin to appreciate why his getting the tailpiece of a turkey is inevitable, why *pošlost'* is a way of life. Ivan Fëdorovič is not contented; contentment is a façade behind which fears are concealed. If so, he no longer lacks depth.

His aunt may scheme endlessly, but she does not know what the reader does. Dramatic irony functions. Even Ivan Fëdorovič may not know what we know, but knowing what we do, he cannot be merely a vegetable. The first of Gogol''s grotesque-pathetic heroes, Špon'ka is, perhaps, because of his dream, more sympathy-provoking than Akakij Akakievič, who delights in trivia because he lives in a world free even of Špon'ka's conscious delights; further, he has no subconscious at all.

If Špon'ka's fictional heart will never beat with the passion known to other men, it will not burst because he is forced to expose himself. He is even tragic in so far as he wants to become but can only be. For him, just being must suffice.

[33] David Magarshack, *Gogol* (London, 1950), p. 161.

Nevskij Prospekt epitomizes Gogol''s total view clearly, is deeply ironic, makes use of a second hero, whose role as foil invites his interpretation as a double, the first in Russian literature. The story is realistic, introduced by those marvelous pages in which Nevskij Prospekt breathes and throbs, and comes alive; and it thereby gains in immediacy. The problem of the ultraromantic hero, Piskarev, is comprehensible even upon a perfunctory reading. He dreams and incubates dreams, and we come to know him better when we expose his subconscious to inspection.

Piskarev is an artist, sensitive, diffident, trembling; Pirogov is a soldier — brusk, confident, nerveless, virile. Together, they watch women pass, Piskarev following an "exquisite lady" down the street, with halting step and palpitating heart: "All he wanted was to see the house, to discover where this exquisite creature lived who seemed to have flown down straight from heaven ...." Pirogov's concerns are more masculine; he chases after a blonde: "We know what you all are". These men, so very different psychologically, separate, never meet again. Piskarev's road leads to complete disillusionment, an agonizing suicide; Pirogov's to adventure, a beating by an irate husband, rebuff, and to a party (after calmly eating two creampuffs) where "he spent a very pleasant evening, and so distinguished himself in the mazurka that not only the ladies but even their partners were moved to admiration".

In Gogol''s world it is the romantic who fares poorly. Gogol''s world is Piskarev's, a should-be world of chivalry and celibacy: "just to touch ... and nothing more! No other desires — they would be insolence".

The girl Piskarev thinks he is following is a divinity; the girl he is following is merely a prostitute. His pursuit is "not aflame with earthly passion"; he is "pure and chaste as a virginal youth burning with the vague spiritual craving for love", imbued with "the sacred duty of chivalrous austerity". His world comes apart at the seams at "the sight of such a beauty touched by the putrid breath of vice". "Alas! by some terrible machination of the fiendish spirit, eager to destroy the harmony of life, she had been flung with satanic laughter into this terrible swamp." The "harmony of life" does not exist in reality; there are too many discordant notes, too many jagged edges that cannot fit into a predetermined pattern. This is what Piskarev is to learn. Prostitutes may indeed look like angels.

Piskarev dreams, and his shattered world comes whole again. He is now a respectable gentleman at a brilliant ball, the girl is surrounded by admirers but eager to be only with him. "Do you hate me?" she asks.

He is overwhelmed and can only mutter. She is about to tell him a secret which, presumably, will explain her appearance in a brothel; but she leaves him, gestures for him to wait, does not return before he wakes up.

"Oh, how revolting was reality! What was it compared to dreams?" Piskarev must solve the enigma of her prostitution or go insane; a "hand, shining white as driven snow" cannot be steeped in the devil's art. There is a secret. It will become clear.

"At last, dreaming became his life. ... he might be said to sleep when he was awake and to come to life when he was asleep". But it is hard to call up her image. "Horrid dreams" interrupt. He takes opium, and "Oh, God, what joy!" She reappears, asking him to think if she could really be "capable of what you imagine". The world of reality encroaches. He awakes, cries out that she should not have lived in this world: "My God! what is our life! An eternal battle between dream and reality!" The problem will not leave; his dilemma is insoluble. Her face appears before him constantly.

Gogol' repeatedly inculcates his conviction of Piskarev's pure motives. He is a knight, Jesus Christ on a mission of mercy. He goes to her again to "restore to the world the loveliest of its ornaments". But the text sometimes jars. He, after all, followed the "lady with the dark hair", the "stunning figure", the "bright-colored cloak". She had smiled at him, told him to be careful, motioned for him to be silent while ascending the stairs. Is this what it is like ascending to heaven? It seems possible that sordidness is not here exclusively the property of the extrinsic world. But perhaps he has, after all, determined to set a sinner on the narrow path. He decides that he will marry her if she but show "herself genuinely penitent and changes her way of life". It is a distinterested deed of charity.

He blurts out an anguished proposal to a disbelieving prostitute. She laughs in his face. "Oh, that was too much!" At home, the razor rights the reeling world as his takes his life.

Piskarev's dreams seem consistent with his periods of wakefulness; they do not contradict the image of the soulful hero driven mad by a soulless world. His artistic sensibility accounts, in part, for his estrangement, and so does his social mediocrity. He too is a "little man". His dreams outline his idea of an earthly paradise, and they are so removed from the realm of possibility that he is more pathetic than ludicrous. His fantasy world existed before the appearance of the girl. She causes it to focus into a hot, white dot, and the pain becomes acute. Piskarev, recognizable as a recurrent type in modern fiction, is an idealist who lives only on the fringe of society, a pariah who cannot enter, one who troubles those of us who live within it because he insists upon living apart. The world of reality cannot begin to compensate for the delights of the world of fantasy.

Piskarev's earthly paradise seemingly has specific requirements, if we judge by his dreams: the girl must be pure but glamorous; other men must fawn over her so that her preference for him is especially meaningful. She is to protect him from society, where court chamberlains with beautiful hair and good teeth are witty and drive "a sharp nail into [his] heart". He is to be humble, forgiving. She is to sit beside him as he paints, her eyes "weary with excess bliss", and to lean her lovely head on his bosom ("He had never had a better dream than that"). In reality, he supports her; in dreams, she supports him.

Piskarev's dream are conventionally romantic, but they are deeply revelatory. They enable us to move him into the capricious and spiteful world of humanity, even if he does not care to enter. He is different from Ivan Fëdorovič Špon'ka, yet he too is afraid.

The story is, then, part tragedy, part comedy. Devoid of the fantastic, there is a brilliantly contrasted clash of different worlds, that of the sensitive artist and that of Pirogov the philistine. Dostoevskij understood the shallowness of Pirogov, the necessity for Piskarevs.[34] Perhaps they are doubles, parts of each in each. Piskarev, the dreams seem to suggest, could become Pirogov; Pirogov must already be partly Piskarev. There is a common denominator — flight. Both run from reality, both dream to escape: Piskarev of what he cannot be, Pirogov of what will make him forget what the world is. His cynicism is as escapist oriented as Piskarev's romanticism. He is perhaps Piskarev turned inside out.

Nevskij Prospekt is a story of doubles, of paradoxes. Primarily, it concerns the threads separating and joining fantasy and reality, a world containing Pirogov-Piskarev, angel-whore, escape-punishment, misery-bliss. The dreams are critical. They make it possible to believe there is a final double, Piskarev-Piskarev.

Nevskij Prospekt is a story of psychologically ill men. It is Gogol''s most profound exposure of his own weaknesses. Piskarev is a tragic figure; he will never belong to established society, but his idealism cannot

---

[34] Dostoevskij loathed philistines and philistinism. His rejection of *pošlost'* is apparently not negative, as it is in Gogol''s grotesques, but is a mystical vision of salvation through suffering.

descend to reality; reality, if ever the worlds truly meet, must ascend to his standards.

In *Diary of a Madman*, Gogol' is perhaps more directly involved with contemporary social reality than in any of the earlier tales, a fact not lost on the Russian censor who cut out several of the original passages, while others he would have objected to got by in disguised form.[35] It is full of references to contemporary society and Western politics, and is, therefore, partly satiric. This is important, for Popriščin's madness is in great measure directly related to the abuses of the society in which he functions.

Popriščin is a destitute clerk like Akakij Akakievič, but he cannot adjust to the same world, and because he cannot he is more sympathetically treated, the grotesque is almost suspended. A "little man", he would be important; unable to be important, he creates a fantasy world which shields him from abuse. His longings are not difficult to comprehend. They can be epitomized in a single phrase: to be important. His demands from the world of reality are not unreasonable in the context of the twentieth century; they were impossible in nineteenth-century Russia, where the civil service hierarchy so precisely positioned a man in a specific rank that his economic situation and social aspirations were absolutely defined. The office where he works has fewer desks than Kafka's fictional office, but the tone is not very different: men are engulfed by the machine. Unseen and unmissed, they drown and disappear.

It is love, pathetic, impossible love, that triggers Popriščin's latent madness — love for his director's daughter. He gives away what remains of his sanity with his heart. Dogs begin to speak a language he can understand. At home he copies lines from Nikolev: "'My life is now a hated task / How can I live this life?', I ask". In the evening he goes out to catch another glimpse of the girl. In the diary entry dated November sixth, we see the primary source of his madness. The head of his department makes it unmistakably clear as he all but destroys him on the spot:

What are you up to? Why, you are over forty. It's time you had a little sense. What do you imagine yourself to be? Do you suppose I don't know all the tricks you are up to? Why, you are philandering after the director's daughter! Come, look at yourself; just think what you are! Why, you are a nonentity and nothing else! Why, you haven't a kopek to bless yourself with. And just look at yourself in the mirror — how could you think of such a thing![36]

---

[35] E.g., the last line originally read "The French king has a boil under his nose", but *šiška* being a colloquialism for trouble, it was changed. In the entry for October the 4th, Popriščin comments on how stupid the French are, probably an allusion to the July Revolution in 1830, etc.

[36] *The Collected Tales and Plays, op. cit.*, p. 457.

The department head has verbalized what Popriščin already knows. From this point on, Popriščin's madness accelerates; he becomes less and less able (and willing) to associate with reality, grows frantic in a search for information which will unlock the benefits of the world for him, but his source is an exchange of imaginary letters between dogs. Completely mad, he convinces himself that he is really a Spanish king in disguise, refuses to work, is taken to an asylum, beaten mercilessly, waits for the Spanish delegation to reveal his identity to all the world. It is to be, of course, an endless wait. But it hardly matters. It is one thing to be beaten because fools cannot recognize royalty, another thing — much more painful — to beat one's head against an inflexible wall of social patterns with no one even to hear the sobs.

The diary is pure fantasy, wildly funny. It is a detailed record of the subconscious because the world of madness is a dream, or rather, a nightmare. Madmen have *carte blanche*, and it would be absurd not to become at least a king; after all, madmen hardly ever wish to become clerks. Popriščin becomes his own double; his double tells us what he needs to become, reflects on the inadequacies and the stressfulness of the world from which he has fled.

He would be a king because he is nothing; he would be loved because he is alone; he would have an identity because he is faceless. His fantasies are hyperbolic because, of course, he is mad. But there is something about his fantasies which should not be lightly dismissed. In parts, they are not unlike those projected by sane characters in Gogol'. The symbolic situation reminds one of the very earliest stories, the symbols themselves suggests that part of Popriščin's madness may be rooted in causes not social. Sandwiched between absolute nonsense ("Spain and China are the same country") and distorted historical allusions (the "English chemist Wellington") there is something else. The moon is back again, and here it seems almost to be defined. I present it without comment:

... I experienced a tremor at my heart when I reflect on the extreme softness and fragility of the moon. ... It was made by a ... barrel maker .... He put in tarred cord and one part of lamp oil; and that is why there is such a fearful stench all over the world that one has to stop up one's nose. And that's how it is that the moon is such a soft globe that man cannot live on it and that nothing lives there but noses. And it is for that very reason that we can't see our noses, because they are all in the moon. And when I reflected that the earth is a heavy body and when it falls may grind our noses to powder ....[37]

[37]   *Ibid.*, p. 470.

Gogol''s depiction of madness is brilliant. The story gains in meaning relative to the degree that Popriščin's subconsciously created world reveals the enormous chasm that exists between what he is and what he desires to be. The pressures of society suppressed, limited, and frustrated him. When he calls for his mother to "drop a tear on his sick head", his flash of sanity is alarming and disturbing. It is good, the reader feels, that the story closed with the totally irrelevant "and do you know that the Dey of Algiers has a boil just under his nose?" because, despite Gogol''s sane allusion to a political situation, it is Popriščin's insane comment, and it informs us that the protective madness has returned.

Popriščin is very much like Dostoevskij's Goljadkin. He too does not belong, is without a niche. He is less than Kafka's insect; a thing without even a place. And there is a darker question beneath the surface: is there a place at all? Perhaps he does not even exist. Perhaps there is no world of reality.

There is about this story an aura of Hoffmann's hopelessness. Popriščin is a puppet, a feeble, wistful nonentity who hardly feels the strings that activate him. He left reality without leaving a trace behind because, after all, he had nothing to leave.

In *The Nose* once more a nose disappears,[38] but this time it walks the streets of St. Petersburg, in full dress. Mirsky notes that in this story "more than anywhere else Gogol displays his extraordinary magic power of making great comic art out of nothing".[39] But Dostoevskij saw its more profound implications, acknowledged that it was important for his own literary development of pathological duality.

The nose is nothing less than Kovalëv's double. A collegiate assessor, Kovalëv is outranked by the nose: "From his [nose's] plumed hat it might be inferred that he was of the rank of state councilor". No one is more conscious of rank than Kovalëv, who insists upon being addressed by the military equivalent, "major". But how, asks an insane-with-grief

---

[38] Popriščin, of course, lost his in the moon; Hoffmann ("not the writer Hoffmann, but ... a great friend of Schiller's") begged to have his cut off in *Nevskij Prospekt*; the sorcerer in *Vij* has a nose that "grew longer and hung down over his lips", and so on. There was a nosology, possibly encouraged by Sterne's *Tristram Shandy*, which appeared in Russian translation in 1807. Noses are to be found in Russian literature of the 1820's and 30's. Nabokov (*Gogol*) notes that the Russian language is singularly rich in expressions dealing with noses, etc. In "The Nose" (*The Slavonic and East European Review*, XXXI, 1952, pp. 207-211), Herbert Bowman argues that "the discovery which may provide the key to Gogol''s story is ... that the nose is perhaps the least important organ of the human body — yet ... the most conspicuous". The traits of the nose, according to Bowman, "provided Gogol' with a humorous representation of his characteristic world of hollow and ludicrous 'appearance'".

[39] *A History of Russian Literature*, p. 159.

man, how is it possible for a nose "which had only yesterday been on [my] face and could neither drive nor walk — to be in uniform"? And how is he to approach his nose if "one can see by everything — from his uniform, from his hat" that he is not to be trifled with? Kovalëv debates how to approach while the nose "was saying his prayers in an attitude of complete piety". Finally gaining courage, he addresses the nose most respectfully, stammering out his dismay: "The matter appears to me perfectly obvious ... either you wish .... Why, you are my own nose!" But the nose, imperious, resplendent in his fine uniform, his eyebrows slightly quivering, gives no ground: "You are mistaken, sir. I am an independent individual". Then, the unkindest cut of all: "Moreover, there can be no sort of close relationship between us. I see, sir [and how patronizing a "sir" this is!] from the buttons of your uniform, you must be serving in a different department". Kovalëv's pursuit of his nose is described in a highly comic succession of outrageous scenes. Finally, and "this took place on the seventh of April", he looks into a mirror, puts up his hands, shouts "Aha!" The peripatetic nose has come home.

The Nose was written especially for the Moscow *Observer*, but it was returned to Gogol' because it was too "sordid". It was finally published in Puškin's *The Contemporary*, with a note by Puškin commenting on Gogol''s reluctance to publish this "joke", and the fact that he found much in it that was original, fantastic, and extremely comic.

The "joke", of course, is obvious, and Gogol' has a good laugh at his own expense, especially in these lines:

... What is more incomprehensible [than how it got into Ivan Yakovlevič's bread] than anything is that authors can choose such subjects. I confess that it is quite beyond my grasp .... No, no! I cannot understand it at all. In the first place it is absolutely without profit to our country ....[40]

but Kovalëv's distress when he is without his nose is too heavily detailed, too acute, not to give away Gogol''s intimate emotional involvement in the situation. Typically, there is distress in the laughter, a voice of muffled panic just beneath the surface hilarity.

Despite the rumors that a nose in disguise has been seen in town, despite its apparent apprehension by a policeman, despite its reality within the fabric of the text, it is impossible to determine how much its existence as a separate entity is a result of Kovalëv's subconscious, for the story is too slight, the details purposely hazy. But it is more than nonsense. The Freudian interpretation is obvious, and there is another implication: the nose is a pathological manifestation. It not only acts

[40]   *The Collected Tales and Plays*, p. 497.

out Kovalëv's desires, it is his alter ego. Its superiority, aloofness, control, are all absent in its psychological source, for Kovalëv is one of Gogol''s empty men, spiritually naked, one who looks into the mirror immediately upon awakening. It rejects him, functions independently. Kovalëv is two people at the same time; he meets himself and, confronted with a consciously incomprehensible *Doppelgänger*, he can only stammer out his distress. But the story is only a hint of what Dostoevskij is so much more fully to develop. Like many of Hoffmann's stories, *The Nose* all but erases the fine line that separates the world of reality from that of hallucination. It implies that there is an aspiration unfulfilled in man that somehow fights its way through the subconscious, only to be rejected. Man's isolation, then, is complete; he is alone even from himself.

It is in *The Portrait*, one of Gogol''s less successful stories, that his use of the subconscious, especially the dream, is most artistically successful and profound. Part of this may be due to the Hoffmannesque quality about it (it is strongly reminiscent of *Die Elixiere des Teufels*), part of this to Gogol''s increasing skill in objectifying and handling the subconscious, part of this to the nature of the story and of its hero; and part of this because the major appearance of the subconscious comes relatively early in the story, and though it is affected by what follows, Gogol' is able to handle it with considerable artistic control. Less charged with personal involvement, it is much less blatantly didactic than the religious allegory that follows (Dostoevskij and Tolstoj almost always artistically surmount the didacticism infused in their works and succeed despite it, or, especially in the case of some of the late Tolstoj — *Ivan Il'ič*, *Master and Man* — almost because of it; Gogol''s moralizing in the later part of this story, because of his lack of objective distance, seems to break its back).

In many ways, the use of the subconscious in *The Portrait* seems closer to the tone and quality of Dosotevskij's use of it than anything else in Gogol'. The depiction of duality in the preceding stories is, of course, one of Dostoevskij's major themes, but its delineation in Gogol' is much more artistically limited, much less profound than it is in Dostoevskij. The implications inherent in the use of the double may be essentially the same in both, but Gogol''s expression of the theme is not only less consistent, but more limited and less effective.

In *The Portrait*, however, the relative complexity of the hero (perhaps the most complex of his heroes), the quality of the interweaving of dream and reality, the symbolism of the dream, the depiction of physical symp-

toms anticipating the dream, its reflection forward, backward, and inward, its creation of a supernatural aura, its use as a symbolic warning
and as a tension-escalating device, all seem to more closely anticipate
Dostoevskij.

Gogol''s attitude toward Čartkov is somewhat ambivalent, much to
the benefit of the story. Being a destitute artist, he is at first positively
depicted, but his comprehension of art is imperfect because his inspiration
is imperfect. He has talent, "but no patience". Gogol''s attitude seems
to be verbalized by the warning of the professor: "Take care. The outside
world begins to attract you. ... forget about fineries ... your own time
will not fail to come". There is something of the materialist in Čartkov.
As the narrator calmly informs us, "the professor was partially correct".
But Čartkov's imperfect inspiration, his desire for money and what it can
buy, are partially born of his very deprivation. Also, he is alienated,
totally without friends or family, and his outcry, "Damn it! What a
miserable world!", is therefore comprehensible. An artist who is something of a fop, talented but impatient, estranged, of "sensitive imagination
and nerves", and destitute, Čartkov has about him the complexity of
humanity, and it is clear that he is a double, in Gogol''s terms. He
contains the seeds of morality, the potential for immorality.

The hyperbolic quality of the eyes in the portrait may be essentially
Čartkov's subjectified view of them. Their major function is to haunt
him to his doom, and "the strange kind of life" in them may represent
the conscience of the artist, one part of him accusing and warning the
other. The eyes, revealingly enough, haunt him not when he is painting
but rather when thinking of money. Again within the context of reality,
their lifelike quality is comprehensible because the narrator assures us
that "the eyes, truthfully, were particularly striking and alive". Also, the
setting itself (e.g., the moonlight playing on the eyes) serves to further
such a conclusion.

The dream, and it flows over from reality, is immediately anticipated
by a feeling of restlessness, thoughts of poverty "and the miserable fate
of the artist". In a sense, then, the dream is a dramatization of his desire
for wealth, a symbolization of wish fulfillment. The horror of the dream
bespeaks Čartkov's own ambivalence; it is subconscious self-punishment.
Most important of all, the dream enables us to see into Čartkov, and,
for the first time, it becomes clear that if he is a dual man, it is yet the
immoral part of him that has the upper hand now and will affect the course
of what follows. This is all expressed in a single sentence: "The gold
glittered, and however great the artist's fear and depression had been,

he could not keep from looking greedily at the gold". The dream serves a double anticipatory role. It not only, by revealing Čartkov's greed, foreshadows his destruction, but the money itself is soon to be found contained in the frame of the portrait.

Čartkov wakes up from this dream no fewer than four times, Gogol' completely erasing the line separating dream from reality; for he not only wakes up in his dream (a common Dostoevskij technique), but even stops, at the conclusion of the first of the three dreams within a dream, to ask himself whether he had been dreaming. Because he dreams he is awake, the horror of the dream becomes reality itself. He runs from it even as the greedy Čartkov runs from the spark of conscience. Three times, waking in his dream, he shrieks, ending it, only to immediately begin the next phase of it.

Dostoevskij's dreamers usually awake shrieking, and it is clear that in Gogol' and Dostoevskij the shriek performs a special literary function — it is the highest point of the tension that has been building, and it is followed by a period of calm. In *The Portrait* this calm is short-lived because the dream is yet incomplete, but it comes immediately after the dream finally ends, when not only is the usually high-strung Čartkov "depressed and sullen as a wet rooster", but even the room is suddenly limp.

Again, as in Dostoevskij, physical distress symbolizes internal conflict. Čartkov too, like Ivan Karamazov, has a headache; he is not sure whether he dreamed or whether it was "the result of delirium" (or, almost gratuitously, of the supernatural). When he had dreamed he was awake from his dream, "the weight on his chest was unendurable"; and this too reminds one of Dostoevskij, where fever and an oppressive feeling of being crushed are consistently used to anticipate hallucinations and acute emotional distress.

In *The Landlady*, the horrible action depicted, viewed with Ordynov's delirium in mind, may never have occurred at all. If Čhartkov's poverty and estrangement conspired to drive him mad, it is possible that even the dreams are delirium-created; in any event, it is conscience being projected.

The anticipatory function of the dream is fulfilled when Čartkov discovers the coins. At this point, because the gold pieces are precisely in the amount and in the shape he had dreamed, he once more asks "Isn't this all a dream?" The original dream, therefore, whether merely a dream or whether a manifestation of delirium brought on by subconscious guilt, continues to directly influence the story. It cloaks what

follows in an aura of unreality. As the predictions implicit in the dream
come true they reflect back on the dream, endowing it with supernatural
prescience, and coloring the story with an aura not so much Gothic as
mystical.

The portrait becomes central again as Čartkov, having bastardized
his talent, realizing in the work of others what he could have been ("to
have ruined [everything] without mercy!"), remembers "that this
strange portrait had been responsible for his errors". He has it removed,
but because he subconsciously knows that he was solely responsible for
his errors, he grows increasingly mad. Haunted by eyes, he slashes all
the portraits he can buy. But guilt is a tenacious disease, and "he died
in a final paroxysm of speechless agony", a man destroyed by himself.

The subconscious, employed as Gogol' employs it here, not only
makes abstractions concrete by dramatizing them, but, aside from those
literary functions discussed, enriches the story because it bespeaks the
complexity of the hero. Functioning on several levels simultaneously,
not only is conflict inherent within him, but must extend beyond him,
shattering the possibility of simple existence, thus making him and the
story in which he appears more dramatic and universally meaningful
than they could otherwise be. The tone of the dream is eminently suited
to the tone of the story.

The first part of *The Portrait*, much superior to the more traditionally
realistic part which follows, indicates an advance in Gogol''s use of
the subconscious, reveals how well it can function when thoroughly
integrated into the fabric of the story being told. Here there is evidence
that Gogol' was employing its manifestations in a most careful and
deliberate way. But in nothing that followed was it ever to be so fully
exploited again by him.

In *The Overcoat* the subconscious is also important but relatively
superficial. The depiction of the hero, Akakij Akakievič, despite its
justifiable fame, is without psychological depth. His importance as a
character depends primarily on his symbolic meaning rather than on the
state of his inner life. Contentment does not breed the conflicts which
incubate the subconscious. It helps, however, elucidate the relationship
between him and his coat, it "explains" the fantastic ending of this
otherwise realistic story.

The coat seems nothing less than a wife to Akakij Akakievič.[41] It

[41] See Leon Stilman's "Gogol''s 'Overcoat' — Thematic Pattern and Origins"
(*American Slavic and Eastern European Review*, XII, 3 (1953), pp. 138-148. Stilman
compares Popriščin's mantle with Akakij Akakievič's "new and glorious overcoat".

intiates a total change in his existence, gives life a meaning it never had for him before. It is cuddled, held, caressed, loved. It is his existence. With its being stolen, its owner begins the decline leading to death.

Gogol' makes Akakij Akakievič grotesque, but he makes him pathetic too; indeed, Gogol''s attitude toward him is ambiguous, passing from one extreme to another. But Akakij's search for his coat, his rejection and humiliation by a heartless and totally indifferent world is treated with compassion: "... who could have imagined ... that he was destined ... to make his presence felt in the world after his death, as though to make up for his life having been unnoticed by anyone?"

Akakij returns as a corpse, not a ghost, a corpse that removes the overcoats "from the shoulders of all passers-by, regardless of grade and calling". Once it is almost captured, but the corpse sneezes, and "while [the policemen] were putting their fists up to wipe their eyes, [it] vanished completely, so that they were not even sure whether he had actually been in their hands". It is the Person of Consequence who suffers most from the return of the corpse. He has treated Akakij worst of all, and when he meets the corpse, it is most lifelike: "The clerk's face was white as snow and looked like that of a corpse". There is special horror; there is no humor in the meeting. There is even "the chill of the grave". The effect is profound. Karolina Ivanovna, a woman with whom the Person of Consequence had an appointment, is forgotten in the panic of the moment. He flees home. The incident had "made a great impression on him. Indeed, it happened far more rarely that he said to his subordinates, 'How dare you? Do you understand who I am?' and he never uttered those words at all until he had first heard all the facts of the case". The remaining paragraph of the story is delightful nonsense, the "apparition" is now "considerably taller and adorned with immense mustaches ...".

Even as imagination made the corpse taller and taller, added the mustaches for good measure, subconscious guilt may have created the wandering corpse. Again the line between reality and hallucination is obscured. But perhaps Akakij, after all, has left something behind other

---

When Akakij is robbed of his mantle, "the illusion [of royalty, importance] vanishes, reality is once more laid bare. The "real" Akaij, stripped of his disguise, is characterized by coprological symbols ...". See also Cyril Bryner's "Gogol''s *The Overcoat* in World Literature" (*Slavonic and Eastern European Review*, XXXII, 79, 1954, pp. 499-509). Bryner traces the frequency and quality of the story's appearance in anthologies, etc., concludes that "Gogol' and his *The Overcoat* have reached us in world literature under the false pretense of realism, mangled by inadequate translations, with his weak points (e.g., 'droll humour') emphasized and his strong ones (e.g., his style) obscured." Bryner, it seems to me, overstates his conviction of Gogol''s "nonrealism".

than "a bundle of quills, a quire of white government paper, three pairs of socks, two or three buttons" and his *kapot*. He has left behind the pathetic image of himself, a sense of guilt in the indifferent world. The socially irresponsible come back to haunt themselves and each other. Unable to fulfill his human needs while alive, Akakij has a hollow triumph after death. He has some meaning in death only because he was so trivial during life.

In Gogol', the conscious use of the subconscious is less developed, less profound, less complex than it becomes in Dostoevskij, though, in many ways, it anticipates Dostoevskij in several most important respects. Part of this is due to Gogol''s level of self-involvement; he too much subjectified his material, was himself too narrowly focused to sustain a theme in depth (even *Dead Souls* is primarily a compilation of vignettes). The intensity so marked in Dostoevskij is not lacking here, but the core of a deep and abiding and universally significant vision of life from which to build a sustained work is. Dostoevskij was extroverted enough, disciplined enough, to convert his experiences and insights into broad and complex works predicated upon a meaningful vision of life. Gogol''s canvas is too small, the sweep of the brush too restricted, the vision too distorted, the self too involved, for such achievement. But these limitations are relative.

Gogol''s works tell us more about their author than do the works of almost any other author I can think of. This accounts in part for their hyperbolic quality. There is a great consistency in his works; patterns emerge, as do attitudes and the separate ingredients of the delightful but disturbing Gogol' brew.

Gogol''s use of the double and the dream is nearly always artistically successful; their appearance is relevant to the literary quality of the stories in which they appear. Almost consistently serving beyond traditional romantic function, the dream and other manifestations of the subconscious not only enrich the potential of the works, but so dominate them that they become necessary for any meaningful interpretation. They reflect backwards, making the preceding ironic; they project ahead, coloring and shading what follows, and, crucially, they reflect inward.

Gogol' surely learned from his predecessors, especially the German romantics, but he is the most original of authors. His distorted vision and total emotional commitment, even as they limit the breadth of his art, account for much of its special brilliance.

Escape from a godless world of *pošlost'* is a central theme in Gogol'. Such a world is found wanting on many levels: it demands the artist lose sensitivity, the celibate be passionate, the humble be obliterated. Hope is possible, but it is only possible through God; refuge from laceration is possible only in dreams or in idealistic fantasies. The paradoxical, so frequent in his work, stemmed from the paradoxes in Gogol': a selfless Christ who was selfish; a loveless man who needed love; an impotent man potent in fantasy; a self-satisfied man disgusted with self; a man who cried when he laughed, laughed even while he cried.

The appearance of the subconscious serves Gogol' very well indeed. It helps us to understand a crucial attitude: "It is a dreary world, gentlemen."

FËDOR MIXAJLOVIČ DOSTOEVSKIJ

Dostoevskij's world view is inherent in his consistent emphasis on the subconscious and its manifestations, and is expressed within subconscious projections integrated into his works. It is clear that Dostoevskij equated the unconscious with the irrational, which, in turn, was equated with the heart and feeling, the parts of man which, in Dostoevskij, stand in direct opposition to intellect and sex, both corrupting forces.

Within the works, the unconscious may, on two levels, serve his characters as an instrument of knowledge. On one, things long forgotten may be returned to the level of awareness; on the other, as the impersonal, pre-personal, or collective unconscious, it may anticipate events (for example, Myškin, upon meeting Aglaja, feels he has met her before. Dreams often predict events which take place in reality). On this second level, it also implies a metaphysical communion between man and the forces beyond him. There is a myth leitmotif in Dostoevskij, but it has never been convincingly argued that he believed in the occult (for unlike Hoffmann, he viewed it with suspicion).

There is also the repressed unconscious, which leads to schizophrenia or, in less dramatic form, to inner division, which, in turn, fosters duality, ambiguous and ambivalent motivation. Raskol'nikov, for example, kills despite himself; Vel'čaninov cannot kill despite himself.

There is even something that might be called the over-unconscious, expressed often in the epileptic seizure, where the oversoul, the paradise within, is revealed in brilliant flashes of light and insight; and epilepsy, in Dostoevskij often the highest expression of the irrational, stands in opposition to schizophrenia, primarily a disease comprehensible within the context of the various pressures exerted by the reality depicted in the works. Schizophrenia, in a sense, labels a character as a man of the world (despite the estrangement it also implies); epileptic seizures move a character beyond the confines of reality, thus establishing him as an anti-world force (I will even argue that Smerdjakov's epilepsy is comprehensible and consistent within the context of Dostoevskijan thought).

Dostoevskij expresses the appearance of the subconscious in several crucial ways: dreams (which may also be supernatural in origin and beyond explanation as a subconscious projection), doubles, hallucinations, delirium, and epilepsy (triggered by the subconscious). There are also other less dramatic symptoms of a psychogenic origin that are consistently used throughout the works to indicate deep emotional distress: chills, sweating, fever, brain fever, headaches, and chest pains (almost invariably accompanied by a feeling of pressure, of being crushed).

The dreams are basically of several kinds: anticipatory (they predict something that is to happen within the context of reality); warning (a projection bespeaking the consequences of an anticipated act, e.g., Raskol'nikov has such a dream before the murder), guilt-born (reflecting the subconscious reaction against a previous act or thought — conscience), anxiety-created (fear of being displaced, loss of identity, extreme poverty, etc.), regenerative (dreams which reveal the incipient or relatively complete moral regeneration of a character). The first two kinds may result from either the subconscious or the metaphysical; the others are primarily a result of the subconscious. All but those of supernatural origin reflect on the dreamer and reveal his inner life.

I have not been trying to set up elaborate and inflexible categories of the subconscious and its function in Dostoevskij. Rather, I have been suggesting the importance of the subconscious in Dostoevskij, trying to establish a general frame of reference, a starting point for discussion.

The peculiar mingling and meshing of diversities, and the merging of disparate elements so typical of German romanticism and Gogol', reaches its most profound significance and expression in Dostoevskij — and it is consistent in him.[1] The Germans had done much to emancipate the fantastic and occult from its traditional setting, to make the double function (as it does in Hoffmann) within the realistic framework, within the urban world in which it was born. Even the use of glamorous Paris as the setting (in *Das Fräulein von Scuderi*, for example), seemingly incidental, is not. The unrealistic achieves a special prominence in the prosaic. It is precisely to the point that the prosaic yield the fantastic, that the commonplace contain the marvelous, that the realistic always contain

[1] Dmitri Čiževsky ("The Theme of the Double in Dostoevsky", *Dostoevsky*, ed. René Wellek, Englewood Cliffs, New Jersey, 1962, pp. 112-129) lists only *The Double*, *The Possessed*, *A Raw Youth*, and *The Brothers Karamazov* as containing doubles. His definition of a double is more restrictive than mine. His article was most helpful.

the potential for the unrealistic, for within the realistic the fantastic threatens the very existence of reality and identity.

In a very fine essay, "The Theme of the Double in Dostoevsky", Dmitri Čiževsky writes that "Dostoevskij's power as an artist lies precisely in his ability to avoid mixing or confusing these sharply contradictory elements [the "naturalistic" and "unrealistic"], and to succeed in weaving them together, fusing them into an organic unity".[2] He further makes the point that Dostoevskij's "'realistically psychological' analysis is at the same time 'transcendentally psychological', 'existential', and that all events and the whole pattern of his theme are always an ideological construct as well".[3]

To understand the significance of the double within Dostoevskij's work, it is essential to appreciate that although his total view of man may be dualistic (i.e., there seems to be a potential for goodness even in evil), it is basically anti-Rousseauistic; man, having fallen, is primarily evil. Nineteenth-century views of man which are optimistic are rejected. Neither science nor socialism nor determinism nor even liberalism (unless it affords man absolute *carte blanche*) can meet the inner needs of man because he is irrational. Materialism cannot serve; the ant heap — that symbol of nineteenth-century progress — is ridiculed because it merely enslaves man's soul. The crystal palace in which man displays his ingenuity merely sparkles in the sun and reflects his shallowness. Bread, therefore, is not enough. There cannot be a self without a metaphysical framework; there cannot be an 'I' without freedom; and there cannot be freedom without suffering. Christ supplies identity.

Goljadkin, the tormented and demented hero of Dostoevskij's second novel, *The Double*, is without a place in the world. His name (from *golij*) tells us that he is "naked". Alone and afraid — as are almost all of Dostoevskij's characters — he has but two companions, his conscience and the projection of his schizophrenia, his double. His double is a manifestation of the repressed unconscious. Despite the fact that Dostoevskij finally came to agree with many contemporary critics, especially Belinskij, that this early novel was a failure, he never ceased insisting that the failure lay in the defects of his art and not in his theme;[4] indeed, as often been pointed out, the implications inherent in the theme were has often been pointed out, the implications inherent in the theme were

[2]   *Ibid.*, p. 114.
[3]   *Loc. cit.*
[4]   Čiževsky (*op. cit.*, pp. 112-113) notes some of Dostoevskij's relevant comments. Dostoevskij's fondness for the theme is apparent if one realizes that Goljadkin is really the prototype of almost all his heroes.

central to Dostoevskij's vision — so central that in "disguised" and more profound form it appears over and over again in his works.[5]

The Double is a story of psychopathology and of man's place (or "placelessness") in society, and the relatedness of the two. Goljadkin is surely a more complex figure than anyone in Gogol', including Kovalëv in *The Nose* and Popriščin in *Diary of a Madman*, his most direct antecedents. A clerk very much like any of Gogol''s clerks, a victim of society as they too are victims, as grotesque as any of them,[6] he is yet very different because, obviously insane from the moment we are introduced to him, a paranoiac running from imaginary enemies ("I have deadly enemies who have sworn to ruin me";[7] "[he was] seeking safety from enemies and persecution";[8] "a persecuting fate",[9] etc.), the first of Dostoevskij's self-lacerating figures,[10] Goljadkin destroys himself from within even as the world crushes him from without. No less vain and pretentious than Kovalëv (he too promptly reaches for a mirror upon awakening), yet diffident almost to the point of disappearing, in "indescribable anguish" upon being recognized (as he rides in unaccustomed splendor in a carriage) by the chief clerk in his office, Goljadkin prepares for his own "execution":

"Shall I bow? Shall I make some response? Shall I admit it's me, or shan't I?" ... "Or shall I pretend it's not me, but someone extraordinarily like me, and just look as if nothing had happened? It really isn't me, it *isn't* me, and that's all there is to it ...."[11]

The visit to Dr. Rutenspitz follows almost immediately, a visit during which Goljadkin is quite incoherent and unable to express the distress he himself cannot begin to understand. He drifts. A pariah who *must* belong — his inability to belong is the root of his dualism — he slips, uninvited, into a party, after hiding amidst the symbols of his nothingness, the garbage. At the party, "as if to spite him, no one was dancing". It

[5] Professor Simmons notes that "many critics ... have pointed out the pervasive dualism of Dostoevsky's characters". Simmons sees Devuškin (*Poor Folk*) as the first of "a type he was to develop with infinite artistic refinement and profound psychological insight in a whole series of more famous characters that followed." (*Dostoevsky: The Making of a Novelist*, New York, 1962, p. 22).

[6] See n. 10, pp. 13, 14.

[7] *The Double*, trans. George Bird (Bloomington, Indiana, 1959), p. 30.

[8] *Ibid.*, p. 71.

[9] *Ibid.*, p. 73.

[10] Devuškin is too passive to be truly self-lacerating. Like Akakij Akakievič, he accepts his fate calmly, almost, at times, seems to enjoy his sweet misery. There is also but little tension in his existence. The social implications in his story are clear, but Devuškin ("maiden") is too innocent and too complacent to rebel, even psychologically.

[11] *The Double*, p. 19.

is a fiasco, as it must be. The rootless creature feeds himself courage, is rejected by all, reels, by accident gets Klara Olsuf'evna to dance with him, and, in the very best Gogol' tradition, "raised one foot, did a sort of bow, gave a sort of stamp, and stumbled". The girl's scream shatters his last hope. Almost the final indignity, it wrenches him from the rest of humanity forever. He rushes out, "demented", running though "he had no more life in him". The St. Petersburg November night beats at him, "gumming up his eyes, cutting him from all sides, chilling him to the bone, and driving him off his path and out of his mind". Further, "he had the look of a man wishing to hide and escape from himself", "... to annihilate himself completely, to return to dust and cease to be". It is now, nature itself supplying the final indignity, that he shudders, thinks "someone had just been standing right there beside him". Someone had. His double had come, never again to leave. From this point on his double interferes with what is left of Goljadkin's life, teases him, mocks him, scolds him, embarrasses him, belittles him, and squeezes him completely out of this world by totally replacing him.

That Goljadkin's double is a result of what might be clinically described as paranoid schizophrenia seems a reasonable assumption. The problem, however, is complex. Having no self, he creates one, but creating a self he destroys himself, for Goljadkin II is in every way superior to Goljadkin Senior. Ironically, however, this superiority consists of guile, deceit, obsequiousness, haughtiness (for example, he wipes his fingers after touching Goljadkin Senior) — of all those artificial social "talents" that Goljadkin Senior has never mastered. Goljadkin, however, is psychologically torn precisely because, consistent with his vanity, he would have liked to, despite his defensive words to the doctor that he does not like "double-dealing", "slander", "gossip", and that "the only time I put on a mask is when I go to a masquerade".

At first Goljadkin's double is as humble as Goljadkin: "What a downtrodden specimen he [Goljadkin II] is!" He even embraces him, warmed, pathetically, by his own company. At the office, however, the takeover begins. Goljadkin II, a social climber, changes and aggressively replaces his host body until even the absence of Goljadkin Senior from the office passes completely unnoticed. He has, with great pain, finally accomplished the desire first expressed in the carriage and later explicit in thoughts of suicide — he has disappeared.

At the end of the story, it is "his abominable blackguardly twin" ("whose face was shining with an unseemly glee that boded ill") who introduces him to the doctor who is to take him to an asylum. He even

helps him get in. The doctor too is a double — and is this double also
Goljadkin's insane creation? Or, because he speaks with an accent absent
in the other Dr. Rutenspitz, is it some mad coincidence? — "not the earlier Dr. Rutenspitz, but another, a terrible Dr. Rutenspitz!" Like Gogol''s
madman, Goljadkin, at the very moment he is forever to disappear, has a
dreadful flash of sanity, even as he rides from a world in which he never
had a place and to which he never belonged: "Our hero gave a scream,
and clutched his head. Alas! He had felt this coming for a long time!"
Dostoevskij's scream echoes too, directed at a world full of madmen
who confuse existing with living, the needs of the ego with those of the
soul.

Goljadkin has a dream, and Čizevsky correctly points out that it is
"the center of the work". Dostoevskij, as always, uses it to serve a literary
as well as psychological function. It symbolically dramatizes the roots
of Goljadkin's mental disorder. It is created by his anxiety, reveals its
nature. In it, Goljadkin, who "had been shaken to the core by the events
of the preceding day", dreams of Goljadkin II "eclipsing him", of him
telling him that "the real Mr. Goljadkin was not real at all but a fraud",
of trying to escape from the "depraved Goljadkin" by fleeing "blindly
wherever fate might might lead", but

as often as his footfalls rang upon the granite pavement, an exact image of
Golyadkin the depraved and abominable would spring out of the ground.
And each of these exact images would come waddling along behind the next,
in a long procession like a gaggle of geese, after Golyadkin Senior. The pitiable
Golyadkin grew breathless with terror. In the end there sprang up so fearful a
multitude of exact images that the whole capital was blocked with them ....[12]

It is also an anticipatory representation of the action which follows.
Goljadkin will soon exclaim "it's happening just like in the dream".
Kafka's monstrous insect has at least a room and a family, belongs in a
sense.[13] Goljadkin never belongs; perhaps he never was. Reality may be
only a dream. In the second sentence of the story we are already prepared for such a possibility as we read of "a man as yet uncertain whether
he is awake or still asleep, whether all at present going on about him is
reality or a continuation of his distorted dreams". He may once have
thought that he was "as well off as the next man" and had "his own place",
and "his own man", but he is not even as well off as his own double; his

---

[12] *Ibid.* pp. 170, 171.
[13] Gregor, despite the revulsion he causes, has yet a mother who can plead "Do let
me go in to Gregor, he is my unfortunate son! Can't you understand that I must go
to him?" (*Selected Stories of Franz Kafka*, trans. Willa and Edwin Muir, New York,
1952, p. 54).

"own place" is inhabited by it; "his own man" will leave because "nice people don't live falsely and don't have doubles".

The social implications are very clear in the story, even if Belinskij was too concerned with thoughts of the betrayal of "naturalism" to find them. The ethical questions are clear: how does one recognize his own individuality? What, after all, is reality?

Goljadkin II, created by anguish, not only replaces our hero, but because he functions so brilliantly in society, even symbolizes all that Goljadkin Senior would be if he could. No less spiritually naked than Akakij Akakievič and therefore already damned despite Dostoevskij's palpable compassion, he would, if he could be what society demands of people as the price of membership, be doubly damned, for even the vestige of conscience evident would no longer be. But perhaps that is, after all, one of Dostoevskij's major points: the metaphysical is the requisite for self; the vestige of conscience in Goljadkin is his only tie to identity. Only a vestige, it cannot support him and prevent his disintegration and dissolution.

The subconscious is the single most important factor governing Goljadkin's life, controlling him not only from within, but flowing over to infect the total context of his life. Repression, initiated by the social demands and pressures of his environment, incubated the schizophrenia. Goljadkin's dream, the center of the work because it dramatically reveals his distress, is fully comprehensible within the context in which it appears. There is little of the supernatural in *The Double*. It focuses primarily on the negative role of society and on the causes, results, and ethical implications of duality. It is an important first step towards comprehending Dostoevskij's use of the subconscious and its function as an expression of his world view.

The dreamer, the madman, the theme of the displacement of man and his pathological disintegration, infuse almost all of even the earliest stories. Dostoevskij's all but consistent psychological approach — already evident in *Poor Folk*, his first work,[14] but long ignored in the search for "naturalism" and "socialist realism" — enables him to verbalize, realistically or symbolically, nonverbal sensations, enables him to direct the reader's vision through the surface of many of his characters and,

---

[14] Simmons (*Dostoevsky*, pp. 22-23) considers Devuškin Dostoevskij's first double, writes that "resemblances have already been pointed out [between Devuškin and Dostoevskij], and it is more than likely that the youthful introspective author unconsciously drew upon the struggle of contending forces in his own nature in portraying the dualism of Devushkin."

hence, accomplishing what Leon Edel has called "the inward turning",[15] to direct it outward.

The psychological description of characters involves him, of course, in the intimate delineation of the subconscious. As we have just seen, the dream, itself a subconscious manifestation, achieves a special prominence and becomes highly significant, even (in such a work as *Crime and Punishment*) almost indispensable. It is the dream, in part, which symbolically directs our attention to the "meaning" of the story, to its reality; representing the reality of "the invisible life", it interprets reality itself.

No less than Tolstoj, Dostoevskij is interested in the semi-conscious, in the state between reality and dream. In Dostoevskij this state, often precipitated by physical exposure and a "chilling", usually takes the form of "delirium", of "fever", consists, in a story like *The Landlady*, of an almost indistinguishable area somewhere between the hysterical and the rational.

Telling us what is going on within his characters, focusing on the internal — especially in the criminal, the psychotic, the epileptic, the "delirious", the hysterical — he describes chaos and disorder. The floating thoughts of the subconscious (which cannot always be hung on a peg of detached logic) have a logic of their own: as in *The Double*, by suggesting the reasons for the pathological, by describing the inner struggle, they supply the keys essential for interpretation, for they contain the essence of one of Dostoevskij's major themes — dual man torn apart by the conflict between the rational and irrational, between his evil impulses and his potential for good.

Mr. Proxarčin repeats one of the central metaphors in Dostoevskij — placeless man "tucked away in his corner". Proxarčin was "a man totally insignificant", sometimes "he looked more like the shadow of a rational being than that rational being itself".

The dualism of Proxarčin also results from the pathological expression of human frustration, but, unlike Goljadkin, he does not see a duplicate self; rather, he is two selves, he is both evil and good (he too, his dream reveals, has a conscience), but the evil predominates. Duality, therefore, need not be externalized. Extreme niggardliness, to the extent of converting man into an insect, is itself an effect of pathology. Proxarčin's "unmistakable parsimony" is highly symbolic.

Having retreated from life and almost completely withdrawn from reality ("if ... anyone, even somebody on friendly terms with him, poked

[15] In his chapter by the same name in *The Modern Psychological Novel* (New York, 1964), pp. 27-34.

his inquisitive nose uninvited into his corner" he "could not endure it"), he was "prone to ill health" — and in Dostoevskij isolation always predisposes to both physical and mental illness, the two being inseparable. His life, in total, consists of nothing more than the contents of his black box (which contained "two rags, a pair of socks, half a handkerchief, an old hat, several buttons, some old soles, and the uppers of a pair of boots ... all sorts of odds and ends, scraps, rubbish, trash ...") and the 2,497 rubles and a half that he had hidden in his mattress.[16] A grotesque creature in life and death ("[his corpse] quite unexpectedly plunged head downward, leaving in view only two bony, thin blue legs, which stuck upwards like two branches of a charred tree"), "the unsuspected capitalist" goes utterly mad at the thought that he might have his money stolen, dies in panic, because, as Okeanov said afterwards, he would not "take into consideration that we all have a hard time".

Money, of course, symbolizes strength and power. As such, the obsession to hoard it and preserve it is clear enough. The money *is* his place in life; it removes him from reality because reality would demand its consumption, hence, the disappearance of his place as its price of admission. He lives in misery so that he will not live in misery. His misery makes possible his fantasy (and though this fantasy life is never described it seems implicit in his character, supplies the major motivation for his hoarding), which, in turn, requires the power represented by the money. He is, then, condemned to lead two starkly contrasting lives, each directly dependent on the other, both possible because Proxarčin is another of Dostoevskij's "rags". Ironically, Makar Ivanovič accuses him, after his death, of not having "enough imagination". The pathology of Dostoevskij's characters rests precisely in their having too much imagination, that is, in their inability to accept nothingness as the final answer. That is why frustration becomes so intense that it represses desire, leading to duality.

Mr. Proxarčin also illustrates Dostoevskij's typical care in preparing for the dream so that its function is at once psychological and literary. The dream in Dostoevskij, even in these early works, is never born just to provide sensational effects. It is never an appendage; rather, consistent throughout Dostoevskij, it is preceded by a most carefully delineated buildup of pressure, as madness is. It reflects back and ahead and in, always adding meaning. It is enlightening to outline the events immediately preceding and leading to Proxarčin's dream.

---

[16] Like Gogol' ("She had exactly three warts ...."), Dostoevskij achieves a sense of reality by specificity.

Having a joke at Proxarčin's expense, one of the boarders tells of a plan to penalize men in the civil service who were "entirely devoid of social graces" by deducting "something from their salary". Proxarčin begins to show "unexpected qualities"; he becomes "scared" and "suspicious", develops "a passion for investigating the truth". Others begin "to discover that there was a great deal that was fantastical about him". The news of his peculiar behavior reaches "him himself at last"; immediately, he goes out into the night, disappears "for an indefinite period"; upon his return, "the lost man was unconscious"; he cries out "at the top of his voice" when put back into bed, his feet "on his sacred box", and he touches the dummy sister-in-law planted there as a joke. He remains "for two or three days closely barricaded by the screen ... cut off from all the world and its vain anxieties"; he is in bed, "lying low ... just as the hare lies close to the earth when it hears the hunter"; he makes an effort to get up and join the other lodgers at tea, sinks back, dreams.

Deeply threatened, growing increasingly insane from the tension surrounding him — and there is in Dostoevskij almost invariably a metaphor of a crushed or hunted animal symbolizing the pressures to which man is exposed — he, as so many of Dostoevskij's characters, makes a final gesture to rejoin humanity; failing, he retreats to the dream, for despite the anguish it often causes, the reliving of its causes is itself a pressure-relieving device. The very first thing he dreams about is the cup of tea he could not have in reality.

The dream supplies information absent from the narrative, dramatically fills in details about Proxarčin's life we did not know before. It also reveals what is essential to an understanding of the story: Proxarčin is tortured by guilt. It suggests the possible cause of the guilt and its degree and quality.

... Prokoyevich ... introduced ... some scheme concerning sisters-in-law and the moral relation of various worthy people to them ... [Proxarčin] was in haste to defend himself .... [He began] dreaming again ... that he was receiving money in his office.

In doing the paper round it ... he looked about him quickly, and made haste ... to subtract half of the lawful wages ... and conceal it in his boot .... he made up his mind ... to give his landlady what was due ... to buy certain necessities, and to show anyone it might concern ... that his salary had been deducted, that now he had nothing left to send his sister-in-law; then to speak with commiseration [of her] ... the next day and the day after ... that his companions might not forget. ... he observed that Andrey Efimovich ... [who] hadn't said a word to him for twenty years ... was [also] counting his silver ... [saying] "Money!" "If there's no money there will be no porridge ...." "And I have seven children, sir." ... [Efimovič gestures] then glances with indignation at

Semyon Ivanovich [Proxarčin] as though it were Mr. Prokharchin's fault that he was the father of seven. ... and though [Proxarčin] was convinced of his innocence ... it seemed to appear that in fact no one else was to blame ... Panic-stricken, he started running, for it seemed the bald gentleman was running after him, meant to take away his salary. ... Prokharchin ran and ran .... Beside him was running too an immense number of people ... jingling their money ... there was the noise of fire engines.[17]

Proxarčin dreams on, and we discover what had happened when he had disappeared a few days earlier. We meet the "drunken cadger" again; Proxarčin feels "just as then in reality". There is a crowd. He is led into the thickest part of it, "squeezed as though in a pincers". "In a whirl of fever and delirium all sorts of strange figures began flitting before him. He remembered some of them". He remembered "a man seven feet high, with whiskers half a yard long", another, a boy, from "whom our hero had received a shove by way of a lift on to another fence, when he had been disposed to climb over it, possibly to save someone". There is an old man "with a sickly face" he had seen before, who now, "with a milk-can and a quart pot in his hands, made his way through the crowd to the house in which his wife and daughter were burning together with thirteen and a half rubles under the bed". Most distinct of all, "was the poor, sinful woman of whom he had dreamed more than once during his illness". She was waving her crutch, shouting "more loudly than the firemen" that her children had turned her out and she had thereby lost two coppers. "The children and the coppers, the coppers and the children, were mingled together in an utterly incomprehensible muddle ...." At last, still watching the fire, Proxarčin is terrified, "for he saw that all this was not, so to say, an accident", and that he would be punished. A peasant with a singed beard began "stirring up the people against Semën Ivanovič. The crowd pressed closer and closer". Proxarčin suddenly realizes that the peasant is a cabman he had once cheated "in the most inhuman way" to avoid paying his fare, "as he ran as though he were barefoot on hot bricks". Proxarčin tries to scream, feeling the "infuriated crowd ... twining round him like a many-colored snake, strangling him, crushing him".

The fire exists in reality too, for when Proxarčin awakes he sees "that his whole corner was on fire, even his precious mattress". He runs, clutching the mattress. He is seized. The only fire is in his head.

It is a very long dream (about one seventh of the total story), and the most consistent thing about it is Proxarčin's need to defend himself;

[17] *Mr. Prokharchin, White Nights, and Other Stories*, trans. Constance Garnett (London, 1957), pp. 304, 305.

for the need bespeaks his guilt. That is why he hides half his money, how he rationalizes his obligation to humanity. Before the isolation immediately preceding the dream, he had shrieked upon touching the very symbols of his duality, the (mock) sister-in-law (humanity), his box (selfishness), and now he defends his righteousness by inculcating the poverty of his sister-in-law in the minds of his friends, as if to say "Would I not help such a creature if I had the means?" Surely, he further rationalizes, he cannot be responsible for the seven children of Andrej Efimovič; even if his money would make their lot easier, is he his brother's keeper? But he runs away, unconsciously recognizing responsibility, for he will not give up his money; after all, look at the number of people, all with silver in their pockets, running too. The world is on fire and he watches. He sees a man's family consumed along with the precious few rubles he had hoarded — a man like him, who had denied himself and the family now burning even a taste of life. There is the old lady who shouts her anguish at losing two coppers, equates coppers and children, confuses greed with humanity. She too is a pathetic, immoral animal. Finally, led by a man he had cheated so that he could add to his money-power, the crowd attacks him — as it threatens Vel'čaninov and Raskol'nikov in their dreams — for even if he has not started the hellish conflagration, he has failed as a human being because he does nothing to assuage the agony of mankind. But he cannot, and this is his agonizing dilemma. It is also man's, as the irrational (spiritual) is repressed and cannot sustain him in his shadowy existence.

The potential for further interpretation inherent in the dream is great. As a literary and psychological device it is illustrative of Dostoevskij's genius. The events of the story, their tempo and quality, cause the dream; and the dream, reciprocally, makes clear the events of the story and their tempo and quality.

Having symbolically clarified the total make-up of a character, the dream also predicts what follows in the story. In Goljadkin's case, institutionalization inevitably follows because utter madness is his only escape. For Proxarčin, because he is strengthened by his money and, thereby, precluded from total psychological withdrawal, death follows. But the dream, precisely because it is born of the character and is integrated with our text-created expectations, must not always lead to negative results. In *Crime and Punishment*, for example, the final dream, reflecting a moral change in Raskol'nikov, predicts his incomplete but substantial return to humanity.

Mr. Proxarčin is only a slight story. It is very early Dostoevskij too.

It contains, however, unmistakable evidence of Dostoevskij's skill with the subconscious and his ability to integrate it within the fiber of his works so that it will meet the literary requirements of fiction. It reveals his ability to reshape traditional devices and use them artistically, profoundly, and compellingly.

The Landlady is both representative and exceptional Dostoevskij. The outrage of the critics ringing in his ears, Dostoevskij never again was to write such a purposely obscure horror story. It stands as the only one of its kind. But it is also Dostoevskijan, not merely because it is the most extreme example of his predilection for the melodramatic, but, more importantly, because Ordynov belongs to the same world from which Goljadkin and Proxarčin and almost all of Dostoevskij's leading characters are estranged. Like most of the others, he has led "a quiet and solitary life"; he has "his heart torn with a sort of unconscious sadness"; he "shut himself up ... as though he had renounced the world"; he was "totally incapable of forcing other people to stand aside when needful to make some sort of place for himself among them".

Goljadkin's strange, shoeless appearance, Proxarčin's incredible and unnecessary shabbiness and filth, represent men at the brink of madness. Ordynov's appearance forces people to look "at him rudely and strangely. He saw that they took him for a madman or a very original, eccentric fellow [which was, indeed, perfectly correct]." Goljadkin shivers and constantly feels the earth "sway beneath him". Proxarčin, late in his story, has "glittering, feverish ... eyes", is earlier described as "delirious". Ordynov "felt overcome by a feverish shiver again; he felt, too, as though the earth were shaking under him". They are all dreamers, and Ordynov seems at times to be almost as mad as Goljadkin, or at least as "feverish" as Proxarčin. But there are problems which preclude a judgment that these characters are all doubles.

The misery of Proxarčin and Goljadkin, within the context of reality, is consistent; not a single ray of hope lights Goljadkin's life, and Proxarčin finds hope only in the fantasies he must have. Goljadkin's warmest moment comes when he reaches out to embrace his own projection, a double who will soon humiliate and totally destroy him. His removal to an asylum is a natural event, only the crowning ignominy of a meaningless existence. Proxarčin, living only with his money, barely exists. Ordynov, on the other hand, at least as we first meet him, can even know "a sensation of gentle gladness and serenity". There was "a faint flush" of life in his cheeks, as "he drew deep and eager breaths of the cold fresh air. He felt unusually lighthearted".

Going back in time, Dostoevskij reveals how three years before Ordynov had been kept waiting "a long while" to be received by his guardian,"then he walked into a dark, lofty, and deserted room". Accepting the pittance left by his father, "he went out into the street". It was the kind of night that had finally destroyed the last traces of sanity in Goljadkin and had precipitated the appearance of his double: "It was a cold, gloomy, autumn evening .... There was a glow of fire in his eyes; he felt feverish, and was hot and chilly by turns". Thereupon, he immediately shuts himself off from the world, and "within two years had become a complete recluse".

We never quite get to know exactly what Ordynov's "fever" consists of. Had he but caught a chill that cold night it could hardly explain the duration and persistence of his "feverishness". Such an oversimplified conclusion is inconsistent with the function of "fever" throughout Dostoevskij, where it is consistently symptomatic of mental distress. In much later works, both Raskol'nikov and Ivan Karamazov, to cite but two examples, are burning up with fever exactly at those times when they are acutely tormented by a conflict between their rationalism and their Christianity. Physical illness *per se* is of little concern to Dostoevskij, and even his attraction towards epilepsy can be explained by the psychic and mystical significance it held for him. There is more than adequate evidence that the cold night also precipitated Ordynov's delirium, and that, symbolically, the night is his rejection by society, reflects his "placelessness", for his only existence consists of finding shelter from the real world in the world of dreams (which explains his lightheartedness when we first meet him). We are told that "he had never known his parents", that "he had to put up with the coarse and brutal treatment from his schoolfellows". But we are also told that "even as a child he had been thought strange".

Immediately after seeing Murin and Katerina, evidence of his delirium becomes ever clearer. As in *The Double*, there is frequent reference to being "weighed down", "crushed", and, almost simultaneously, to a state of "upheaval and chaos". His delirium erupts from within. Contact with life, emphasizing his isolation from it, makes him feel "as though his life had been broken in half". The aura of insanity engulfs him: his sleep "was not sleep but the agonizing unconsciousness of illness"; "the room seemed to him to be going round".

It is precisely one of the difficulties of this often difficult story that we cannot determine the moments when his mind is clear and how much is "read" and how much imagined. If the incredible events which follow are to be believed as happening outside his mind, then the story must be relegated to the Gothic genre, perhaps dismissed as an unsuccessful fantasy. Belinskij's judgment that it is "monstrous" would then carry some weight. But surely there is another potential in the story, one which should not be ignored.

If my argument that Ordynov is either mad or close to insanity has validity, it becomes possible to maintain that the fantastic may be delirium-created, that the subconscious needs of Ordynov perform before us in the story. Such an explanation cannot make total order of chaos, nor need it (though the weakness of the story consists, I think, primarily of the mystery Dostoevskij seems to have so deliberately and, on occasion, unconvincingly, infused into it). There is a major piece of evidence to support my contention. Like Goljadkin, Ordynov also has a dream. I think it is no less revealing than Goljadkin's. Typically, Ordynov's dream flows so naturally from the narrative, is so consistent in tone with it, that it becomes clear that he has been dreaming and is not delirious only retrospectively, when we arrive at the point where he "uttered a shriek and woke up".

The dream is initiated by Katerina's "burning kiss", the first time he has ever been kissed, the first time he has ever belonged; and the anguish of his estrangement from life and his fervor to claim a place in it manifests itself as the kiss becomes "like a knife thrust into his heart". A "faint shriek" follows, he sinks into unconsciousness, and "then a strange life began for him".

In moments when his mind was not clear, the thought flashed upon him that he was condemned to live in a long, unending dream, full of strange, fruitless agitations, struggles and sufferings. In terror he tried to resist the disastrous fatalism that weighed upon him, and at a moment of tense and desperate conflict some unknown force struck him again and he felt clearly that he was once more losing memory, that an impassable, bottomless abyss was opening before him and he was flinging himself into it with a wail of anguish and despair. At times he had moments of insufferable, devastating happiness ... when a hope beyond words falls with life-giving dew on the soul; when one wants to scream in ecstacy. ... his whole soul was swooning in continual, irresistible yearning .... But to what end, what led him on and tortured him, and who had kindled this terrible flame that stifled him and consumed his blood, again he did not know .... Often he greedily clutched at some shadow .... Someone's moist and uneven breathing passed over his face, thrilling his whole being with love ... all existence ... seemed standing still ... and everything seemed shrouded in a long night of a thousand years ....[18]

[18] *The Landlady, The Gambler, and Other Stories*, trans. Constance Garnett (London, 1957), p. 266.

And he dreams of the "tender, calmly flowing years of early childhood ... the first sweet wonder of life", of a mother who held and kissed him — though we have been told by the narrator that "he had never known his parents" — then of a "wicked old man", "unknown", who suddenly appeared and shattered his childhood, followed him about, mocked him "like a spiteful evil gnome", setting the child's "inhuman schoolfellows against him". He begged the evil man to leave him, but he "sat by his pillow ... he drove away the bright spirits, told him unintelligible, thrilling fairy tales, tormenting him with terror and unchildlike passion". The old man went on until the child "sank into numbness, into unconsciousness". Suddenly the child awakes, a man; "the years passed over him unseen, unheeded. He suddenly became aware of his real position. He understood at once that he was alone, an alien to all the world, alone in a corner not his own, among mysterious and suspicious people ....." And he "saw himself borne along like an atom in this infinite, strange world, from which there was no escape ... crushing and oppressing him...". But he finds "no corner in all the universe to hide him". He shrieks and awakes.

Ordynov is a "rag", as Goljadkin and Proxarčin are "rags", an infinitesimally small and impotent atom in an infinite and suspicious and hostile world. Without self, he falls with a last shriek of despair into the endless black pit of life, pummeled by forces he cannot comprehend. Life is devoid of meaning; he cannot shape his destiny, nor even scratch his identity into it. Yet the life force — always powerful in Dostoevskij — would emerge. The creature would live. There is, whispers a voice, a chance for happiness, a possibility of being, of belonging. But the yearning is shattered by the reality of his fate. Love only tortures. He reaches out, his soul struggling for emancipation; but everything stops, the "long night of a thousand years" shrouds everything. Gogol''s Popriščin shouts for his mother as he is beaten in the asylum, Ordynov evokes the memory of a mother he has never known as he is beaten by life. But soon even the fantasy-created delight of childhood is destroyed by the appearance of evil, of cruel classmates who glory in their destructive powers as they mock him because he is somehow different and drive him further into himself. Evil turns paradise into hell, brings the horrors of reality to the innocuous visions of the innocent, makes men of children by shattering their pathetic little illusions about the goodness of life. It is a most painful education. Its meaning is clear enough: the world is insensitive to your needs; you are nothing; you can never be anything; you are condemned merely to squint at life from its periphery, and even the corner in which you huddle for comfort is not yours for you do not even exist.

It is possible that Murin has become the evil man of Ordynov's dream; it is even possible that the evil man of Ordynov's dream has become Murin. But how does one even begin to interpret Murin? He may be a double. Surely, our final impression of him as a humble protector of an epileptic and insane wife — and at this point in Dostoevskij's career epilepsy is not yet related to an oversoul and its function is primarily melodramatic; indeed, there is no *internal* evidence that Katerina is epileptic — is in extreme contrast to our earlier view of him as necromancer, mystic, hypnotist, corruptor, assassin, "murderer". Is his role as one "thoughtful and dignified" merely a "farce"? Perhaps he seems to be a double only because we see him through Ordynov's eyes, eyes so steeped in despair and so feverish that they paint those who stand in their way black. Or, then again, is Murin, like Hoffmann's Cardillac, a double whose evil is dominant?

I know no one who has convincingly answered all the problems inherent in the text. But, at the conclusion, a point of view which becomes consistent in Dostoevskij is described as Jaroslav Il'ič speaks of a gang of thieves having been discovered, and having for their leader "that pious, respectable, worthy-looking old man [the master of the house]". A question is then asked which I have already tried to answer: "What is one to think of mankind?" From Dostoevskij's bias, that deception is hardly surprising because man cannot, without faith, surmount the evil within him. Jaroslav Il'ič, naïve and optimistic, walks into the woods of life as does Hawthorne's Goodman Brown; both emerge deeply shaken by what they see there.

Ordynov had seen it all while still a child. But the perverse need of man to live even as he is tortured, and the enormous tenacity of the life force condemn Ordynov to live on. He returns again to the world of fantasy, dreams of an innocent Katerina mysteriously bound to a mystic. She becomes, once more, a "poor defenseless creature". Like Piskarev in *Nevskij Prospekt*, he cannot live with the idea that ideals are but illusions. Like the prostitute Piskarev would rehabilitate, Katerina is envisioned as a "free soul that had been clipped of its wings till it was incapable at last of resistance or of a free movement towards free life ...".

Ordynov cannot slash his wrists, but he walks aimlessly at twilight, through "remote, secluded and unfrequented places". His heart has turned almost to stone. Only when meeting his former friend, Jaroslav Il'ič, does he even feel the need for sympathy. He would believe that Murin had been a part of the gang that had been apprehended, but Jaroslav

Il'ič says that "Murin could not have been one of them. Just three weeks ago he went home with his wife to their own parts ...." What may have been left of Ordynov's world simply collapses into the dust.

The story is strangely reminiscent of Gogol''s *A Terrible Vengeance*. Here two men also vie for a woman named Katerina. Here there is also more than a hint of an incestuous relationship, of the mysterious power exerted by a sorcerer upon a sensuous woman. It is partially unsuccessful, not because Dostoevskij may have had Gogol' in mind while writing it, or Hoffmann or Balzac, but because it is hopelessly muddled and deficient as art.

Whatever merit *The Landlady* has results primarily from Dostoevskij's use of the subconscious. Dostoevskij was very early convinced that the delineation of the pathological and the psychological could not only serve the ends of literature but could encompass and express the philosophical and ethical, and even the least successful pieces he wrote are therefore necessarily of some profundity. Implications inherent primarily in the later works of Gogol' become realities even in the earliest works of Dostoevskij.

In these early stories there is no recourse to the collective unconscious, to epilepsy (except in Katerina, in a most perfunctory way). The repressed unconscious initiates the schizoid personality. Guilt or anxiety, causing the dreams, serve to elucidate their own motivation and function. Goljadkin, Proxarčin, and Ordynov, despite their apparent differences, are bound together by common denominators: frustration, estrangement, "unusualness", fervent imaginations, psychological agitation, fever, and mental illness. Also, their neuroses must be viewed against the background of intense social pressures. It is only later that blame (guilt) is to be primarily internalized (for example, in Raskol'nikov and Trusockij). Even Proxarčin's guilt stems primarily from social conditions, whereas, despite the acute destitution of Raskol'nikov which is surely a contributing factor to his own duality, he comes to recognize *his* responsibility. Trusockij, of course, gregarious, a man of means, cannot even use social pressures as a rationalization for his guilt.

The metaphysical is not involved. Even Goljadkin's anticipatory dream may be explained as a subconscious prediction of what the repressed unconscious recognized as inevitable. But in Ordynov's dream there is already an anticipation of the "Golden Age". His "irresistible yearning" is followed by someone "thrilling his whole being with love ... all existence ... seemed standing still ... and everything seemed shrouded in a long night of a thousand years ...". Seventeen years later, the Underground Man talks of the Golden Age, ridicules it because it is the plan of the utopists; but later, in *The Possessed*, for example, where it is described as the acme of bliss, it becomes a crucial part of Dostoevskij's vision. Ordynov's dream is ambiguous; I am merely suggesting that inherent in the lines I have just quoted is the seed of the promise of miraculous regeneration which is later to flower.

Netočka Nezvanova is not only an unfinished novel, but an extremely uneven one. The first two parts, very well done, are of interest here because they focus so minutely on the psychology of Netočka, the impact of the focus being enhanced by the first-person narrative.

The very last line of the novel ("But perhaps that was my fancy".) symbolizes the singular dream-reality aura of life as viewed from within a guilt-ridden, sensuous, imaginative, neurotic girl, a precursor of all of Dostoevskij's female characters torn apart by love-hate ambivalence: Nataša (*The Insulted and Injured*), Nastas'ja (*The Idiot*), Lise and Grushen'ka and Katerina (*The Brothers Karamazov*), for example. Her stepfather is deeply distressed psychologically too, for he "saw clearly that all his jerkiness, his inability to advance his talent, feverish haste and impatience were nothing but unconscious despair at the thought of his wasted talent".[19]

Efimov, punished by guilt, and by his placelessness in society, drives himself inexorably to total ruin, dies a madman. He lives with a woman who is the rationalization of his failure, and his guilt is rooted in his idea (shared with Netočka, who both revels in it and is anguished by it) that "when he had buried his wife *who had ruined him* [Dostoevskij's italics] all would go well again". It is a myth of course, one which enables failure to be exorcised by externalizing its causes.

Viewing everything from Netočka's perspective, one must suspect the "reality" described by her no less than the reality colored by Ordynov's delirium. The completely subjectified point of view, admirably suited for interweaving fantasy and reality, also precludes a determination as to where one stops and the other starts.

It is clear that Netočka is also "feverish".[20] Her feverishness, as a manifestation of her own guilt, is born in part of what she several times labels a "morbid" attachment for her stepfather. So perverse is this attraction for her stepfather that even after she witnesses him murdering

---

[19] *The Friend of the Family* (and *Nyetochka Nyezvanov*), trans. Constance Garnett (London, 1957), pp. 214-215.
[20] At different times, she is described as "delirious", "extremely distressed", "uneasy", "morbidly obsessed", etc.

her mother she desires to go off with him. Her guilt incubates in her toleration of the abuse of her mother.

But it is also a result of her frustrated longing that she be loved, that she and her stepfather be removed from the world of the destitute. She believes in the genius of her stepfather, broods because the world will not recognize it. Further, during an argument between her parents, her mother "began hotly and bitterly saying something to my father and pointing at me". From her point of view, she is somehow responsible for the misery pervading the house.

Netočka's emotional involvement with her stepfather ("He was painfully reflected in [her] earliest impressions".) grows in relation to her increasing awareness that there is "laughter on other faces". He is the prince who is to lead her from the dark forest.

Netočka feels that she attached herself to her stepfather because they were both suffering from the "same cause" — ostensibly, social deprivation and her mother's lack of love (and there is some truth in this) — but the mother is the cause in a different way too, for she stands between the girl and her stepfather and a dream of "paradise": "the more attached I became to my father, the more I grew to hate my mother".

In an internalized, dream-like atmosphere, Netočka reports having many dreams, often merely mentioning them in a single line. There is one dream-hallucination-delirium that is central to the book, but it is preceded by another dream which is not described.

Having been painfully lifted up (she was bruised) to look through a window, she sees the red curtains of a house belonging to glamorous people. That night she dreams of them, goes the next morning to see them again, later asks Efimov if they are going to live in the house with the red curtains.

On its most basic level, the curtains surely symbolize the world Netočka has never known, wealth, security, peace. Her stepfather is inextricably connected with them, and her relationship with him grows more and more fervent. She dreams of him after she dreams of the curtains (later, the aura of the red curtains spreads over what she calls her "abnormal" love for Katja, who belongs with them, and the relationship between the two girls strongly suggests lesbianism, Dostoevskij describing this relationship in more graphic terms than he ever uses to describe normal sex).

Netočka's sensuality reflects on her need to be made secure, and thus bespeaks her estrangement.

It is after her mother's death that Netočka, spoken of as an orphan, can no longer repress thoughts of her. Sobbing, she is invited to pray

but cannot ("I was overwhelmed, even terrified."). She recalls her stepfather's words that last night beside the already-cold body of her mother
and has a "nervous seizure". Flooded by memories which burst into consciousness, and remembering dreams she once had, she becomes delirious, has a "sick brain". She walks (or thinks she walks) through the lush
rooms, the perfumed air fanning her face "like a hot wind". It all seemed
as if she had seen this "somewhere in a dream ...". Thoughts of the
garret, the red curtains, then:

So here, here was that paradise! flashed through my mind. This was where I
wanted to go with my poor father .... So it was not a dream .... Yes, I had seen
it all before in my dreams, in my fancies! My imagination, inflamed by illness,
took fire, and tears of inexplicable rapture streamed from my eyes. I looked
about for my father: "he must be here, he is here ...." [21]

Behind a curtain, her stepfather's violin interpreting his despair, she
rushes to find him, is seized instead by a man with black eyes and bony
hands. The musician was not her father. "It was his murderer". The
people who just before had seemed, like her, to be "suffering agony"
as the playing went on, now laugh. She loses consciousness.

It is a "vision" of considerable interpretive possibilities. Two are
crucial. Convinced of her stepfather's genius, she holds the world responsible for his death because his wailing went unheard and he went
unappreciated. He is replaced, effaced, murdered. Her frenzy here is
palpable evidence of her blaming society for her stepfather's failure, and
her own impotence to help is one area of guilt. It suggests what may be
other guilt too — Oedipal guilt. At the very moment her father had run
from her after her mother's death she had chased him in panic, had felt
"as though something hideous was happening". That too seemed like a
dream, like a sensation she had had in dreams "that she was running away
from someone". She wants to run away, but to stay; to stay, but to run
away. Having witnessed her mother's death, she let it happen, thus
shares responsibility for it. She had a dream of paradise even while her
mother deprived herself of tea.

The intensity of the parts of *Netočka Nezvanova* stem from its narrator.
Painted with the colors of fever, neurotic love, and guilt, the real becomes
part of a dream.

The dream of the curtains clearly anticipates her removal to the house
containing them (where the love for Katja substitutes for the love for her
father). The rooms, the lushness, the "paradise" of the house had also
been anticipated by the dream, the anticipation being rooted in the

[21] *The Friend of the Family*, pp. 271, 272.

subconscious and in the metaphysical. Having seen the curtains from a window, her recognition of them is fully comprehensible, but the impression that she had seen everything in a dream is not. They stem from irrational sources, perhaps warning her of what is to follow — another "love affair" which will also be abruptly terminated.

Once more the repressed unconscious has led to a schism. Netočka's guilt could never be assuaged, but she is only seventeen at the end of this unfinished novel, and the rest can only be conjecture.

The pressures leading to her duality are both internal and external, born of guilt and poverty and frustrated longing and the terrible relationship between her mother and her stepfather.

Netočka Nezvanovna presages the subconscious in the works to follow in three ways: love-hate ambivalence, internal responsibility as a major cause of duality, the appearance of the metaphysical in dreams which are themselves anticipatory.

In Dostoevskij, dreams, an irrational part of man, place him in communion with the metaphysical, even, I shall show, as does epilepsy. The subconscious, therefore, has implicit in it a promise of another world.

Uncle's Dream is different from anything that preceded it. It is often Gogol'ian, with its interrupting narrator, its social satire, its externalization, its ironic humor which coats tragic implications, its bittersweet quality.

The dream of the old prince (whom Simmons, in an inspired moment, calls a "mechanical corpse"[22]) is, of course, the center of the work, leading to an unmasking of hypocrisy and to the moral regeneration of Zina. It also illustrates how dreams can be utilized to perform comic functions. The prince's inability to even distinguish between what happened and what he thought had happened only in his dream and the content of the dream itself are grotesquely comic. The comedy, however, stems not merely from what is explicitly in the dream, but from its implications.

The senile old man, vain beyond the point of foppery, perfumed, bedecking himself in a plethora of artificial contrivances (surprised when someone is not shocked by his baldness), after having been seduced to mumble a drunken proposal, dreams of a "very dreadful bull with horns", of Napoleon ("they all tell me I am like Napoleon"), of a woman's curves ("such a figure"). Somehow, from a subconscious fountain of youth, inspired by the proposal, he projects a wish fantasy in which he

[22] *Dostoevsky*, p. 70.

is no longer aged, but a bull equal to any task. Unable to determine how much he has dreamt and how much happened, he prefers his new role to the old, can mutter that she has "such contours ... and if I really had to be married ...".

The discrepancy between his longing and his capability is funny, and on one level becomes outrageous when he soon dies, thus retrospectively revealing the extent of his former decrepitude. But on another level, just as there are implications that, unable to exist in reality after his luscious "dream", the prince, despite physical symptoms to the contrary, died of a broken heart, there are implications that others in the novel have also been dreaming rather than living. Vasja, for example, moments before his death, says that "all my life has been a dream. I was always dreaming; forever dreaming, but did not live". The metaphor of life as a dream spreads, and we see how little the pretentious and crass social climbers have ever really lived.

But Vasja is separate from the others. He has only dreamed of living because he too late has come to understand that his despising the "herd", his separateness, was but "romantic foolishness!" And he too late understands "how much vanity there was in it!"

The dream metaphor thus serves Dostoevskij beyond the immediate needs of the novel, for it expresses another part of his vision: humility, involvement, moral commitment, suffering with humanity, and suffering for humanity — this is the price which must be paid for life to take on meaning and not be merely a dream. Suffering must not be evaded. It is an inextricable part of living; it makes possible the freedom dreams can only hint at.

Zina, another of Dostoevskij's dualistic women, is purified by suffering with Vasja as he dies. Sleepless and torn by grief, she emerges a different woman, a better woman.

The uncle's dream, then, funny yet tragic, affects the total setting. It stems, of course, from his repressed unconscious, but it bespeaks, from Dostoevskij's point of view, the shallowness of all who are touched by it.

Nataša, in a key passage in *The Insulted and Injured*, expresses Dostoevskij's concept of repentance:

I don't know [when the time for repentance will come] .... We shall have to work out our future by suffering; pay for it somehow by fresh miseries. Evething is purified by suffering....[23]

The first epileptic fit described in Dostoevskij — and seizures are crucial

[23] *The Insulted and Injured*, trans. Constance Garnett (London, 1957), p. 75.

parts of most of the later, more major, works — is Nellie's, in *The Insulted and Injured*. We are told that it is "the third fit this month" by the virago "caring" for her, even as Nellie is picked up from the ground. Much later in the book, upon finding Nellie in delirium, we are told that she must have had a fit in Vanja's absence.

Nellie's epilepsy, unlike Kirilov's or Myškin's, for example, is not preceded by a startling light, a euphoric inner vision, a state of transforming rapture (but in Dostoevskij, the fit implies the "light"). Epilepsy, from Dostoevskij's bias, is a holy disease. It is man at his most irrational, and the ecstasy of the fit presages the Golden Age, for experiencing the fit is as close as man comes to bringing paradise to earth.

For Nellie it serves a different function too: it removes her from the rational world at the precise moment when its agony becomes totally unbearable. I am not suggesting that she can consciously will herself into an epileptic fit; rather, that such fits are subconsciously triggered (they are so dependent upon subconscious "coloring" that tranquilizers are a vital part of the modern therapy offered epileptics).

It is hardly accidental that preceding the fit Nellie is accused of being a "damned slut", a "bloodsucker", a "louse", a "leech", a "rattlesnake", an "obstinate limb of Satan", and so on. These words she must have heard often enough to have become immune to them, but they have a singular horror now because Vanja — compassionate, meek, self-effacing Vanja — hears them too. The outside world, a part of existence which cannot be repressed, is witness to her utter degradation, and this makes it all too unbearable to be countenanced. Being herself beaten, Nellie, despite being "petrified with horror", can yet tolerate it. But at the precise moment when the shrew rushes at Vanja, the "inhuman shriek" is heard.

"Inhuman" is an important word. It is always used in Dostoevskij to describe the onset of a seizure. It is "inhuman" because it is beyond humanity — at the exact moment it erupts from the contracting throat the sufferer no longer suffers but is in blessed communion with the source of his immortal soul. It wrenches man from rationality and offers him a small promise of the glories that are somehow to come. In Nellie's case, it is as if metaphysical powers, feeling her distress, call her to them.

Not only does the fit remove her from reality, but, later, we are told that "after a violent epileptic fit she was usually for some time unable to collect her thoughts", and "that at such times reality is mixed up with delirium". Vanja adds to this last line, "and she had certainly imagined something awful", but that is because he has forgotten his own bout with delirium, when

"I woke up several times and always saw Elena's ... little face leaning over me. But I remember that as in a dream, as through a mist, and the sweet face of the poor child came to me in glimpses, through my stupor, like a vision, like a picture."[24]

I am suggesting that delirium, another expression of the irrational, often has a positive function of its own. It too removes one from the context of reality.

Nellie has a dream, and Vanja is correct in saying "that was a dream ... that comes from illness, for you are ill". But her dream of her grandfather bespeaks her need to belong; by dreaming that she must stay "here and look after grandfather" she creates a pretext for being needed. Also, her dream of grandfather bespeaks the treatment she received from him, when "he wouldn't listen to [her] and kept shouting, 'You've stolen a penny!'" It is the repressed unconscious projecting a source of her misery.

The great novels were yet to be written. Six years later, *Crime and Punishment* appeared as a book, in two volumes, and the apprenticeship served with the subconscious was to pay full dividends.

Dostoevskij most sublimely and profoundly exploited the literary and philosophical potential of dreams in *Crime and Punishment*. This novel is different from the works already discussed. There is a notable shift in emphasis, a more artistically controlled and functional use of psychological tension and setting. The focus, as in most of the mature works, has, most significantly, shifted from the primarily social to the primarily moral and intellectual. The heroes are no longer destitute clerks reacting against, disintegrating before, running from, inimical society, and their behavior cannot be explained essentially in terms of the immediate effect of extrinsic reality, as it can be explained in the early Dostoevskij and in Gogol'. There is, therefore, a new profundity not before possible. It is not man's society which is alone responsible for the oppression of man and for his suffering and perverseness, but his selfishness and his conscious demands to live outside moral law, beyond Mother Earth, which initiate psychological disintegration. It is, I think, a critical shift, for in internalizing the blame, Dostoevskij moves his art across the chasm separating the pathetic from the tragic (That is why what has lately become "naturalistic" seems not to succeed as tragedy. The tragic genre demands a freedom of choice and responsibility, a freedom to fail and suffer which is antideterministic).

[24] *Ibid.*, p. 151.

The choice Dostoevskij's characters make — and they have one — is essential. Even economic deprivation, such as that suffered by Raskol'nikov, cannot be viewed as final responsibility; it is a contributing motivational factor, but it cannot explain nor replace his lack of moral commitment to humanity (as it is also in Tolstoj, and the absurdity of placing this "naturalist" between Strindberg and O'Neill is unfortunately often lost on the compilers of anthologies).

It is precisely in the area of intrinsic guilt that psychological delineation achieves its highest potential in Dostoevskij, because internal reaction to uncontrollable external forces carries with it its own rationalization for neuroses, while the acceptance of responsibility—and flight admits this acceptance — is not only inherently more tragic, but more dramatic as well. Man tortures himself.

Raskol'nikov (as his name indicates) is, to be sure, another "split" man. Razumixin, Raskol'nikov's Horatio, says that he alternates "between two characters", and Svidrigajlov insists that he and Raskol'nikov are really counterparts. Like Ivan Karamazov, there is a part of him that is poisoned by intellect, that sees utilitarianism as man's highest goal. Ivan Karamazov's "all-is-lawful" idea exists in Raskol'nikov too, but in different form. For him, everything is permitted the supermen of society; they are the titans among pygmies, and they can be ruled only by ego. Murder, then, becomes acceptable, even salutary, for it is merely the weeding out of the weakest.

The characterization of Raskol'nikov, however, is in many ways more complex than that of Ivan Karamazov. Raskol'nikov's motivation is not clear. His deprivation — he is another of the alienated men — is partially responsible for his titanism. It is even strongly suggested that his estrangement from humanity has made him mad — he is already "feverish" when we first meet him. Indeed, much of the book's greatness rests on Dostoevskij's insistence upon the multiplicity of human motivation. Like Ivan Karamazov, Raskol'nikov, however haltingly, moves in the direction of faith, toward partial regeneration.

Raskol'nikov has four dreams, three which are described by the narrator, one which he himself describes and in which he does not appear, even symbolically. The first three dreams are tied together by the common denominator of violence, and each reflects light on the other and, in turn, is itself illuminated. As always, the dreams project backward, forward, and inward. The final dream is similar in function to that of Dmitri Karamazov's: it provides a central insight into his regeneration and into Dostoevskij's concept of it; but I take up Svidrigajlov's dream

first so that I need not later break into the discussion focusing on Raskol'nikov.

Svidrigajlov is evil. Dostoevskij, in the notes, described him as "conscious of mysterious horrors within himself .... He has convulsive,
animal-like urges to rend and kill. Coldly passionate. A wild beast".[25]
But there is something more. The evil in Svidrigajlov is precisely that
evil which Dostoevskij so strongly condemns, sexual evil. But in Dostoevskij, sexual evil is not merely a physical disease, for it is born primarily
of duality and thus bespeaks alienation and estrangement from Mother
Earth. It is a perversion of love which, of course, is a unifying experience,
treating and healing duality and uniting one with Mother Earth. Self-
willed, amoral, Svidrigajlov would appear to have somehow transcended
conscience, but the dream reveals that he could not, despite himself; and
his suicide is the natural culmination of the consciousness of his inability
to function beyond man. The dream destroys a myth he fostered, a
myth of his noninvolvement, one around which he has constructed his
life. The dream, which he must have recognized as the symbolization of
repressed guilt, erodes the foundation of his existence, and it crumbles
before him. It is a revelatory dream in a double sense. It tells both the
reader and Svidrigajlov of his inability to surmount his lechery.

It is anticipated by his attempted rape of Dunja, his "wandering between
various taverns and brothels". The weather reflects his own oppressiveness
("sultry and overcast"); he is soaked by the rain. He gives money to his
fiancée, takes a filthy room, grows feverish (and his being soaked offers
an ostensible reason for his fever, but, of course, it is symptomatic of
internal duress). Immediately preceding the dream are thoughts of
Dunja, and we even have a hint of a potential for regeneration in
Svidrigajlov ("But she might indeed have re-moulded me somehow ... ").
Then the dream.

The symbolism of the dream is clear: the body of the child who killed
herself because he violated her; a horrible five-year-old whore who disgusts
even Svidrigajlov, a man with a penchant for young girls. His cry of
"Accursed creature" is intended for the smiling courtesan, but it is
also Svidrigajlov's subconscious accusation against himself. He can no
longer rationalize his debauchment. The bullet he soon fires into his
body is his passing sentence on himself.

Raskol'nikov's first dream is incubated by accelerating emotional
distress. It follows several crucial scenes: his painful meeting with Marmeladov and his introduction to his wretched family (which leads to his

---

[25] Quoted in *Dostoevsky*, p. 165.

giving them the kopeks he had received from the moneylender); his receiving the letter from his mother (which "tortured him", made his "thoughts wildly agitated", made him claustrophobic, craving "more space"); his witnessing the molestation of a drunken girl (again giving money). Also, flitting through his mind, just out of the reach of full consciousness, are thoughts of "when *that* is over ...". He counts his kopeks, falls, completely exhausted, to the ground, dreams.

It is an excruciating dream. Like Ordynov, Raskol'nikov seeks out childhood as the period affording the greatest peace and security, and like him he finds only horror there. The letter received from his mother, that warm symbol of home and youth, was instrumental, of course, in effecting this return in time. The father, mentioned in the letter, appears in the dream; his role is to defend the boy (and it is his impotence which adds to the anguish of the dream). The setting is ominous, brooding. There is a church (the one he so loved as a child), the cemetery (tranquility), the tavern, which displaces both church and cemetery (he had met Marmeladov in one).

The mare being senselessly beaten with such unrestrained violence takes on special significance in light of Mikolka's three times repeating "my property", for Raskol'nikov had already met Sonja, herself "property", he has seen the other girl abused in the street, he knows his mother is "selling" his sister to help finance his education. Ruth Mortimer is correct in noting that the mare "symbolizes a whole class of sacrificial victims".[26] There is, however, another symbolic meaning.

Having already thought about the crime, Raskol'nikov is subconsciously warning himself not to commit it, and that is why the accent is so completely on violence. He is Mikolka, and the savage beating of the mare foreshadows his own axe murder of the moneylender and her sister. He even uses the butt end of the axe to kill the old woman, as Mikolka uses a blunt crowbar to kill the horse, thereby prolonging death, as if to spite himself with the recognition of the enormous will to live inherent in all life (and when he uses the sharp edge on Lizaveta it is only because he is totally surprised by her appearance, reacts in panic).

Mikolka and Raskol'nikov are both motivated by perverse maliciousness. The crowd — and there are almost inevitably crowds in the dreams in Dostoevskij — is like a Greek chorus, for it comments on the action, interpreting its meaning. Over and over again it reviles Mikolka as Raskol'nikov has reviled himself. The mood of the men, their sheer

[26] "Dostoevski and the Dream", *Crime and Punishment*, ed. G. Gibian (New York, 1964), p. 646. A good essay to which I am indebted.

recklessness, their gross corporality ("thick neck and fleshy face"), their hysteria to beat and destroy (the impotence of the church and the tranquility of the cementery providing an ironic backdrop), the determination of the horse not to die, this total scene of chaos symbolizes the tone and quality of Raskol'nikov's internal struggle and, later, the tone and quality of the murders.

The old man in the crowd, the leader of the chorus, the voice of conscience, shouts at Mikolka, but his shout is really Raskol'nikov's self-accusation: "You're more like a brute beast than a proper Christian!" The grotesque beating goes on, Christianity in the shadows, unable to control or even affect the evil of the tavern, even as Raskol'nikov's conscience cannot prevent his foul crime. The father, the intended protector, fails because he will not involve himself. His comment that "it is none of our business" is the voice of utilitarianism (Raskol'nikov's voice) disowning humanity. Had it been another voice, had it involved itself, perhaps the crime could have been prevented. The boy smashes at Mikolka for killing the horse, but it is Raskol'nikov beating the animal within his own breast. The boy fondles the dead horse and sees the blood; Raskol'nikov will see blood not only during the murder, but, compulsively, he will return to the place of the crime to see if it is still there.

The dream predicts the future. Raskol'nikov's comments immediately upon awakening — he cannot even scream — would seem, at first, to contradict the possibility of the murder taking place:

"Thank God it was only a dream ...." "God!" he exclaimed, "is it possible ... that I really shall take an axe and strike her on the head, smash open her skull ... that my feet will slip in warm, sticky blood ...." [27]

and is even followed by "'No, I shall not do it, I will not do it!'" But the dream contains the clue to Raskolnikov's ability to surmount this initial horrified reaction. It is not that Raskol'nikov wants to murder, but that he *must*. Just as Mikolka is a man possessed of a demon and cannot hear the voice of Christian sanity, so too will he be driven by internal forces which are inexorable, which he cannot control. Mikolka is drunk with spirits; Raskol'nikov is no less drunk with power.

Even fate joins the conspiracy. Distressed by the dream, Raskol'nikov wanders off his accustomed path, by pure chance happens to overhear a discussion of the old woman's evil nature, becomes again agitated and feverish as he hears of her being "stupid, senseless, worthless, spiteful,

[27] *Crime and Punishment*, trans. Jessie Coulson (New York, 1964), p. 57.

sick, horrible". His resolution not to commit the crime melts and disappears at precisely this point, and he prepares for the murder. The dream, then, aside from its symbolic warning, ironically directly influences the murder. Then again, it is perhaps inevitable, and the conversation about the old woman merely supplies additional "justification" for her destruction.

Aside from its function as a warning, as an anticipatory and revelatory device, the dream is the culmination of what preceded. It halts the action, forces the reader mentally to return to the previous pages of the text and review and reinterpret their meaning. We are not to be told until the following chapter that the idea of murder had entered Raskol'nikov's head the previous winter. Now, when we are told, the telling is acutely meaningful. The pieces begin to fit together, we even begin to understand what the anguish was that Dostoevskij very early in the novel tells us "had started long ago".

The following chapter also tells us about Raskol'nikov's superstition, which "is of recent origin". Retrospectively, the dream now assumes even more meaning, for Raskol'nikov's inability to heed the dream's warning bespeaks the intensity of the criminal drive in him; he kills despite everything, despite his superstition, despite the omens the superstitious seek out and interpret; the dream is surely a most potent omen the superstitious can hardly ignore. In a sense, the dream is not only born of the subconscious, it is his superstitious nature speaking to him. But, of course, it is all to no avail. Even his call for God's help is without lasting effect because he has repressed the *meaning* of the dream, and it flounders in his consciousness and cannot make itself heard.

The dream, further, becomes totally integrated into his life, not only because he henceforth acts out what it symbolized, but, rather, because the dream initiates his confusing dream and reality more and more. As he steals the axe, for example, he is suddenly aware of the "unreality" of it all.

Having dramatized his internal battle, the dream not only anticipates the immediate, but colors all that follows. Some four hundred pages after the dream, as Raskol'nikov kneels before his mother, we are suddenly reminded that in this very first dream the boy had been in his father's arms. In both cases he turns to the very symbols of warmth and security; in neither case does he find peace, for the resolution of his intense dilemma must be internally accomplished.

The second dream, colored by the first, takes place after the murder.

It is preceded by "a disordered state of mind", by fever and chills, by "semi-delirium", by the appearance of the police officer and Raskol'nikov's breathless, trancelike visit to the police station (only to discover that it is a summons from his landlady that is the cause of his being sought), by his overhearing a discussion of the murder, his fainting, his ultimate terror. He wanders again, buries the stolen articles, has a painful experience at Razumixin's (cursed as he leaves). Lashed by a coach driver, given a coin by a woman affected by his appearance (and his giving and receiving kopeks highlights the influence of poverty on his behavior), only to throw it into the river, he goes home, has a nightmare.

Less than one fifth the size of the first dream, this one is also primarily about murder, but, taking place after the act, the violence is even more concentrated and hyperbolic. It is the landlady who is being beaten now, by the very police officer who so threatens Raskol'nikov. By juxtaposition, Raskol'nikov and the landlady have changed places (both are destitute, driven creatures). There is again a crowd, a world of conscience which engulfs him and knows of his evil (despite his having convinced himself that no one knows of it). The landlady has taken the place of the horse too, the police officer the place of Mikolka. The murder scene is reenacted again, in all its "rage and fury". There is noise, "howling, shrieking, wailing ... an uproar", seemingly in exact contradiction to the relative silence of the actual murder, but it is Raskol'nikov's emotional behavior during the murder which is here being symbolized. The uproar recaptures its tone, not its action.

The dream enables us to see how little like the titan he thinks he is he really is. He identifies himself with the landlady because they are both beaten by life, and he "trembles like a leaf" at the voice of Ilja Petrovič because the officer, symbolizing justice and retribution, represents Raskol'nikov's own subconscious awareness that he has committed a crime and must, despite his deprivation and inconsequence, pay. The first dream anticipated the crime; this one anticipates the punishment. Its interpretive potential, is, in part, directly related to the first dream. The first one, a warning, had resulted in a temporary resolution to abandon the plan for murder; this one contains a line, once more invoking God's name, which answers the warning by posing a question: "God, how can all this have really happened?"

The terrorizing dream, despite (perhaps, because of) being followed by four days of semi-delirium, once it is over, relaxes the anxiety in Raskol'nikov, the tension of the story. The dream and its termination (and this holds for all the dreams) result in a tension-filled, tension-easing order, and, as such, duplicate the very rhythm of the book, as Raskol'nikov and the police officer engage in a duel which also results in rhythmic swings from tension to release.

The third dream is preceded by his strange confrontation with a fat man who has been asking about him. Chasing him, catching him, Raskol'nikov plays tortured host to the only thing he says: "Murderer". "You are a murderer". Some hundred pages later a rational answer is given for this man, but it is clear that from Raskol'nikov's view it is nothing less than his double, the voice of his conscience. He is accusing himself and can no longer rationalize the crime away. In the context of reality, the accuser then walks calmly away while Raskol'nikov, numb, weak, totally miserable, can only return to his room, where even the appearance of Razumixin cannot mitigate his agony; and he pretends to be asleep so that he can lacerate himself undisturbed.

His laceration, even as the dream will indicate, is the very beginning of regeneration. His accusations against himself are elaborate, but here is the heart of it:

"Oh, aesthetically speaking, I am a louse, nothing more .... Yes, I really am a louse", he went on, clinging to the idea with malicious pleasure, burrowing into it, playing with it for his own amusement .... "I've been importuning all-gracious Providence for a whole month, calling on it to witness that it was not for my own selfish desires and purposes that I proposed to act (so I said), but for a noble and worthy end ... ha, ha!" [28]

In this third dream, Raskol'nikov relives the actual murder, and the stranger who had called him a murderer is juxtaposed into the murder scene itself, perhaps, as it has been suggested, so that Raskol'nikov "might discover what evidence he might have for his sinister charge".[29] What is crucial is that for the first time Raskol'nikov can see himself commit the crime, in relatively undisguised fashion, without the mitigation afforded by symbolic representation. His victim only laughs at him ("overcome with noiseless laughter") as he strikes her again and again, and he is unable to kill her in his dream. This is surely because Raskol'nikov cannot stand to see himself actually kill again, that is, he is emotionally unable to project the crime in its full detail because he is different now. This, then, is the major clue to his regeneration. He relives the experience to admit its having happened and to admit his responsibility for its having happened, but he is so ashamed of its having happened that he cannot

[28]   *Ibid.*, p. 264.
[29]   "Dostoevski and the Dream", *op. cit.*, p. 650.

even face his previous act. He sees now that "she [was] afraid", that the "worthless creature" was a human being and that in ending her life he became a "worthless creature", or, as he put it earlier, "a louse".

Raskol'nikov only partially awakes from this nightmare. Svidrigajlov flows right into dream-reality, and Raskol'nikov must ask himself whether his dream is continuing.

In a sense, it continues, as do the others, for the remainder of the novel. The new attitude now revealed in the dream is what the rest of the book is all about. Dostoevskij, however, far too sophisticated to ever write a "rags-to-riches" story, well aware that duality never completely resolves itself into singleness, describes the positive influence of this spark of conscience, but Raskol'nikov, although he repents, never really repents, not even in frozen Siberia with Sonja, Christ's angel, at his side to show him the way. Tolstoj's peasants come to see the light too, and it enters into them completely as they burst into joyous song exalting Him who gave the Sermon on the Mount, but after reading the mature Dostoevskij and his profound insight into the incredible complexity that is man, Tolstoj's art, as magnificent as it usually is, seems somehow naïve because the philosophy which underlies it refused to accept dualism as part of man's inheritance. But, then, Tolstoj believed Rousseau and Dostoevskij never could. Raskol'nikov, I am trying to say, sees the light. Like Ivan Karamazov, he begins to mount the ladder; but even as he looks down from his new height he knows how much of him still belongs below. He renounces his theory, but he cannot renounce his heritage. When he makes his confession he does not even quite know why he makes it.

The final dream, in "The Epilogue", is only one of "the dreams that had visited him while he lay in his fever and delirium [in the prison hospital]". It is a dream about "unknown pestilence which was moving on Europe", about parasites which invaded men's bodies, infected them with a concept of their own invincibility, and about the slaughter that resulted when these men, "everyone putting forward his own ideas", were unable to come to any agreement about anything. Everything is destroyed in the conflagration that follows.

Allegorically depicting Raskol'nikov's prior belief in titanism, the dream is the final renunciation of this belief. Raskol'nikov is now aware of the end results of everyman being a law unto himself, the inevitability of society crumbling before the onslaught of intellectuals who, knowing no reason but their own, bring not heaven to earth, but chaos.

Carefully read, the dream also contains the ingredients of the miracle Dostoevskij envisaged as somehow occurring to cleanse the earth:

The plague grew and spread wider. In the whole world only a few could save themselves, a chosen handful of the pure, who were destined to found a new race of men and a new life, and to renew and cleanse the earth.[30]

It is a chilling vision, for like the story of Noah it requires almost total destruction before rebirth.

The first three dreams result from guilt; they are comprehensible within the framework of subconscious projection. The last dream, however, must be considered part of what Ivanov means when he speaks of this novel as being Dostoevskij's "first great revelation to the world, and the main pillar of his subsequent philosophy of life".[31]

The last dream cannot be explained as a subconscious projection; it stems from the collective unconscious of man, for it is mythic. It is a mystical projection of knowledge and insight which stems from the dawn of man's existence. Even as the plot of the novel concerns Raskol'nikov's estrangement from his immediate world, it concerns his estrangement from Mother Earth herself, for his crime bespeaks this estrangement, and the suggestion of regeneration implicit in this dream bespeaks the fact that repentance (albeit incomplete) is the first necessary step towards a reunion with Mother Earth. There is, from Dostoevskij's point of view, a pact between man and Mother Earth; it is unbreakable and eternal. It binds and commits him. It is a pact made before he existed and a pact that will continue after his death. Honoring it is essential to being.

The need to cling to Mother Earth, so clearly expressed in later works, is explicit in the lines Dmitrij Karamazov quotes from Schiller's "Eleusinian Festival":

> Would he purge his soul from vileness
> And attain to light and worth,
> He must turn and cling forever
> To his ancient Mother Earth.[32]

Raskol'nikov, at the moment he becomes aware, through the collective unconscious, of his abrogation of the pact with Mother Earth, is visited by her and made heir to a holy secret.

As one gets into the mature works, it is clear that dreams in Dostoevskij are not restricted to traditional functions. They are sometimes the medium through which man becomes aware not only of Mother Earth but, concomitantly, of the existence of God.

[30] *Crime and Punishment*, p. 524.
[31] Vyacheslav Ivanov, *A Study in Dostoevsky*, trans. N. Cameron (New York, 1960), p. 78.
[32] *The Brothers Karamazov*, trans. C. Garnett (New York, 1958), p. 105.

Dostoevskij's apotheosis of subconscious manifestations must, then, in great measure, have been born of his insight into its dramatic potential for the expression of his philosophical conceptions. It is through the irrational parts of man that irrational forces speak and teach. Dostoevskij's belief in the power invested in Mother Earth, bespeaks his commitment to the mythic, man's commitment to powers which he recognizes only through the irrational.

There are no dreams described in *The Idiot* — only things that seem like dreams — nor are there doubles in the traditional sense, that is, there are no subconscious projections of self functioning as characters, and guilt is not personified. There are doubles however, foils such as Myškin and Rogožin. Also there are internally identical characters, Nastas'ja and Ippolit; and there is duality, characters being "split" in the most extreme fashion: Myškin and Nastas'ja.

I am, however, especially interested in Myškin's epileptic fits, not only because seizures, as already noted, may be subconsciously triggered, but also because I think they serve a literary function heretofore reserved for the dream; besides, unlike Nellie's seizures, the aura immediately anticipating them is now for the first time described, giving us insight into the ability of this "holy" disease to efface reality and bring a glimpse of paradise on earth, and insight into its immediate relevance to the conception of Mother Earth, for even as the seizures lift Myškin above the context of reality, they return him to a more primitive and meaningful context, unite him again with primordial consciousness.

There is an enormous amount of psychological detail in *The Idiot*. Dostoevskij's minute presentation of states of mind is overwhelming. Externalized dialogue is often reported — and Dostoevskij's method is essentially dramatic; he shifts scenes quickly, does not long hold up the action for elaborate analysis — in a manner suggesting that there is still a residue of repressed and non-verbalized psychological activity, and that the inner life is not committed to social exposure: "that at least was what she [Nastas'ja] said; she did not perhaps utter all that was in her mind". This "holding back" invests the characters with most diverse potentials, for the suggestion that what we know of a mental state is incomplete prepares the way for even contradictory behavior to be rationally acceptable, such behavior stemming from the dark part of the psyche which has not been exposed.

If Dostoevskij the moralist had succeeded in making Myškin "a truly beautiful soul", "a positively good man", Myškin would have been a failure as a character, but he did not, and Myškin's success as a character is directly related to his complexity, his ambiguity. When he is merely Christ-like he is as contrived and unconvincing as anything in Dostoevskij, but the moralist made way for the artist (as he often did even in Tolstoj's most didactic pieces).

In many ways, Myškin is Christ: he is a rarefied and transparent individual; he has great intuitive insight; he is clairvoyant, pure, naïve, simple, humble, guileless. Further, he look like Christ as imagined by the nineteenth century ("... very fair thick hair, with sunken cheeks and a thin, pointed almost white beard ... eyes were large, blue and dreamy; there was something gentle [about them] ...".), loves children, has a great capacity to suffer, and so on. He is even, he seems to tell us ("I have no knowledge of women"), sexually innocent.

But the Christ image breaks down after a careful reading, or, more correctly, there is a different Myškin too. He has been withdrawn from the world before we meet him, will withdraw from it again at the conclusion of the book; his humility is vitiated by transcendent pride; his epilepsy is his mark of Cain, for although it represents his mystical unity with Mother Earth, it also symbolizes his deficiency as a sexual human. Moreover, he is attracted to the physical, becoming first interested in Nastas'ja after having seen her photograph in General Epančin's office ("'So that's Nastas'ja Filippovna!' he observed, looking attentively and curiously at the photograph. 'Wonderfully beautiful', he added warmly at once"); and Carr, standing almost alone, may even be correct in writing that Dostoevskij's intention "is surely to represent him as sexually innocent rather than sexually impotent."[33] Myškin admits that there is something selfish in him; and, like Rogožin, he seems to be obsessed with a death wish.

Myškin is both passive and active. He is an "idiot" with great intellect, a dependent man to whom others cling, an "innocent" man who attracts and is loved by two women. He is divided. He admits as much:

"The two thoughts came together; that often happens. It's constantly so with me. I think it's not a good thing, though; and, do you know, Keller, I reproach myself most of all for it. You might have been telling me about myself just now. I have sometimes even fancied ... that all people are like that; so that I was even beginning to excuse myself because it is awfully difficult to struggle against these double thoughts; I've tried. God knows how they arise and come into one's mind."[34]

As Krieger correctly points out, "in part ... this is God's humble man

[33] E. H. Carr, *Dostoevsky* (New York, 1962), p. 166.
[34] *The Idiot*, trans. Constance Garnett (New York, 1958), p. 300.

seeing in himself the weaknesses of others in order not to be the self-righteous judge. But Myškin is indeed concerned about his own 'double thoughts'".[35] Several pages before, we read that Myškin

of late ... had blamed himself for two extremes, for his excessive "senseless and impertinent" readiness to trust people and at the same time for his gloomy suspiciousness.[36]

From their first meeting in the train ("thank you [Rogožin] very much for liking me ... I like you ... myself") there is the very strong attraction of opposites drawing Myškin and Rogožin together. Rogožin, obsessive and demonic, seemingly is Myškin's extreme opposite, yet there is something unifying about the failure of both to be able to deal with a rational world. They are both irrational men and, despite the obvious differences of intention, they both create havoc. There is something grotesquely comic about them both too. Rogožin is the personification of passion, Myškin, of meekness, yet there are scenes in which the roles seem somehow reversed, when Myškin, echoing Dostoevskij's sentiments, gets so carried away delivering philippics that we might confuse his passion for Rogožin's: "Myškin was positively trembling all over. Why he was suddenly so agitated, why he was in such a state of ecstasy and emotion quite irrelevant and as it seemed out of all proportion with the subject of conversation, it was difficult to decide".[37] And when discussing Roman Catholicism, for example, Myškin is not only in "extreme agitation", but he exhibits "excessive abruptness", becomes so emotional that he grows "pale and breathless".

Myškin and Rogožin are both mentally sick men. Myškin's description of Rogožin could well fit himself: "I fancied there was a great deal of passion in him, and even a sort of morbid passion ... he seems still quite ill".[38] Both men are described as feverish, both act on impulse, both overreact. Further, even as there are negative qualities in Myškin, there are positive ones in Rogožin.

The first meeting in the train culminates, of course, in the final meeting of the two men over the dead body of Nastas'ja. It is clear that Rogožin has ultimately succeeded in destroying what was left of Myškin's sanity; it is also clear that the chain of events leading to Nastas'ja's murder was at least in part initiated and accelerated by the very presence of

---

[35]   Murray Krieger, "Dostoevsky's 'Idiot': The Curse of Saintliness", *Dostoevsky*, ed. René Wellek, p. 42.
[36]   *The Idiot*, p. 292.
[37]   *Ibid.*, p. 525.
[38]   *Ibid.*, p. 29.

Myškin. The merging is at its most complete stage as they sleep together on the floor by the corpse, two madmen who have found the world unprepared for them because neither could belong to it. Rogožin escapes the horror of reality through lunacy. Myškin, no less delirious, withdraws into himself and once more becomes an "idiot".

Nastas'ja, very much like Nataša in *The Insulted and Injured*, is inherently ambivalent, and Harkins is correct in calling her "the most dramatic of all Dostoevski's double heroines".[39] She is torn between pride and humiliation; masochistic, she immolates herself, goes off with Rogožin for pure spite, subconsciously aware that she will die for it. Her enforced role as a mistress and the guilt inevitably associated with it destroy her capacity to survive life, even as her corpse finally destroys Rogožin and Myškin.

Ippolit is Nastas'ja's psychological double. He is no less ravaged by a frustrated ego in revolt, no less irrational and intelligent, no less debilitatingly spiteful and self-lacerating than she. Myškin's perfection destroys him as it leads to the destruction of Nastas'ja. Living proof that Ippolit's theories are wrong, Myškin drives him into an ever-shrinking corner, just as Myškin's representation of the ideal accelerates the frustration of Nastas'ja, drives her to symbolic suicide.

Dostoevskij's view of the inherent duality of all men is nowhere more fully illustrated. Because there is the irrational behind the rational, the potential for irrational behavior creates a tension of its own, a suspense which, at times, is all but unbearable, for the reader's frame of expectancy is almost boundless. "What will happen next?" cannot easily be anticipated. Further, the use of contrasting yet similar doubles like Myškin and Rogožin enables us to view ambivalence dramatically: the two-sidedness of a single man being represented by himself and his double. Crucially, irrational man is motivated by his subconscious, and if subconscious drives are ignored by the reader, the plot reduces itself to absurdity, becoming a parody of itself. It must be absolutely clear that Nastas'ja wants to die, that Rogožin, despite his marriage to her, must kill her on their wedding night because he knows he cannot ever fully possess her, that Myškin must create havoc, for only then can he once more retreat to where he really wants to be.

Myškin has two seizures. The seizures, it is clear, function on several levels. Psychologically, they are cathartic, coming as they do exactly at that point when emotional involvement has become most intense, and

---

[39] William Harkins, "Dostoevski", *Dictionary of Russian Literature* (New York, 1956), p. 87.

even as Smerdjakov consciously uses his epilepsy as a weapon and an alibi, Myškin subconsciously uses his fits totally to remove himself from the intolerable. That the seizures also function on a literary level is manifest if we merely observe that, as in his use of dreams, Dostoevskij prepares for the seizures most carefully. The action, both internally and externally, is accelerated, internal conflict is exposed, external oppressiveness grows, self-accusation and doubt become more pronounced. The fits are beautifully integrated into the fabric of the story. They are dramatic culminations of an ever-increasing tempo, halt the action even as they intensify it; the concomitant scream, as in the dream, is the very apex, and what follows is a period of relative calm and readjustment. Then there is again the gradual buildup of tensions which will culminate in either another fit or Myškin's lapse into "idiocy". The fits, of course, cannot supply insight into the subconscious as the dream can, but the specific moment of their appearance points to both conscious and subconscious motivation, and, therefore, they "describe" the subconscious condition of their host even as do the dreams used in Dostoevskij's other novels.

At the conclusion of Chapter 4, Part I, Myškin's anxiety, which had been relieved as he earlier had talked most passionately to Rogožin about religion, had exchanged crucifixes with him, had even been taken to be blessed by Rogožin's old mother, is, ironically, immediately reactivated by Rogožin's conciliatory comment, "'Well, take her [Nastas'ja] then, since it's fated! She is yours! I give in to you! ... Remember Rogožin!'" Rogožin slams the door, and Myškin, tortured by ambivalent feelings and fresh insight that he causes unhappiness even as he seeks to bring bliss, in extreme distress, begins wandering in search of humanity and peace — for him, an impossible combination. Rogožin had asked to be remembered, and it is Myškin's inability to forget him and how much these two are alike and attracted to one another, that precipitates the fit.

He goes to find Kolja, but he is away. "Myskin went out and walked away mechanically". He "wandered aimlessly", he "was painfully strained and restless", but "felt an extraordinary craving for solitude". He "was pursued by something, and that something was a reality", and "he had at intervals begun suddenly looking for something". He wonders whether he had dreamed about the shop window. We learn that he felt "almost as he used to in the past when an attack of his old disease was coming on". Then "he caught Rogožin's eyes fixed upon him", feels himself pursued by his evil double. Leaving, he debates whether or not he is indeed Rogožin's rival, whether he is honest or deceitful. He thinks of the "higher moments" afforded by epilepsy, then of the "stupefaction, spiritual darkness, idiocy [that] stood before him conspicuously as a consequence". Driven, almost to spite himself, he goes to Nastas'ja's home. Revealingly, it is exactly here that he once more feels Rogožin's eyes burning into him. Tormented by a guilt he cannot express, "an irresistible desire seized Myškin to go straightway to Rogožin, to wait for him, to embrace him with shame, with tears, to tell him everything and to end it all at once". But he is already standing before his hotel, and he need hardly go in search of Rogožin, for he is hidden in the niche, and "those two eyes, *the same two eyes*, met his own". They look at each other, Rogožin prepares to murder Myškin, "then something seemed torn asunder before [Myškin]; his soul was flooded with intense *inner* light". A scream. "Then his consciousness was instantly extinguished and complete darkness followed". It was the fit.

It seems to me that the eyes following Myškin may be his inner eyes, his subconscious, for his internal debate about his treatment of Rogožin serves the same function as the dream and reveals his emotional torment, and its roots. Myškin has been "offered" Nastas'ja, but if his motives in wanting her were less altruistic than physical, his guilt can be explained without difficulty. Does he not perhaps attempt to see Nastas'ja primarily because he wants to reassure himself of his pure motives? It seems possible that he would embrace Rogožin "with shame" for precisely this reason. Rogožin's eyes, projected from Myškin, burn, I think, with accusation, not jealousy, and it is the accusation that most anguishes Myškin: "Are you different from me?"

I am not certain that it is fear for his life that immediately precipitates the seizure, for upon finding Rogožin in hiding, "Myškin seized him by the shoulder and turned him ... nearer to the light; he wanted to see his face more clearly". Then comes the flash of "*intense* inner light". It is almost as if Myškin had suddenly seen his own frailty paraded before him, and the fit, at the moment of vision, bespeaks not fear but intense horror and, paradoxically, relief in the discovery. He shouts "I don't believe it!" and not for help. He had "felt an extraordinary craving for solitude" yet searched for Nastas'ja, perhaps hoping to find Rogožin and be murdered, but he finds only the eyes. Rogožin's inability to kill him makes the other alternative almost simultaneously operative, as the fit itself becomes the solitude he sought.

The pace slows down tremendously, and the following chapter is the calmest of any in the book. Almost well, Myškin chooses to remain in seclusion. To become again a part of the world is to become again hurt

by it, but, with Lebedyev driving him out of himself, he has no choice.
The action begins its inevitable acceleration again as Lebedyev introduces
four men to Myškin who "have gone far beyond the nihilists". Myškin
is once more "agitated" and "uncomfortable".

Myškin's peace of mind is directly related to the peace he hopes to
bring. The stream of accusations against him wells up: Ippolit shrieks
that he hates him, describes Myškin as a "Jesuitical, treacly soul, idiot
..."; Aglaja, with whom he is very much in love, supplies the unkindest
cut of all, as she tells him that rather than kind, he is cruel, that he is
devoid of tenderness, that he seeks only harsh truth and judges unjustly.

Immediately prior to the fateful party, Myškin is crushed by Aglaja's
"becoming every hour more gloomy and capricious", and he becomes
aware that she is afraid that he will disgrace her because of her vehement
protests to the contrary ("Why should I be afraid on your account, even if
you...disgrace yourself utterly?"); he is afraid of precisely the same thing
("I shall begin talking and break the vase.") Here, some twenty pages
before the description of the events immediately prior to the fit, we see
Myškin's emotional condition:

Myshkin was in a fever all night. Strange to say, he had been feverish for
several days running. That night, when he was half delirious, the thought
occurred to him: what if he should have a fit tomorrow before every one?
He had had fits in public. He turned cold at the thought. All night he imagined
himself in a mysterious and incredible company among strange people ....[40]

He waked up at nine o'clock with a headache, with confusion in his mind and
strange impressions. He felt an intense and unaccountable desire to see Rogoz-
hin, to see him and to say a great deal to him — what about he could not
himself have said ....[41]

Again it is Rogožin he cannot erase from his thoughts. Before the first
seizure he wished to embrace him, now he must talk with him. His double,
the representation of his guilt, is the only one who can relieve the pressure
of it, but Myškin is too confused to seek him out, goes to see Ippolit
again, the very man who has already so tortured him (and this is one
reason why I wrote before of Myškin's subconscious death wish, his need
to lacerate himself). His fever, of course, is synonymous with his
emotional distress. His fear of having another fit helps precipitate it,
for he can at once punish himself and remove himself.

At the party, he breaks the vase, even as he and Aglaja had predicted
he would. The total absurdity of his position, the utter hopelessness of

[40] *The Idiot*, p. 511.
[41] *Ibid.*, pp. 511, 512.

his claims to humanity are symbolized in its shattering; his reaction is as intense as the guests' is mild. Speaking with abandon before it was broken, he is now swept away by hysteria, compulsively pours out words in a heavy stream, in an impossible attempt to "explain everything, everything, everything!" He must make his position clear or remain forever estranged from society, but he cannot. The metaphor of fever becomes traditionally adjectival now, as Myškin speaks in "feverish outburst". He must convince others that he cannot understand how "'one can talk to a man and not be happy in loving him!'" But he cannot express it. "'Look at God's sunrise!'" he says, "'Look at the grass, how it grows! Look at the eyes that gaze at you and love you! ...'" It is Christ who speaks, but a Christ who has seen eyes that do not contain love. The seizure comes precisely now, his last conscious thought of love. Dostoevskij verbalizes the root of Myškin's fit: "she [Aglaja] heard the wild scream of the 'spirit tearing and casting down the unhappy man'".

Myškin suffers the fate of all "perfect" men. If he insists upon his perfection he is precluded from involvement with humanity; if he wants to involve himself he also contaminates himself. He cannot have the best of two very separate worlds. Involvement, further, reveals his own fragility. This most innocent man is educated, but his enlightenment presages darkness, for he comes to know that there is much of the demonic Rogožin within his own breast. Billy Budd unwittingly destroyed himself because perverse humanity could not tolerate goodness. Othello is doomed because innocence cannot survive amidst deceit. Myškin does not die, but he is defeated by civilization. His defeat is intrinsic in his retreat to the sanitarium. Like Cervantes' "pure knight", Myškin had come into the world to succor the distressed, but he learns that "it was not that 'the Russian soul was a dark place', but that in his own soul there was darkness".[42]

After the second seizure, the pace slows down again. Another peak has been reached and what follows in this tortured, diffuse, yet intense novel, often seems merely bathetic. The seizures, critically positioned, not dividing but unifying the novel, accelerating and then slowing the action and tension, pace it. The major symbol of Myškin's internal agitation, Myškin's fits project ahead to his ultimate confinement, reflect back and elucidate the strange behavior preceding them. In a sentence, by illuminating Myškin's subconscious, they serve, concomitantly, to illuminate his behavior and the novel. But they do more. They focus our attention on the mythic element again, for they represent

[42]   *Ibid.*, p. 212.

the entry of Christ, and I need to examine them more closely. The first seizure, immediately preceding Rogožin's murder attempt, is described as follows:

"Parfyon, I don't believe it!" Then suddenly something seemed torn asunder before him; his soul was flooded with intense *inner* light [Dostoevskij's italics]. The moment lasted perhaps half a second, yet he clearly and consciously remembered the beginning, the first sound of the fearful scream which broke of itself from his breast and which he could not have checked by any effort. Then his consciousness was instantly extinguished and complete darkness followed.[43]

The second is not described at all. "Love you!" is followed by the seizure, but the "*inner* light" must be taken for granted; besides, earlier in the evening, before the seizure actually takes place, Myškin thinks it has begun, for "there was light, joy, and ecstasy".

I have mentioned that upon seeing Aglaja for the first time Myškin recalls having seen her before. He has, but not in the immediate world that surrounds them at the moment; rather, it is in his primordial memory that she is indelibly impressed, in his pre-existence consciousness. He is, then, clearly rooted beyond the confines of earth; and part of his reason for idiocy is apparently his inability to adjust to dual memory; that is, primordial memory becomes somehow indistinguishable from contemporary memory, and, if this is truly the case, it is inevitable that his memory, transcending earth experience, often makes him appear an idiot to others because he is indeed different. He is, in fact, clairvoyant, but clairvoyance, viewed externally, at the moment of its expression, before fulfillment, seems merely the babble of an idiot.

Even as clairvoyance is confused with idiocy, the epileptic seizure has in it the potential for misinterpretation. It too has a façade and a core. Primordial sources are the core of Myškin's clairvoyance, idiocy the façade; inner light (intense communion with the metaphysical) is the core of the fit, and ugliness and pain are the façade behind which it hides.

That which is "torn asunder before him" is precisely the invisible wall separating him from his spiritual origins, and, at that exact second, the barrier removed, the flood of light can enter, even as he can rush to meet it. The "fearful scream" is not of agony, but of immediately imminent ecstasy, spontaneous and beyond the power of will. It is the intensity of the light, its incredible concentration, that blinds, overwhelms, exhausts, and leads to the darkness that follows. It is the flesh that trem-

---

[43] *Ibid.*, p. 227.

bles before the spiritual, and Myškin, representing the descent of spirit into flesh, is for "half a second" called back by both his parents, not only by Mother Earth but by Father God as well, and, for that infinitesimal moment of time, he goes home.

Before the second seizure, as Myškin grows more and more agitated, he not only presents some of Dostoevskij's strong biases, he also reaches to the very heart of part of his world view:

"There's no reason to be troubled because we're absurd, is there? You know it really is true that we're absurd, that we're shallow, have bad habits, that we're bored, that we don't know how to look at things, that we can't understand; we're all like that, all of us, you, and I, and they! And you are not offended at my telling you to your faces that you're absurd? Are you? And if that's so, aren't you good material? Do you know, to my thinking it's a good thing sometimes to be absurd; its better in fact, it makes it easier to forgive one another, it's easier to be humble. One can't understand everything at once, we can't begin with perfection all at once! In order to reach perfection one must begin by being ignorant of a great deal. And if we understand things too quickly, perhaps we shan't understand them thoroughly. I say that to you who have been able to understand so much already and ... have failed to understand so much. I am afraid for you now."[44]

And it is here too:

"Oh, what does my grief, what does my sorrow matter if I can be happy? Do you know I don't know how one can walk by a tree and not be happy at the sight of it? How can one talk to a man and not be happy in loving him!"[45]

In fact, it is everywhere in *The Idiot*: primordial memory, Mother Earth, freedom through suffering, the epileptic's oversoul, man's duality and love as the unifying forces within man and with forces beyond man, the spiritual through the irrational, the apotheosis of the soul and the condemnation of the body, the denigration of schizophrenia and the glorification of epilepsy. Through Myškin Dostoevskij reveals how man's unconscious may be a great instrument of knowledge, and how irrational man is motivated by his subconscious.

Less dense and diffuse than anything of comparable length ever written by Dostoevskij, there is a restraint, a singular crispness about the prose of *The Eternal Husband*. There is even a disarming lightness. I find no evidence to contradict Simmons, who attributes its "unusually well-constructed plot and smooth narrative style" to Dostoevskij's having had time to carefully revise — an unaccustomed luxury — and "its comparative lightness of tone to a retreat from the serious work of *The Idiot* ... as

[44] *Ibid.*, p. 536.
[45] *Ibid.*, p. 537.

something of a relaxation".[46] Its "lightness", however, only throws its tragic implications into sharper relief, and its tight construction enables us to view Dostoevskij's treatment and exploitation of the subconscious in unusual clarity.

Trusockij is, like Myškin, "a man of property"; Vel'čaninov, his double, is "a man who had lived ... in grand style", one "who had command of himself". Trusockij and Velčaninov function within the framework of society. If, hiding from guilt, Velčaninov retreats from society, his exile is wholly self-imposed. If Trusockij is another of Dostoevskij's underground men, and he is, it is not because he jeers from society's periphery, but because he enjoys torturing himself from within it. He shares, with the other underground men, certain key features: he is inflamed by hatred and fury, is self-examining and hypersensitive; he resents yet courts and thrives on humiliation. But he is a different kind of underground man. Even as his name tells us, he is a coward, not a revolutionist. He cannot sustain himself by jeering because he is a sniveler. He cannot avenge himself because he is not only impotent, but ambivalent — he must love and succor even as he hates and would murder; he must run from shame yet he must court it and search it out if he is to survive. He is a psychological double. He is a natural cuckold destined to kiss the hand and admire the friend who betrayed his trust, and even the infidelity of his wife was predestined, being no more than the price he knows he must pay for his own absolute unattractiveness and mediocrity. Not only is his agony no less acute than Velčaninov's, it is more acute. He cannot ever change his position in life, for he is an eternal cuckold.

Velčaninov, on the other hand, assured and confident, lacking bile and malice, regretting the affair which resulted in the birth of Liza primarily because he cannot convince himself that he was in love with his lover, "had long [presumably for nine years, since the termination of his affair] been subject to hypochondria", "his vanity too began to change its character in solitude", "he was worrying about some sort of *higher* causes of which he would never have thought twice in earlier days". Velčaninov is also a double, divided in mind, a moral criminal who cannot expiate his moral crime without being exposed, and he reacts to Trusitsky in two contradictory ways precisely because of his subconscious need to be exposed — he runs from him, and he runs towards him. Liza, no less a symbol of his guilt than Pearl is of Hester Prynne's, alleviates guilt because the feelings she stirs in him convince him that he had been

[46]   Simmons, *Dostoevsky*, p. 221.

in love with her mother, but he cannot tap it all by pouring love on her because she too soon dies. He cannot even reveal it to Trusockij, because he prefers his own suffering to causing him further anguish. Master and slave trail each other, but the guilty one is the master, the wronged the slave. They need each other; the distress of each forcing them to become each other's double. Trusockij's anguish is mitigated by showing Velčaninov that he knows of his guilt; Velçaninov's is assuaged when he knows that Trusockij has known. The letter represents the catharsis. Trusockij haunts him till almost the very end of the novel, and Velčaninov's residual guilt makes him uneasy, but it can no longer distress him, for when Trusockij appears with a wife again Velčaninov has not only already thought of how eminently seducible she seems to be — even before he knows she is Trusockij's wife — but, eyeing the "unfortunate young" soldier in their company, recalling that such a young soldier had already once cuckolded Trusockij, Velčaninov can even think that "to be sure, everything is in order; the picture's complete". Men such as Velčaninov perform a service as lovers of such wives.

Kovalëv's "nose" is his superior. Goljadkin's double is too. Velčaninov, representing all that Trusockij would but cannot be — and he replaces Trusockij even as the other doubles crowd out their host bodies — is the projection of Trusockij's ego, just as Trusockij is the projection of Velčaninov's guilt. *The Eternal Husband* is about a duel, one removed from the external world to Dostoevskij's favorite battlefield, the psychological.

As always, Dostoevskij prepares for the psychological personification of guilt and anguish with meticulous care. It is not only that the events and emotions described grow more and more intense in anticipation of the appearance of the double, but that the third-person narrative, in Dostoevskij's hands, achieves a unique intimacy, creates, from the very first sentence of the novel, a subjectified setting, that is, it is presented outside of Velčaninov, yet it not only complements his mood, but is created by it. The promise implicit in the coming of summer ("the summer had come") is immediately nullified by: "and, contrary to expectation, Velčaninov remained in Petersburg". The dichotomy is immediate. The aura of unfulfilled promise permeates the early pages, ostensibly comprehensible within the context of the surface reality of the story. The setting, besides its normal function in literature as a backdrop before which the action takes place, is, in Dostoevskij, intimately related to the psychological action itself. Its mood-creating function is, of course, important, but Dostoevskij focuses on its density, and, critically, on its degree or lack of heat, for the external temperature is a concomitant of psychological withdrawal or involvement.

External heat precedes internal fever, which always anticipates the dramatization of emotional crises. It is for these reasons that we are early told that Velčaninov was enjoying "the dust, the stifling heat ... that always fret the nerves", and the almost immediate reiteration of his hypochondria converts dust and heat to psychological metaphors. Dust and heat are converted into anxiety too: "he was becoming overanxious about everything", and they precede his awareness that "'higher things' are mere illness". Serving as catalysts, the heat and dust accelerate Velčaninov's "illness". We learn now that he had been suffering from a loss of memory — and how thoroughly Dostoevskij prepares an external rationalization for Velčaninov's failure to recognize Trusockij. We know, of course, that it is not his memory but his repressed guilt that makes recognition impossible — that there are "inward tears", that "apropos of nothing" Velčaninov suddenly recalls figures he has wronged: a clerk he had once insulted, a woman he had seduced and had a child by and then abandoned. A parade of misdeeds follows. Not because he would consciously undo them, but because he cannot control his subconscious, and because he is spiteful enough to say "I'll stay here, even if I burst!" He is punishing himself. And it grows hotter and hotter. What had been "stifling heat" soon becomes "insufferable" heat, delirium and stuffiness — the metaphor of man weighted down is operative again. Despite the ever-increasing temperature, Dostoevskij, aware of the function of food as a neurotic's substitute gratification, as a tension-relieving device, has Velčaninov's appetite increase, till he recognizes that "there's something morbid about it". His agitation grows, and when he can objectify the cause of his distress as a man wearing a "damned bowler hat" which he had seen two weeks before, and which had peculiarly arrested his attention, it suddenly becomes clear that the acceleration of heat and oppressiveness and appetite all stem from that "strange encounter", and that the strange encounter symbolizes a previous encounter which is tearing him apart. Finally, in a frenzy of frustration, "he had strange dreams such as one has in fever", and the promise implicit in the heat is fulfilled.

The dream content is not very different from the other dreams discussed, except in literary function, for it is a dream that is to be repeated a month later. Both dreams not only do not stop the action of the story by merely filling in details and presenting information about subconscious activity, but they are so integrated into the action that they are a part of it, and their contents immediately flow over into the context of reality. They are, then, accelerating devices, and, as such, serve uniquely. Their role is not cathartic; they continue the acceleration of pace, of heat. They are terminated, as are most of the dreams in Dostoevskij, by a shriek, the apogee of despair.

There is again a threatening crowd; there is a "strange person", once an intimate friend of his, who was "dead", whom everyone expected to "decide on [his] guilt or innocence". Again there is noise. The "judge" is silent. In a fury, Velčaninov strikes at him again and again, in rage and terror but in "infinite delight". All shriek, turn towards his door. The bell rings. Velčaninov, awake now, rushes to the door, finds no one, cannot understand how such a "real ring" could be part of a dream, but, after all, dreams are "always a sign of fever with [him]". The face of the man with the crepe on his hat becomes somehow more distinct; he seems to know some "former great secret of [Velčaninov's]". The man is outside his window now. The "dream seemed to have merged with reality". The handle turns; the man, unable to get past the locked door, turns to leave. Breathless with terror, Velčaninov flings it open, almost falls on Pavel Pavlovič Trusockij. Only now does the tension ease. Only now can Dostoevskij, the pace suddenly relaxed, begin to prepare for the psychological duel. The crescendo is complete. A new chapter begins immediately, and from its very beginning there is again an acceleration which will culminate only in the second dream, the moment of greatest and final crisis; and what follows will be essentially anticlimactic.

Aside from its function as psychological and extrinsic narrative, the dream supplies substantiation and focus. We know what we had only surmised: Velčaninov cannot expiate his guilt, and he cannot rationalize it away; we know that he failed to recognize Trusockij because he subconsciously wanted to fail. The dream tells us he wishes him dead to alleviate his own suffering. He beats at Trusockij because he is but a foolish sheep who cannot even accuse him and, thereby, by exposing guilt, lessen hidden sin. The "infinite delight" is the sadistic pleasure of a superior man reveling in the fruits of his superiority, the sheer joy of making an inferior creature the brunt of morally initiated frustration.

Trusockij must show Velčaninov that he is capable of being a man. Velčaninov must face up to Trusockij's accusations. But Trusockij fails when he brings Velčaninov to see his intended bride, and Velčaninov, ostensibly, never has to really face up to Trusockij's accusation, for it comes only by mail. But until it does come, he lacerates himself.

The second dream is the culmination of this laceration. It follows

Velčaninov's destruction of Trusockij's plan to marry. Trusockij reminds him that he had called him "the eternal husband", and that he had never forgotten it. Velčaninov finally says that "we are both vicious, underground, loathsome people". There is an intense pain in his chest. The tension is relaxed at the intrusion of Lobov, but never broken because the pain does not leave for an instant. The interlude over, the pain becomes so intense that Trusockij, "as though it were a question of saving his own son", treats it, relieves it. Just before he falls asleep, Velčaninov mutters "you are better than I am! I understand it all, all …. Thank you".

He dreams he is in a "waking delirium". It is like the dream he had before, only everything is heightened. Now he can recognize the "judge". He cannot determine whether it is real or delirium: "But if this is not delirium, how is it possible that the clamor should not have waked Pavel Pavlovič?" And he even sees him as he sleeps on the sofa, as he is, in reality, on the sofa. The crowd presses about him, others "were bringing something in with them, something big and heavy". All eyes are on Velčaninov. Convinced it is reality, he stands on tiptoe to see what is being carried up the stairs. Again, "as in the earlier dream", the doorbell rang violently. He screams, wakes up, leaps out of bed, and, with his hands before him, "rushed straight toward the place" where Trusockij had been asleep, touches hands stretched out above him, realizes that Trusockij had been standing over him with a razor to murder him.

Velčaninov's humiliation of Trusockij at the Zaxlebinins', the recollection of other pains he had caused him, Velčaninov's incredibly selfless attempts to relieve his painful chest — ostensibly the result of a liver condition, but of course, the weight of sin that crushes Velčaninov — the love of a humiliated creature who fawns on him and its implications ("I understand it all"), this steady procession of events creates the "waking delirium".

This dream which is not a dream saves Velčaninov's life, for he could not consciously have anticipated his murder, even as Trusockij did not prepare for it. The doubles had spontaneously come to the conclusion that there would be an attempt, that there *should* be an attempt. It is Velčaninov's guilt that warns him of the upraised hands even though he cannot see them, for the guilt anticipates and reacts independently. Velčaninov, subconsciously, excepts to be murdered, now, at the height of his humiliation of Trusockij. The metaphysical is not involved.

The duel is over, so is the oppressive duality. Truscockij has tried to do what he had to do. Velčaninov, in pain from his torn hand, has expiated his sin, and the weight lifts from his chest. It remains only for the letter to make him what he had been over nine years before. At the final confrontation, Velčaninov shows Trusockij his hand; Trusockij whispers "Liza". They part forever. Momentarily disturbed, Velčaninov "did not turn off to the right to visit the provincial lady of his acquaintance", but it is but a very temporary setback. The psychological confrontation is over. More than nine years have passed, and, having come full circle, all is as it then was. Trusockij will be cuckolded again, Velčaninov will find another lover. It is a comic conclusion to a story in which the repressed unconscious has led to duality and to the manifestations of the subconscious which reveal the guilt that is at the heart of it.

In the chapter called "Analysis", in which Dostoevskij quite brilliantly analyzes the motivations of Velčaninov (through Trusockij), there is ample evidence of Dostoevskij's conviction that the unconscious can serve as a source of knowledge. Also, interestingly enough, he understood that the conscious part of the recipient of unconscious information must convert the irrational to the rational before it becomes meaningful in terms he can readily accept. For example, Velčaninov had a "positive conviction, which suddenly grew strong within him" that he would call on Trusockij. "Why? What for? He had no idea, and, with repugnance, refused to know". But this conviction, surely irrational, cannot be dismissed; hence, it must be converted:

This madness [the positive conviction] however — he could give it no other name — did, as it developed, take on a rational, as it were, appearance, acquired a fairly legitimate pretext: already the day before he had been haunted by the idea ....[47]

The Possessed, at times almost unintelligible, contains so much of Dostoevskij's overflowing bile that there is hardly a single figure in it who is positive. Satire was surely not Dostoevskij's bent, but here the sting of scorn is very widespread.[48] In fact, so much detail is devoted to political allusions and satire that it is possible to underestimate Dostoevskij's concern for the moral and ethical. The epigraphs, however, from Puškin and from St. Luke, leave no doubt that Dostoevskij is once again involved with his most consistent theme, the evil within man, his estrangement from Mother Earth.

Part of the difficulty in discussing this book from my bias is that the

[47] *The Short Novels of Dostoevsky*, trans. Constance Garnett (New York, 1945), p. 448.
[48] A most extensive list of things and people being satirized could be drawn up, e.g., bluestockings, atheists, bureaucrats, revolutionaries, intellectuals, etc.

sections most directly concerned with the subconscious were expurgated by Dostoevskij's editor, and "Stavrogin's Confession", so essential to understanding Stavrogin's motivation and psychology, cannot be considered an integral part of the novel.

Without the unexpurgated text, there are no neurosis-born doubles, but, as in *The Idiot*, there are foils, and there is duality. Strangely lacking in conscience — Stavrogin, for example, seemingly torn between good and evil, is yet beyond them — the characters are relatively devoid of guilt; hence, subconscious projections would be inconsistent. Perhaps this is one of the reasons why Stavrogin's "demon" was dropped when the novel appeared in book form; or perhaps, as Čiževsky writes, "it [the demon-double] might simply have changed the tragedy of Stavrogin into a psychic illness".[49] As such, it would have better suited my theme. In any event, the unexpurgated text would have irreversibly subverted Dostoevskij's stated purpose — as outlined in his notebooks — to make Stavrogin a "shadowy figure",[50] a determination Dostoevskij achieves only if we allow the novel to remain in the form which he approved.

"At Tixon's" aside for a moment, there are sections of the novel which are so obscure that they are dream-like, but no dreams are detailed. Dostoevskij even seems less concerned with "fever" than previously. Its earliest appearance, however, is vital, for it appears in the young Stavrogin, as "brain fever", when "behold — the wild beast suddenly showed his claws". Dostoevskij immediately thereafter raises the major question, even supplies the anticipatory answer:

Yet, how had it [Stavrogin's outrageous behavior] happened? It is remarkable that no one in the whole town put down this savage act [biting the governor's ear] to madness. They must have been predisposed to expect such actions from Nikolay Vsyevolodovich, even when he was sane.[51]

Thus are we early prepared for Stavrogin's incredible career.

Stavrogin is "split". "Real people follow him, but they take him for something totally different from what he really is ... he is 'split into two', he has no face, or many faces, or even all faces".[52] He exists, then, on two very different levels; whether he is "black" or "white" depends on the angle of vision, on whether the vision stems from an internal perspec-

[49] "The Theme of the Double in Dostoevsky", *op. cit.*, p. 121.
[50] He even remind himself not to explain Stavrogin, to "keep the reader in a quandary", etc. See Simmons' *Dostoevsky*, p. 249.
[51] *The Possessed*, trans. Constance Garnett (New York, 1961), pp. 65, 66.
[52] "The Theme of the Double in Dostoevsky", *op. cit.*, p. 119.

tive or whether it depends upon the other characters to supply insight.

Stavrogin believes in nothing, is protected from deep emotion by an impenetrable shell. He too is a nihilist. But he is also an underground man; no one else in all of Dostoevskij is so inexorably fated to remain forever on the periphery of humanity. His alienation, in great part, accounts for what Simmons calls his "psychological amoralism".[53] Šatov, who, like Dostoevskij, would "raise the people to God", points this out:

"You're [Stavrogin] an atheist because you're a snob, a snob of the snobs. You've lost the distinction between good and evil because you've lost touch with your own people. A new generation is coming, straight from the heart of the people, and you will know nothing of it .... Attain to God by work; it all lies in that; or disappear like rotten mildew ...."[54]

And when Stavrogin asks "What sort of work?" Šatov's answer, "Peasants' work", makes it clear that Stavrogin's estrangement from the earth and its people precludes morality; nevertheless, he is, like Kirilov, to whom he is externally linked by membership in the conspiracy, a tragic figure because his failure to make a distinction between good and evil (he gets "pleasure" from both) does not preclude his awareness of good, even his striving for it. It is just that he seems unable to overcome what is called "acedia", that is, "that torpor of the spirit which provides the greatest resistance to God because it lacks the power to resist anything".[55]

But the problem of Stavrogin is complex, for if there is about him that which "provides the greatest resistance to God", there is also about him that which is godlike. Dostoevskij, always conscious of the significance and effect of symbolic names, has derived Stavrogin's name from the Greek for "cross", hardly accidentally.[56] What is more, it is clear that Stavrogin's attraction for those with whom he comes in contact far exceeds anything attributable to personality or position. Their devotion to him can only be metaphysically rooted. His appeal stems from the fact that, through the collective unconscious, Stavrogin is inextricably bound to them and they to him. Indeed, the mythic element is very strong in this novel, and Stavrogin's followers may, because of it, be viewed as parts of his own soul. Further, even if he is a nihilist, he is a prophet too, and this contradictory role leads to ambivalent results: even while

[53] Simmons, *Dostoevsky*, p. 250.
[54] *The Possessed*, p. 273.
[55] See Muchnic, *An Introduction to Russian Literature*, p. 138.
[56] *A Study in Dostoevsky*, p. 63.

incubating and inculcating atheism, he is incubating and inculcating
Jesus Christ. His failure to distinguish between good and evil demands of
others that they make such a distinction. His amoralism is eminently
suited to initiate or encourage faith or atheism. He brings faith because,
through a powerful reaction against him, he fans sparks of belief to
white-hot flame. And the atheism he brings cannot be equated with
amorality, for Dostoevskij knows that the atheist is reacting against a
belief in God, and that the very reaction bespeaks consciousness of
His existence and power. It is only the amoral man who cannot be reached,
and Stavrogin is the only truly amoral figure in the book.

Šatov and Kirilov represent the polarization of a single obsession —
God. Having been long together, having suffered together, they live
together in absolute hostility, in two different worlds, curtained by silence.
Kirilov, who has moments of Myškin-like bliss (and his epilepsy con-
firms that he is only an atheist and not amoral, for it is his insight into
God through the irrational, and, anointed by the "holy" disease, it is
small wonder that he must strive so desperately to convince himself of
his godlessness), kills himself to prove that there is no God precisely
because he knows there is.

Because the doubles are primarily ethical rather than psychological
counterparts, because Stavrogin's duality is, in the cut text, merely inherent in his make-up, in the mythic element intrinsic in the text, and not
primarily a result of psychological tension, a manifestation of his subconscious, further discussion is, from my bias, relatively pointless unless
I turn to "At Tixon's", the suppressed chapter, and note other deleted
scenes. Here we find the mythic, hallucinations; here we read of Stavrogin
dreaming; here we meet his demon-double (who later turns up as Ivan
Karamazov's devil); here we even have a suggestion of another epileptic
seizure (the monk's) — in a sentence, "At Tixon's" is about the subconscious. I must, however, tread lightly, conscious of the fact that it is not
an integral part of the book — the Penguin edition, for example, excludes
it — and that to insist that it does more than supply an interesting footnote is to make a different book of *The Possessed*. Further, because the
chapter is not integrated into the whole (it had probably been intended to
follow Chapter 8 of Part 2), it cannot, of course, serve a literary function.
It should be noted that despite the plethora of reasons advanced for
its continuing exclusion during Dostoevskij's life, the most obvious seems
to have been overlooked: Dostoevskij could not restore the chapter
after 1875 because in that year its most crucial part appeared in *A Raw
Youth*.

In one of the scenes cut from the text, Stavrogin talks to Daša about his double:

"I saw him again ... at first here in the coner, there near the stove and then he sat next to me, all night, and stayed there even after I left the house .... Now begins a series of his visitations. Yesterday he was stupid and impudent ... I got angry that my own demon could appear in such a miserable mask ... I don't believe in him. I don't believe in him as yet. I know that it is I myself divided in different ways and that I speak with myself. ... he terribly wanted to be an independent demon and that I would believe in him as a reality."[57]

And he tells Tixon that "he was subject, especially at night, to certain hallucinations, that he sometimes saw or sensed beside himself a malicious creature, mocking and 'rational'", that "of course, I see him. I see him as I see you ... but sometimes I see him and I'm not sure I see him, although I do see him ... and sometimes I don't know what's real: me or him .... But can't you possibly suppose that it is in fact a devil!"[58]

"At Tixon's" emphasizes Stavrogin's crime, and if we interpret his hallucinations, his "vision" of the little girl with her fist upraised, the confession itself, as guilt-born symbols of his recognition of having sinned, it would indeed, as Čiževky wrote, change "the tragedy of Stavrogin into a psychic illness", despite Stavrogin's insistence that he was always in "full control" of himself. But Tixon, whom Stavrogin calls a "damned psychologist!" because of his insight, recognizes that without God there cannot be expiation, that feeling himself to be a Byronic hero, Stavrogin seeks martyrdom, not forgiveness, that he will commit another crime "solely in order to *avoid* this publication of the little sheets [the confession]". Yet, despite Tixon's insight, if Stavrogin had earlier committed a great crime — and Lizaveta Nikolaevna tells him that she has suspected that there was something "loathsome" on his conscience — it surely would demand that we re-evaluate our concept of Stavrogin. That Stavrogin is on every level of consciousness aware of guilt is very clear in those sections cut from the text.

It is, first of all, clearly represented by his demon; it is clear in his dream of Matrësha:

I caught sight of her, emaciated and with feverish eyes, just exactly as when she had stood in my room on the treshold and, shaking her head at me, had raised her tiny little fist at me.[59]

Stavrogin himself asks whether this is "called remorse of conscience or

---

[57] Quoted in "The Theme of the Double in Dostoevsky", *op. cit.*, p. 118.
[58] *The Possessed*, p. 702.
[59] *Ibid.*, p. 721.

repentance?"[60] He insists, further, that he could "get rid of Matrësha even now, if he wanted to", but that he does not want to.

Even within this slight chapter, Dostoevskij prepares for the dream brilliantly. It is preceded by Stavrogin's having two years previously bought a picture of a little girl "very much like Matrësha". Stavrogin makes the point that he could so well "dominate his recollections" that he forgot about the little picture. It is a year later, after riding "absent-mindedly" past his station, stopping in a little town, that he dreams.

His dream, however, is not wholly the result of repressed guilt. It offers confirmation that the mythic is functioning here, for it stems, in part, from the collective unconscious of humanity. Stavrogin dreams of the 'Golden Age'. It is, in essence, a dream that not only appears again in *A Raw Youth* and in *The Dream of a Ridiculous Man*, but permeates, in one form or another, almost all the later works as well because, as I have been trying to indicate, it is so central a part of Dostoevskij's world vision. This is part of the dream, it is of a time during which

beautiful people lived [in a corner of the Greek archipelago] .... They got up and went to sleep happy and innocent; the groves were filled with their merry songs; their enormous surplus of untouched energy went into love and open-hearted joy .... I finally loved them .... for the first time in my life [my eyes] were literally wet with tears ....[61]

He then sees a spot which takes on form, becomes a spider, a spider which the reader recalls is very much like the one he had seen while waiting for Matrësha. What he had insisted he had been able to repress, awakened once more from the subconscious, bursts through the surface, and the little girl's appearance shatters his dream of the 'Golden Age' (even, I shall show, as it reinforces it).

Unless what I have been saying about the collective unconscious is true, the dream of the 'Golden Age' is merely a *tour de force*, for it otherwise seems to be not only artistically inappropriate but a meaningless appendage to the rest of the dream, which can be interpreted within the context of the subconscious. But Stavrogin has, albeit unwittingly, been heralding Christ, hence, as his disciple, is no less than the other disciples in Dostoevskij inevitably attuned, through the unconscious, to the metaphysical. This being the case, his "lofty delusion" is Dostoevskij's miraculous promise of a world to come to all men; but it must come through the heart and not through the brain. Socialists can never build it, and the best of intentions cannot make it a reality. Even those lines

[60] *Ibid.*, p. 722.
[61] *Ibid.*, pp. 720, 721.

I have quoted from the part of the dream focusing on the 'Golden Age' present Dostoevskij's unformulated conception of "paradise" — and, because his concept of faith is essentially (like Tolstoj's) anthropocentric, it is a paradise on earth and not in heaven. What this part of the dream details is no more important than what it excludes.

The "beautiful people" are beautiful because they are not rationalists. They are creatures of spontaneity, they thrill to feeling and, in turn, are intensely feeling. They sing their merry songs because through feeling they have come to know God; they feel Him more completely than they could ever rationally come to know Him. Their "open-hearted joy" bespeaks their uninhibitedness, for they have cast off the shackles of thought; and the energy once expended on useless thinking, no longer so expended, ever-replenished amidst love and selflessness and common devotion and exaltation, is directed outward, and, hearts overflowing, all join a magnificent *Gloria in Excelsis Deo*.

There is, of course, an intimate connection between the 'Golden Age' and Mother Earth, a connection perhaps most explicit in a short story soon to be discussed, *The Peasant Marey*. As in Tolstoj, the peasant, in his naïvete, in his primitivism, in his lack of intellectuality, is the apotheosis of feeling, and, dirt under his fingernails, he is closest to paradise; indeed, God is already in him.

The two parts of Stavrogin's dream are hardly separate, each is intimately dependent upon the other. The subconscious recognition of guilt indicates that conscience does exist, and it is precisely because it exists that the promise of the 'Golden Age' is offered to Stavrogin; and, once having been offered, it must accelerate the feelings of guilt, thus further igniting the spark of conscience.

Tixon's seizure is only hinted at (He "stood in front of [Stavrogin], his hands folded, palms out, and an unhealthy convulsion, as if from extreme fear, seemed to cross his face for an instant". "... I see ... I see ..."[62]). His insight into Stavrogin has come from God, for his epilepsy, of course, bespeaks his mystical union with heaven.

I have shown, then, that *The Possessed*, even without "Stavrogin's Confession" is, because of the mythic element within it, much more than a political melodrama. As a whole, the novel illustrates what becomes clear after reading all of Dostoevskij: after his return from exile in Siberia, the works, almost without exception, contain within their irrational elements his most profound ethical and philosophical concepts.

Almost without exception, every work that follows is infused with

[62]   *Ibid.*, p. 734.

manifestations of the subconscious. *The Brothers Karamazov*, of course, must be discussed in detail, but I need first pause for some comment on *A Raw Youth, Peasant Marey*, and *The Dream of a Ridiculous Man*, primarily because the collective unconscious manifests itself in the first two, serving as an instrument of insight and knowledge, and forgotten memory functions in the last, bringing peace and insight, hence, also serving as an instrument of knowledge.[63] I have already made some comment on dualism and its implications and its consistency in Dostoevskij (and will need to make some further comment on the matter as it affects *The Brothers Karamazov*). Seeking not to be redundant, I quite ignore its appearance in the stories. There is, however, one part in *A Raw Youth*, "Conclusion", where, through Dolgorukij, Dostoevskij comes very close to epitomizing part of his conception of duality, and I quote several of the lines without further comment:

"But I repeat again: though that scene at mother's and that broken ikon were undoubtedly partly due to the influence of a real 'second self', yet I have ever since been haunted by the fancy that there was in it an element of a sort of vindictive symbolism, a sort of resentment against the expectations of those women, a sort of angry revolt against their rights and their criticism. And so hand in hand with the 'second self' he broke the ikon, as though to say 'that's how your expectations will be shattered!' In fact, even though the 'second self' did come in, it was partly simply a whim .... But all this is only my theory; it would be hard to decide for certain."[64]

In a good paper, "The Golden Age — Dream of a Ridiculous Man?",[65] Elizabeth Trahan correctly finds the dream of the 'Golden Age' a common denominator in *A Raw Youth* and *The Dream of a Ridiculous Man*, but she does not make a connection between the 'Golden Age' and Mother Earth, does not concern herself with the mythic element, the implications inherent in the collective, primordial unconscious; hence, further comment seems appropriate.

Versilov's vision, so much in contrast to the rationalistic part of him, at once bespeaks the potency of the collective unconscious, its purpose, and the insight it offers, for through it we know beyond doubt that there is a part of Versilov that has been infected with the holy light represented by Makar Ivanovič. He has been selected to receive the vision of the

---

[63] Of the other stories, the subconscious figures most prominently in *A Gentle Spirit* (*Krotkaja*) and *Bobok*, but I have not discussed these because, in the first, its use is traditionally Dostoevskijan, and, in the second, it serves primarily a grotesque function and, as such, is relatively superficial.

[64] *A Raw Youth*, trans. Constance Garnett (London, 1957), p. 548.

[65] *The Slavic and East European Journal*, XVII (1959), pp. 349-371.

'Golden Age' because he is already being regenerated. His vision is almost identical with Stavrogin's:

"I picture to myself, my boy", he said with a dreamy smile, "that war is at an end and strife has ceased. After curses, pelting with mud, and hisses, has come a lull, and men are left alone, according to their desire: the great idea of old has left them; the great source of strength that till then had nourished and fostered them was vanishing like the majestic sun setting in Claude Lorraine's picture, but it was somehow the last day of humanity, and men suddenly understood that they were left quite alone, and at once felt terribly forlorn. I have never, my dear boy, been able to picture men ungrateful and grown stupid. Men left forlorn would begin to draw together more closely and more lovingly; they would clutch one another's hand, realizing that they were all that was left for one another! The great idea of immortality would have vanished, and they would have to fill its place; and all the wealth of love lavished of old upon Him, who was immortal, would be turned upon the whole of nature, on the world, on men, on every blade of grass. They would inevitably grow to love the earth and life as they gradually became aware of their own transitory and finite nature, and with a special love, not as of old, they would begin to observe and would discover in nature phenomena and secrets which they had not suspected before, for they would look on nature with new eyes, as a lover look-ing on his beloved. On awakening they would hasten to kiss one another, eager to love, knowing that the days are short, and that is all that is left them. They would work for one another, and each would give up all that he had to all, and by that only would be happy. Every child would know and feel that every one on earth was for him like a father or mother." [66]

It is replete with images of earth, of earth as a source of spiritual strength, of earth as protector, of earth as parent. It is earth that succors her "terribly forlorn" children, and she that precludes a belief in immortality, for she offers glorious love in the context of immediacy. Mother Earth offers her bosom through the irrational, and the irrational offer flows over into reality, reinforcing and redirecting man's walk through life. It is not an impotent vision. The very clarity of its recall indicates not only its special origin, but its special ability to shape and channel thought; it is, therefore, wholly consistent that Versilov's following words make abstract impulses concrete:

"... it's noteworthy that I always complete my picture with Heine's vision of 'Christ on the Baltic Sea'.[67] I could not get on without Him. I could not help imagining Him ... in the midst of His bereaved people. He comes to them, holds out His hands, and asks them, 'How could they forget Him?' And then,

[66] *A Raw Youth*, pp. 466, 467.
[67] Mrs. Trahan points out that Dostoevskij is in error, that Heine speaks of the North Sea (*The Slavic and East European Journal, op. cit.*, p. 356).

as it were, the scales would fall from their eyes and there would break forth
the great rapturous hymn of the new and the last resurrection ...."[68]

The clarity with which he sees Christ is a concomitant of his vision of
the 'Golden Age'. He too has been taught through the irrational.

In all of Dostoevskij, there is no clearer example of how the subconscious and the collective unconscious may serve supplementary functions
than in *The Dream of a Ridiculous Man*, for the ridiculous man, as he
says, "is ... the only one who knows the truth", and he comes to know
it precisely on the third of November, the very day two things happened
to him, each inextricably related — he refuses to help a little girl (after
all, a man who has just decided to finally kill himself can hardly be blamed
for being selfish at such a time), and he has a remarkable dream.

The dream is incubated by unaccustomed feelings of guilt, by the ridiculous man seeing "clearly that so long as I was still a human being and
not nothingness, I was alive and so could suffer, be angry and feel shame
at my actions".[69] Immediately before epileptic seizures, the curtain
separating man from Christ is rent asunder; feelings of guilt, because
they are concrete evidence of conscience (hence morality), tear this curtain
too, albeit less dramatically. Long estranged not only from Christ but
from himself and, because of his defensive ridiculousness, from society,
the ridiculous man's guilt now heals him, making him whole.

Soaring through space, approaching a planet, "a feeling of great and
holy jealousy glowed in [his] heart":

"How can it be repeated and what for? I love and can love only that earth which
I have left, stained with my blood, when, in my ingratitude, I quenched my life
with a bullet in my heart. But I have never, never ceased to love that earth,
and perhaps on the very night I parted from it I loved it more than ever. Is there
suffering upon this new earth? On our earth we can only love with suffering
and through suffering. We cannot love otherwise, and we know of no other
sort of love. I want suffering in order to love. I long, I thirst, this very instant,
to kiss with tears the earth that I have left, and I don't want, I won't accept life
on any other!"[70]

Now alone, on "this other earth", the "Golden Age" spreads before him;
"everything was exactly as it is with us, only everything seemed to have a
festive radiance, the splendor of some great, holy triumph attained at
last".[71] On this other earth was the fulfillment of the potential inherent in

[68]   *A Raw Youth*, p. 467.
[69]   *The Dream of a Ridiculous Man, An Honest Thief and Other Stories*, trans.
Constance Garnett (London, 1957), p. 387.
[70]   *Ibid.*, pp. 393, 394.
[71]   *Ibid.*, p. 394.

his earth. Like the other visions of the "Golden Age", it was "the earth untarnished by the Fall".

Once more Dostoevskij's conception of paradise has familiar requisites: "their [its inhabitants] knowledge was gained ... by intuitions"; "they did not aspire to knowledge of life ..."; "they without science know how to live"; they were without "that *cruel* [Dostoevskij's italics] sensuality which overcomes every man on earth ... and is the source of almost every sin of mankind".

The ridiculous man is a contaminating force, and in paragraphs which almost duplicate Raskol'nikov's last dream of the plague infecting and destroying earth, the ridiculous man, perverted by experience and need fostered on his earth, sows the evil seeds which shatter the love and peace and joy known before he came. He brought his earth to them: "corruption, contamination and falsity".

Even as the guilt associated with the child incubated this dream, his responsibility for despoiling paradise incubates another sense of guilt, one much more profound; and having seen Christ through the irrational, he awakens from his dream a new man. Thoughts of suicide disappear and are replaced by overflowing love. Laughed at, ridiculed, the ridiculous man, no longer really ridiculous, becomes Christ's prophet on earth, for he has "seen the truth":

"The chief thing is to love others like yourself, that's the great thing, and that's everything; nothing else is wanted — you will find out at once how to arrange it all. And yet it's an old truth which has been told and retold a billion times — but it has not formed part of our lives! The consciousness of life is higher than life, the knowledge of the laws of happiness is higher than happiness — that is what one must contend against. And I shall. If only everyone wants it [paradise on earth], it can all be arranged at once."[72]

The brilliance of this story (and I cannot agree with Mrs. Trahan that "ambiguity in viewpoint ... renders its conclusion questionable and unconvincing"[73]) is due, in part, to the fact that the ridiculous man's "conversion" to Christ is fully comprehensible within the context of his psychology — guilt is an awesome purgative — and, even as the dream, it is not really dependent upon the influence of the collective unconscious. But the mythic *supplements* the purely psychological, helps explain

---

[72] *Ibid.*, pp. 404, 405.
[73] *The Slavic and East European Journal, op. cit.*, p. 353. Part of Mrs. Trahan's difficulty in resolving this "ambiguity" stems from a self-created problem. She views the ridiculous man as both prophet and madman, but Dostoevskij's point seems more clear to me, i.e., he is not a madman because he is too positively depicted. His religious zeal precludes insanity.

the degree of the ridiculous man's conversion, its completeness. For his experience, in part, has surely been beyond himself; it has surely been existential.

In *The Peasant Marey*, a strongly autobiographical piece (the narrator mentions *"The House of the Dead* I wrote fifteen years ago"), a prisoner who has found no meaning to life recalls a peasant he once knew, for his much earlier adventure with Marey had "lain hidden in [his] soul though [he] knew nothing of it, and rose suddenly to [his] memory when it was wanted".[74] The forgotten memory, another part of the unconscious, another part of irrational man, comes from its hiding place and shows the light to the prisoner.

The peasant Marey is a symbolization of Mother Earth, of paradise on earth. The prisoner recalls not only his unsophistication, his good-heartedness and spontaneity, but he "remembered particularly the thick earth-stained finger with which he softly and with timid tenderness touched [his] quivering lips".[75]

The peasant, through the earth, has seen Christ, and through the peasant and the irrational forgotten memory, the prisoner has seen him too. He must have, for he tells us as much:

"And when I got down off the bed and looked around me, I remember I suddenly felt that I could look at these unhappy creatures with quite different eyes, and that suddenly by some miracle all hatred and anger had vanished utterly from my heart. I walked about, looking into the faces that I met. That shaven peasant, branded on his face as a criminal, bawling his hoarse, drunken song, may be that very Marey; I cannot look into his heart."[76]

In *The Peasant Marey* we see that forgotten memory is another manifestation of the subconscious which serves as a medium between Christ and man.

The Brothers Karamazov, for which Dostoevskij had been preparing all his adult life, is his greatest novel. In Ivan Karamazov, the most brilliantly depicted of the doubles, the ambivalent personality sublimely symbolizes the profound struggle between the head and the heart, between the "all-is-lawful" rationalism of what Ivan himself calls the "Euclidean mind" and Zosima's simple faith; between intellect and compassion; between atheism and Christianity; between life as a scientific experiment and life as a meaningful experience; between "nothingness" and "somethingness".

---

[74]　*The Peasant Marey, An Honest Thief and Other Stories*, p. 318.
[75]　*Loc. cit.*
[76]　*Ibid.*, pp. 318, 319.

The Karamazov heritage, at its most extreme, is lustfulness and, at its least, is an almost unbounded joy for living. Fëdor Karamazov, the very personification of debauchery, is yet capable of most subtle reasoning, an almost incredible insight into the tangled motives of the human mind. Having been beaten by Dmitrij, he yet asks Alëša "Where's Ivan?" Told he is outside, that he has a headache, he can already anticipate his own murder:

"What does Ivan say? Alyosha, my dear, my only son, I'm afraid of Ivan. I'm more afraid of Ivan than Dmitri. You're the only one I'm not afraid of." [77]

Alëša, the personification of humility and Christianity, Ivan's foil, Dostoevskij's answer to Ivan's rationailty, is yet almost shaken from his belief by the stench emanating from Zossima's corpse, reels before Ivan's arguments; he is a Karamazov too. Hearing Dmitrij detail his "wild life", he blushes:

"I [Alëša] wasn't blushing at what you were saying or at what you've done. I blushed because I am the same as you are." [78]

Dmitrij is unconvinced ("That's going a little too far!"):

"No, it's true", insisted Alyosha (obviously the idea was not a new one). "The ladder's the same. I'm at the bottom step, and you're above, somewhere about the thirteenth. That's how I see it. But it's all the same. Absolutely the same. Anyone on the bottom step is bound to go up to the top one." [79]

Dmitrij Karamazov, the most lustful of the brothers, is confused by the "breadth" of man, his potential for ambivalence. He is a Karamazov, but he can not accept Ivan's rationality as an answer to life. He is kind and generous, devoid of shrewdness and guile, in many ways the most unsophisticated of the brothers:

"Beauty! I can't bear the thought that a man of lofty mind and heart begins with the ideal of the Madonna and ends with the ideal of Sodom .... Yes, man is broad, too broad. I'd have him narrower. The devil only knows what to make of it! What to the mind is shameful is beauty and nothing else to the heart. Is there beauty in Sodom? ... the awful thing is that beauty is mysterious as well as terrible. God and the devil are fighting there and the battlefield is the heart of man." [80]

Smerdjakov, the bastard brother, a grotesque epileptic without original thoughts, ignored for the most part as an inarticulate thing, involves

[77] *The Brothers Karamazov*, p. 136.
[78] *Ibid.*, pp. 107, 108.
[79] *Ibid.*, p. 108.
[80] *Ibid.*, p. 106.

himself in the discussion taking place in "The Controversy". Scoffed at when he begins to speak, he can yet cause an uproar with his casuistic reasoning, as he shows that there are situations in which it is not sinful to renounce God.[81] "Grigorij was thunderstruck". Fëdor Karamazov, that attractive and infernal well of life, shouts: "Alëša! Alëša! What do you say to that! ... He must have been with the Jesuits somewhere .... Don't cry, Grigorij, we'll reduce him to ashes in a moment".

The women, too, cannot escape "doubleness": Katerina is another of Dostoevskij's women torn between meekness and pride. Nastas'ja had gone off with Rogožin to lacerate herself; Katerina, loved by Ivan, prefers to be tortured by her hopeless love for Dmitrij. Her pride demands she refuse to yield to reality; her refusal involves her in an almost endless love-hate ambivalence which Ivan, himself a double, can understand. He tolerates her anguish because he understands its irremedial roots.

Grushen'ka, too, is not unlike Nastas'ja, for she shares in common with her an early traumatic experience that warped her life, and, like Katerina, her life revolves about a love-hate axis; unlike Katerina, however, she, at the conclusion of the novel, is committed to an affirmation of life.

Lise, who takes pleasure in crushing her finger in the door, is the most extreme example of duality in the book. Her passion for suffering and self-torture is beyond the most elastic bounds of normality. It is for good reason that Dostoevskij calls her chapter "A Little Demon". Alëša, immediately upon asking "Why did you send for me today, Lise?" is told:

"I wanted to tell you of a longing I have. I would like someone to torture me, marry me and then torture me, deceive me and go away. I don't want to be happy."[82]

His question is diagnostic: " 'You are in love with disorder?' "

Her attraction to Ivan, so utterly incapable of fulfillment, is exactly based on her luxuriating in masochism. It is no less clear that she likes Alëša primarily because she can, in turn, torture him.

A plethora of doubles and duality. The German Romantics had used doubles too; they had also described man torn apart, *zerrissen*, and I have shown that much of Dostoevskij's insight into the working and literary effectiveness of the subconscious was part of his heritage, but nothing that preceded him conveys the impact and the implications of

---

[81]   See Book III, "The Controversy", pp. 125, 126.
[82]   *Ibid.*, p. 527.

duality with such artistic success. Dostoevskij's consistency and intensity are unique, and never before (or since) were ethical and philosophical questions so dramatically and forcefully raised, and, within the text, even answered, at least by implication.[83]

Dostoevskij's dualistic view of man also invests his works with a singular electric quality, for inherent in it is a supreme potential for a dramatic confrontation between good and evil. In *The Brothers Karamazov* this potential is fully realized. Further, the German romantics make us wait to discover evil beneath respectability. Dostoevskij, because the potential for regeneration is in Everyman, makes us wait to discover if it will be fanned into life. Dostoevskij, then, is not only necessarily more dramatic than the Germans (even if we discount his technique), but, I feel, eminently more rewarding. Evil fascinates, but, regardless of the brilliance of its depiction, it cannot inspire.

Very late in the novel, Dmitrij Karamazov is "educated" by a remarkable dream. Three hundred and fifty pages earlier, before any crime, speaking with Alëša, Dmitrij had sought peace but could not answer the riddle posed by "beauty in Sodom". His impulses are good, but he does not know how he is "to cling forever to Mother Earth":

"I don't kiss her. I don't cling to her bosom. Am I to become a peasant or a shepherd? I go on and I don't know whether I'm going into darkness or to light and joy. That's the trouble. Everything in the world is a riddle."[84]

At the very moment he discovers that he had not indeed killed Grigorij, he thanks God, leaps in ecstasy. At the trial, as "evidence" piles up against him, he gradually becomes resigned to his fate as he recognizes moral responsibility for the crime, for he had wanted to kill his father (and parricide for Dostoevskij symbolizes man's decay and degeneration). As Dmitrij's soul suffers, so is it cleansed. More selfless than ever before, he even begs mercy for Grushen'ka. She, the last witness, is interrupted on the stand to hear him swear his innocence. She crosses herself and praises God. Dmitrij is at peace.

The dream is the culmination of what preceded; it is the central scene of regeneration. In it, he does cling to Mother Earth. He is a peasant.

---

[83] I have heard it stated repeatedly that the major function of literature is to diagnose and not to prescribe, and, of course, I agree that literature need not supply answers to problems it raises. It is interesting, however, that both Dostoevskij and Tolstoj strove to be didactic, and their didacticism, unless (especially in the late Tolstoj) it completely overwhelmed their artistic sense, serves a positive function. It actually imbues the works with an aura of sincerity, with "convincingness".

[84] *The Brothers Karamazov*, p. 105.

The babe, the representation of humanity, suffers (and he likes the word "babe" because "there seemed more pity in it"). Pity floods his own heart, "he wanted to do something for them all". Grushen'ka's voice is heard, speaking the hopeful words spoken before. There is a "new beckoning light" toward which he struggles.

Dmitrij has exorcised evil from his bosom. With "his whole soul ... quivering with tears", he announces that he will sign anything: "'I've had a good dream, gentlemen', he said in a strange voice, with a new light, as of joy, in his face". God has come to him, and even as the dream had been anticipated by his gradual regeneration, so it inevitably leads to his final confession of his evil, as, "impelled by uncontrollable feeling", he accepts "the torture of accusation", announces that he wants "to suffer because by suffering I shall be purified". He has seen the light because Mother Earth has come to her son to welcome him. Once more she reaches out through the primordial unconscious, speaks through the irrational.

As a symbol of regeneration, the dream is a singularly effective literary device, for its contents are intimate, unprotected, "true". The subconscious does not lie, and Dmitrij's dream not only reveals the depths of his "new" feeling, but his absolute sincerity. Further, because the dream is not controllable by will, because it is spontaneous, no less than an epileptic seizure does it epitomize man's communion with the metaphysical. In both cases, the metaphor of light is important.

Ivan Karamazov, in some ways Dostoevskij's mouthpiece, in other ways his arch antagonist, is complex. A man who dissects life rather than lives it, he, above all, lusts for justice. He does not reject the existence of God, but he cannot reconcile this existence with suffering, especially the suffering of guiltless children. He demands justice on earth, insists there can be no eternal harmony without it: "'It's not God that I don't accept, Alëša, but I most respectfully return Him the ticket.'"

Dostoevskij, of course, takes enormous care to allow Ivan's ideas to be aired (and the novel consists primarily of ideas as actions); Ivan's ethical position can be summarized in a single phrase — "All is lawful", a position diametrically opposed by Alëša and Zosima and their major tenet — "forgiveness is all". It has been pointed out that Dostoevskij seems to have spent his life convincing himself that Christ would not have joined the socialists;[85] Ivan Karamazov would have.

Ivan's insistence that there is only nothingness and, therefore, that there is no law, is inculcated into Smerdjakov, Ivan's philosophical heir.

---

[85]   By Helen Muchnic, for example, *op. cit.*, p. 148.

Smerdjakov is the very symbol of Ivan's ideas, and, as Ivan confesses when he later meets his devil, there is in his own bosom the base, the contemptible, the mean. There is, then, an evil self within him, and it is represented, in reality, by Smerdjakov, another demon.

Ivan is not able to master his ideas, for they imprison him even as Smerdjakov activates them and thereby tears Ivan apart. In murdering Fëdor Karamazov, Smerdjakov does no more than he thought that Ivan wanted done; after all, parricide is consistent with lawlessness. Shocked at first, then distraught, then tortured, then feverish, then hallucinatory, Ivan finds a modicum of peace only after he too, like Dmitrij before him, accepts the guilt for a crime he did not commit but for which he was nevertheless responsible.

Once more, it is a subconscious projection that is the very apex of a critical part of a work. Ivan's meeting the devil is the culmination of an elaborate acceleration of an awareness of responsibility and guilt. It begins to develop even before the murder of his father. This growing consciousness of evil within him is, of course, diffused through the text, but there are five major scenes which anticipate the ultimate appearance of the devil, and, revealingly, they all involve Smerdjakov.

Ivan, "had lately come to feel an intense dislike for Smerdyakov", had begun to hate him for reasons not clear to himself. He tries to ignore him: "he tried to go through the gate without speaking or looking at Smerdjakov." Nothing had yet been said about a crime, but Ivan subconsciously anticipates disaster. Smerdjakov's wink intensely irritates Ivan; he reacts vehemently: "Get away, miserable idiot. What have I to do with you?" A strange verbal duel follows. Ivan cannot understand why Smerdjakov talks of having a fit, "a long fit", the next day, nor his talk of being thus unable to defend Fëdor Karamazov from murder. He is disturbed by what Smerdjakov seems to be suggesting, but cannot consciously define what he is hinting at. He is about to fling himself on Smerdjakov when he turns to leave. Smerdjakov smiles a "revolting" smile. Ivan laughs, "and went through the gate still laughing":

Anyone looking at Ivan's face at that moment would have known that he was not laughing from lightness of heart. But he could not have explained what he was feeling at that moment. He moved and walked as though in a frenzy. [86]

On his way to Čermašnja, very happy at first, Ivan then thinks of Smerdjakov and what he had said when he had heard of Ivan's intention to go there ("It's always worthwhile speaking to a clever man"), and he is

[86]   *The Brothers Karamazov*, p. 252.

wracked by foreboding: "'I am base', he whispered to himself". This is the beginning of his insight.

After the murder, there are five visits with Smerdjakov, three "interviews". During the first one, Ivan tries to determine whether Smerdjakov did feign his seizure; he is told it was genuine. Smerdjakov, obviously sparring with Ivan — though it is a one-sided match, for Ivan, defensively, cannot become involved — hints that Ivan had left the house because he was afraid of what would take place there. Upon leaving Smerdjakov, there are several most vital sentences that reveal Ivan's subconscious awareness of his guilt:

His feeling was one of relief at the fact that it was not Smerdjakov, but Dmitri who had committed the murder. He did not want to analyze the reason for this feeling, and even felt a repugnance at prying into his sensations. He felt he wanted to forget something. In the following days he became convinced of Dmitri's guilt, as he learned of all the evidence against him. [87]

Surely Ivan's relief is born of his self-exoneration, and the very fact that he needs to exonerate himself bespeaks his moral involvement. He becomes convinced of Dmitrij's guilt not because, on a conscious level, he learned of evidence pointing to his having committed the murder, but because, subconsciously, the sacrifice of Dmitrij cleanses him. Smerdjakov, the "disgusting idiot", is, hence, exonerated, and Dmitrij, the beloved brother, is made the sacrificial lamb.

It is hardly accidental that Ivan now becomes more intensely involved with Katerina than ever before. Clearly, he seeks to escape, but he cannot. He meets Alëša and, no longer able to repress his distress, he asks him whether he thought that he wished for his father's death and wished for Dmitrij to kill him. Alëša answers in the affirmative, and "from that time on Alëša noticed that Ivan began to avoid him". He must avoid one accuser, but he cannot avoid the other. He is driven to see Smerdjakov again.

Smerdjakov drives Ivan into absolute rage by telling him that he must have condoned the murder since, expecting Smerdyakov to commit it, he had nevertheless left. Ivan leaves, and walks into complete self-awareness, but he is still capable of partially rationalizing, shifting the blame:

"Yes, of course, I was expecting something. He is right .... Yes, I expected it then, that's true! I wanted the murder, I did want the murder! Did I want the murder? Did I want it? I must kill Smerdyakov! If I don't dare kill Smerdyakov now, life is not worth living!" [88]

[87]   *Ibid.*, p. 553.
[88]   *Ibid.*, pp. 559, 560.

And the unvoiced threat to kill Smerdjakov occurs again. It is now Ivan's only possible way to pass off guilt, but he is already punishing himself. His distress is expressed in illness, for "during the last week of that month Ivan himself began to feel very ill". The illness has internal roots. It will result in the final hallucination, remain forever a part of Ivan.

At the last interview, Smerdjakov no longer cares to carry out what he considers to be an absurd farce. He confesses to the murder, insists that he was merely Ivan's instrument. Ivan, now fighting desperately for his sanity, at first refuses to acknowledge his responsibility, then declares that he will give evidence against Smerdjakov and himself.

Smerdjakov is an epileptic, and, if I am to be consistent, I must try to explain his epilepsy in light of what I have been saying about it, for he is, to be sure, nothing but a revolting parasite, and it seems strange that one so seemingly beyond regeneration should have the "holy" disease.

Smerdjakov, I hold, is without identity. He is only the worst part of Ivan, and being a part of Ivan, his epilepsy is Ivan's. A parasite who draws nourishment from Ivan, he yet unwittingly nourishes him. Smerdjakov creates the crisis that directly precipitates the change in Ivan and the total moral commitment of Dmitrij. He is, as he himself says, an instrument, but he is an instrument of regeneration. Even as his epilepsy supplies him with an alibi which enables him to commit the murder, it supplies Ivan with a basis for moving towards moral responsibility. Smerdjakov, through Ivan, serves God, and it is his God-given epilepsy that lights the way.

Dostoevskij, after Ivan's acceptance of responsibility, once more employs setting to create a dramatic confrontation. Ivan is now beaten by a raging snowstorm, but even as he staggers he becomes more and more resolved, for "something like joy was springing up in his heart". Exactly at that moment, symbolizing his partial return to humanity, he lifts an almost frozen peasant in his arms, carries him to a police station, stays to care for him — at the conclusion of the purifying "nightmare", Alëša comes to him out of the snow. He is satisfied that his interest in the peasant, his ability to stay with him, indicates that he is not going out of his mind. But the self-satisfaction quickly wears off:

As he entered his room he felt something like a touch of ice on his heart, like a recollection or, more exactly, a reminder of something agonizing and revolting that was in that room now, at that moment, and had been there before ....

There was evidently something there, some object that irritated him, worried him and tormented him.[89]

Ivan Karamazov, an amazingly resourceful rationalizer, a rationalist who refuses to be hounded by irrational guilt, can run away no more. Stavrogin's devil has finally come. It is compounded of shame and guilt, of the clear awareness that that which Smerdjakov represents is in his own bosom. Because Ivan is finally able to recognize that guilt is not exclusive, that no man is an island, that all men are mutually responsible for evil, he is on the way to becoming a moral man. The devil, Ivan's emancipated guilt, is the symbolization of the crisis. Dostoevskij has so carefully prepared for the devil that his comments about Ivan's "illness" immediately preceding the appearance of the double ("he was at the moment on the verge of an attack of brain fever") are almost gratuitous.

The devil, a genteel Russian gentleman in unhappy circumstances, has, we discover, appeared before:

"I sometimes don't see you and don't even hear your voice as I did last time, but I always guess wha tyou are saying, for it's I, *I myself speaking, not you.*"[90]

The devil speaks the stupidest thoughts Ivan has had, and Ivan's cry of "Fool!" reflects only upon himself. But it is a strangely gay and bantering devil too ("Listen, in dreams ... a man sometimes sees such vision ... as I swear Lev Tolstoj had never invented", and, being no less literate than Ivan, he knows of Xlestakov too). Ivan, despite himself, despite his attempt to convince himself that the devil is only a dream (hence within the realm of normality), verbalizes its origin and import:

"Never for one minute have I taken you for reality", Ivan cried with a sort of fury. "You are a lie, you are my illness, you are a phantom. It's only that I don't know how to destroy you and I see I must suffer for a time. You are an hallucination. You are the incarnation of myself, but only of one side of me ... of my thoughts and feelings, but only the worst and most stupid of them."[91]

There are two sides to Ivan Karamazov. The cosmic struggle for his soul is not here resolved; here we see only the seeds for future regeneration, the spark of awareness that was to have burst into a flame of belief in a sequel never written. But the recognition of guilt is the crucial first step up the ladder to heaven. Ivan can now begin the slow and painful ascent.

It is in the courtroom, delirious and feverish and giddy, near hysteria,

[89] *Ibid.*, pp. 574, 575.
[90] *Ibid.*, p. 577.
[91] *Ibid.*, pp. 577, 578.

that Ivan confesses that he, like all men, desired his father's death and is guilty of it. He thus climbs another rung on the ladder, but he is involved in a titanic struggle, and he is screaming out his agony as he is carried away.

The dramatization of Ivan's subconscious struggle elucidates his dualism, even as his dualism effectively dramatizes the philosophical debate encompassed in the novel. There is a part of Ivan that is the Grand Inquisitor (and the book itself seems to try to answer its most brilliant chapter). The answer to this part of Ivan is to be found precisely in the other part of Ivan, for he comes to learn that just being cannot be enough; that existence itself demands not the cool rationalism of science but the total commitment of heart. All men must be the keepers of their brothers' and must join them in their frightful search for answers. The search is devoid of security and immediate rewards; it leaves man exposed to a hostile world sated with comfort and the ephemeral joys of utilitarianism, but it is a search which must be undertaken if man is truly to discover that his existence is not merely another hallucination, that he does, in fact, exist.

Dmitrij's dream has come to him through the medium of the collective unconscious. Ivan's hallucination is wholly explicable within the context of the subconscious. Both the dream and the hallucination, however, serve the same function, for neither is more irrational than the other, and through the irrational both Dmitrij and Ivan are no less attuned to God than Zosima. They do not need to take holy orders, for the irrational path to God is part of their heritage.

Before I summarize my findings on the subconscious in Dostoevskij, a brief comment on his possible indebtedness in this area is in order.

Aside from the Germans and Gogol', his most direct literary influences, he was, of course, exposed to many other literary works, to many philosophies, and to occult and scientific works concerned with the subconscious. The nineteenth century witnessed an enormous outpouring of fiction; it was an age of thought and writing, some of it inevitably resembling something in Dostoevskij.[92] Dostoevskij waded in it all, but aside from

[92] Here, for example, is a section from Schopenhauer, which seems strikingly Dostoevskijan, yet, although we know that Tolstoj and other Russians knew it, there is no concrete evidence that Dostoevskij did. I quote *merely* to illustrate that much of what we consider "Dostoevskijan" thought was all-pervasive: "Our brains are not the wisest part of us. In the great moments of life, when a man decides upon an important step, his action is directed not so much by any clear knowledge of the right thing to do, as by an inner impulse — you may even call it instinct — proceeding from the deepest foundations of his being ....

It may be that this impulse or instinct is the unconscious effect of a kind of prophetic

the German romantics, Gogol', Carus, and the all-pervasivè interest in the subconscious which he could hardly avoid, it is difficult and, I think, unwise, to make specific determinations as to where he caught his choicest philosophical and literary fish, or precisely how much of his thought is a result of synthesis, how much is original.

Among others, we know (even restricting ourselves to his contemporaries or near contemporaries) that he had read Dickens, Thackeray, Balzac, Hugo, Sue, Poe, Turgenev, Tolstoj, Flaubert. Further, he knew the Gothic novel from childhood and he knew *le roman terrifiant*. He knew Shakespeare and Cervantes and Richardson and Goethe and, of course, the Bible. He knew some German philosophy, and he knew Rousseau too. In a word, he knew what every sensitive and intelligent nineteenth-century author knew.

I have taken care to present his possible heritage in a broad and, hopefully, a meaningful way. If, with the exceptions discussed, I have desisted from being specific, it is only because having read much that Dostoevskij read, I have experienced flashes of insight that tempt one to trumpet his "discovery" to the world; but, recollected and evaluated in tranquility, the leads evaporate or, at the least, are so cloaked in the heavy shadow of doubt, that one is reluctant to begin building a castle with bricks of dust.

Dostoevskij's debt to the Germans (especially Hoffmann) is manifest; so is his debt to Gogol', but he is a greater writer (I am reticent to call him a philosopher) than they, and in his works the subconscious is apotheosized.

I have shown that the various manifestations of the subconscious serve literary as well as ethical and philosophical ends, for without the first, the others are essentially irrelevant. Dostoevskij is a writer of fiction and must be judged as such. The dreams, for example, regardless of their type and origin, not only dramatize the abstract, not only inform us, not only, because they cannot lie, show us the very soul of the dreamer, but they anticipate action, pace action, terminate action, and, when they

---

dream, which is forgotten when we awake — lending our life a uniformity of tone, a dramatic unity, such as could never result from the unstable moments of consciousness, when we are easily led into error, so liable to strike a false note. It is in virtue of some prophetic dream that a man feels himself called to great achievements in a special sphere, and works in that direction ... out of an inner and secret feeling that this is his true path .... This is the impulse [which is] the great power of moral discernment: it is something that a man instinctively feels to be his salvation, without which we are lost." (Arthur Schopenhauer, *The Complete Essays of Arthur Schopenhauer*, trans. T. Bailey, New York, n. d., p. 48).

flow over into reality, they may even accelerate action. So too, the whole concept of the double would fail if it remained but an unfulfilled conception, but it does not; eminently dramatic, it creates suspense and complexity, epitomizes the struggle within man, raising it to cosmic significance. Even epilepsy serves a literary function, not because it is essentially melodramatic, but because, in the absence of dreams, it is no less carefully prepared for, no less paces and terminates action, no less does its occurrence determine the very rhythm of the work in which it appears. Delirium and hallucinations serve brilliantly too. They are not only acute symptoms of internal distress (as are a plethora of other symptoms: fever, headaches, chest pains, chills, etc.), but they often efface the very line separating fantasy from reality and, by so doing, add not only to the complexity of the work but enrich its implications, even as they create implications.

I have shown that within the works the unconscious teaches on two levels: through the return of things long forgotten, and, as the impersonal unconscious, through the knowledge it offers from the very dawn of man; the repressed unconscious, stimulated by guilt or anxiety, leads to schizophrenia or less dramatic inner division; the over-unconscious (epilepsy) establishes the epileptic as an over-world force, and as such he stands in direct opposition to the schizophrenic, an anti-world force; dreams are anticipatory, warning, guilt-born, anxiety-created, or regenerative, the first two resulting either from the purely subconscious or the metaphysical, the others primarily from the subconscious.

I have, all this aside, tried to make it clear that the subconscious was apotheosized by Dostoevskij not only because of its inherent literary potential, but because he could, within its manifestations, implant his ideas. This being the case, Dostoevskij's unformulated conception of the subconscious contains the very heart of his world view.

Dostoevskij equates the unconscious with the irrational because the irrational represents feeling. As such, it is the part of man closest to Christ. It follows, then, that the unconscious is not only a mode of communication but, in every sense, an instrument of knowledge. Christ comes to man in dreams, in hallucinations, in delirium, in forgotten memories, in premonitions, through every part of his irrational being, and, at its most forceful expression, through the over-unconscious, through the epileptic seizure and its blinding light. And He comes to teach and to warn and to illuminate regeneration. He comes through the mythic, through Mother Earth, through primordial unconscious, collective unconscious. He seeks man's heart, and he can only reach it through the irrational. The unconscious not only would show man how to live but, implicitly or explicitly, it even takes him to paradise, a paradise built around the soil, where Mother Earth instills in her children feeling, love, and unbounded joy.

Thus does Dostoevskij's conception of the subconscious, never formulated by him, serve us as an instrument of knowledge too: it teaches us about his important conceptions concerning Man, Christ, and paradise. From these conceptions I now draw my idea of Dostoevskij's ten commandments: Thou must be moral; Thou must love life; Thou must have freedom of will; Thou must enjoy suffering because it is an expression of freedom; Thou must trust the heart and be a creature of feeling; Thou must distrust the brain and the intellect; Thou must be humble; Thou must be compassionate; Thou must not be lustful; Thou must seek Him and heed Him through the irrational.

CONCLUSION

The awareness that there are in human beings invisible forces which manifest themselves in different ways and, in one way or another, influence lives, dates back to most primitive times. As early as the sixteenth century, the level of sophistication could accommodate considerable insight into psychogenic disorders, hence, into the very meaning of the subconscious. In Shakespeare and his contemporaries (not to speak of Plautus and other earlier writers), the subconscious and its projections were integral parts of their works.

Even as occultist and scientific insight into the workings of the subconscious grew, literature become increasingly sophisticated in its delineation of the psychological and became increasingly dependent upon the implications of the psychological content to supplement its meaning.

The psychological, I have argued, is an important part of the sentimental and the Gothic novel (in France, England, and the United States). Influenced by Mesmer and occultist thought and science, the German *Schauerroman* exalted subconscious manifestations, and the psychological became an indispensable part of it. In Tieck and Jean Paul and, especially, in E. T. A. Hoffmann, the double and the dream reached sublime heights. What is more, the Germans infused their view of life into even their most fantastic pieces, thus made them serve far beyond the traditional restrictions of the genre. Also, the singular mingling and meshing of diversities, of dream and reality, the fantastic and the realistic, so typical of the German romantics, had a profound influence on Gogol' and Dostoevskij. Hoffmann seems to have had a strong influence on the American Gothic novel and on the two Russians. The possibility of the influence of the other Germans on them has been raised. Tieck, for example, seems to have directly influenced some of Gogol'.

I have pointed out the quality and quantity of the general heritage to which Gogol' and Dostoevskij were heirs, dealing not only with scientific and occultist doctrines, and with literature, but with thought that was all-pervasive.

In Gogol', subconscious manifestations are an important part of the works in which they appear; indeed, I have indicated, they are often so central to his works that to ignore them and their implications is to invite distorting the meaning of the works. Gogol' excels in the use of the dream and the double, and he anticipates Dostoevskij's use of the subconscious in these most important areas. But Gogol''s use of the subconscious is less developed, less profound, less complex than it is in Dostoevskij. I have suggested that this is partly due to the level of Gogol''s self-involvement, partly to the narrowness of his focus, partly to the fact that he is primarily an external writer, and partly to the lack of a core of deep abiding and universally significant vision of life which could be artistically integrated into his works. Gogol', despite his brilliance as a writer, was too provincial and too neurotic to accomplish with the subconscious what Dostoevskij did.

Dostoevskij, if not a philosopher, was a thinker, and his apotheosis of the subconscious is primarily a result of his concept that it would serve to illuminate his thought, even, of course, as it served literary functions. I have described these literary functions in some detail, have shown that, in their various forms, subconscious manifestations anticipate, reveal, illuminate, complicate, pace and direct action, elucidate and create meaning.

I have stressed that the irrational was equated by Dostoevskij with the unconscious. As such, within his use of the subconscious, his world vision is contained, albeit unformulated. I have drawn his unformulated concepts of the subconscious from his works, have shaped them, hopefully, into a meaningful whole. My stress on the metaphysical, on the over-unconscious, the impersonal unconscious, on the mythic elements so prominent in his use of the unconscious, has, then, been purposeful. Nor have I ignored the repressed unconscious which leads to duality, which bespeaks guilt or anxiety, or estrangement, or, indeed, any combination of these.

The subconscious has a most primitive history, and, with great success, was long a traditional part of literature. It is a vital part of the works of Gogol', an indispensable part of Dostoevskij, for, in the latter, it serves far beyond its function in other writers; and it serves brilliantly.

BIBLIOGRAPHY

Alexander, Franz and Helen Ross, *The Impact of Freudian Psychiatry* (Chicago, 1961).
Allen, Walter, *The English Novel* (New York, 1954).
Baake, A. M. *Die Verwendung des Traummotivs in der englischen Dichtung bis auf Chaucer* (Halle, 1906).
Baring, Maurice, *Landmarks in Russian Literature* (London, 1910).
Baxtin, M., *Problemy poetiki Dostoevskogo* (Moskva, 1963).
Béguin, Albert, *L'âme romantique et le rêve* (Paris, 1946).
Belinsky, Vissarion, "Letter to N. V. Gogol", *Belinsky, Chernyshevsky, and Dobrolyubov*, ed. Ralph E. Matlaw (New York, 1962), pp. 83-94.
Belyj, Andrej, *Masterstvo Gogolja* (Moskva-Leningrad, 1934).
Bem, A., *Psixoanalitičeskie etjudy* (Praga, 1938).
Berdyaev, Nicholas, *Dostoevsky*, trans. D. Attwater (New York, 1957).
Berlin, Isaiah, *The Hedgehog and the Fox* (New York, 1953).
Besoushko, Volodymyr, "Nicholas Gogol and Ukrainian Literature", *Ukrainian Quarterly*, XVI, 3 (1960), pp. 263-268.
Bettenstin, Martin, "Introduction", *Joseph Andrews and Shamela* (New York, 1961)
Boswell, James, *Life of Johnson* (London, 1960).
Bowman, N. E., "The Nose", *Slavonic and Eastern European Review*, XXXI, 76 (1952), pp. 204-211.
Bräuchli, Jacob, *Der Englische Schauerroman um* 1800 (Weida i. Thür., 1928).
Braun, M., "Gogol als Satiriker", *Die Welt der Slaven*, IX (1959), pp. 129-147.
Bryner, Cyril, "Gogol's *The Overcoat* in World Literature", *Slavonic and Eastern European Review*, XXXII, 79 (1954), pp. 499-509.
Carr, Edward, *Dostoevsky* (London, 1931).
Cazamian, L., "Richardson", *The Cambridge History of English Literature*, X (London, 1952).
Čiževsky, Dmitri, "Gogol: Artist and Thinker", *Annals of the Ukrainian Academy of Arts and Sciences in the U.S.*, IV (1952), pp. 261-278.
——, "The Theme of the Double in Dostoevsky", *Dostoevsky*, ed. René Wellek (Englewood Cliffs, New Jersey, 1962), pp. 112-129.
Cobb, Palmer, *The Influence of E. T. A. Hoffmann on the Tales of Edgar Allan Poe* (Chapel Hill, 1908).
Cross, Wilbur, *History of Henry Fielding* (New York, 1918).
Descartes, René, *Selected Writings of Descartes*, ed. N. Kemp Smith (New York, 1952).
Dickenson, G. L., *The Greek View of Life* (Michigan, 1960).
Dolinin, A., *Materialy i issledovanija* (Leningrad, 1935).
Dostoevsky, Fyodor, *The Brothers Karamazov*, trans. C. Garnett (New York, 1963).
——, *Crime and Punishment*, trans. Coulson (New York, 1964).

——, *The Double*, trans. George Bird (Bloomington, Indiana, 1958).

——, *The Eternal Husband and Other Stories*, trans. C. Garnett (London, 1947).

——, *The Friend of the Family and Nyetochka Nyezvanov*, trans. C. Garnett (London, 1957).

——, *The Gambler and Other Stories*, trans. C. Garnett (London, 1957).

——, *The Honest Thief and Other Stories*, trans. C. Garnett (London, 1957).

——, *The House of the Dead*, trans. C. Garnett (London, 1957).

——, *The Idiot*, trans. C. Garnett (New York, 1958).

——, *The Insulted and Injured*, trans. C. Garnett (London, 1957).

——, *Letters of Fyodor Dostoevski*, trans. E. C. Mayne (New York, 1964).

——, *Poor People, Three Short Novels of Dostoevsky*, trans. C. Garnett (New York, 1960).

——, *The Possessed*, trans. C. Garnett (New York, 1961).

——, *A Raw Youth*, trans. C. Garnett (London, 1957).

——, *The Short Novels of Dostoevsky*, trans. C. Garnett (New York, 1945).

——, *White Nights and Other Stories*, trans. C. Garnett (London, 1957).

Edel, Leon, *The Modern Psychological Novel* (New York, 1964).

Ehlich, E. L., *Der Traum im Alten Testament* (Berlin, 1953).

Eixenbaum, Boris, "Kak sdelana 'Shinel'' Gogolja", *Poètika* (Petrograd, 1919).

Elton, Oliver, "Samuel Richardson", *A Survey of English Literature: 1730-80*, I (London, 1928).

Erlich, Victor, "Gogol and Kafka: a Note on 'Realism' and Surrealism'", *For Roman Jakobson* (The Hague, 1956), pp. 100-108.

——, *Russian Formalism* (The Hague, 1955).

Forster, E. M., *Aspects of the Novel* (New York, 1954).

Foster, James R., *A History of the Pre-Romantic Novel in England* (New York, 1949).

——, ed., *The World's Great Folk Tales* (New York, 1953).

Frazer, J. G. Sir, *Folklore in the Old Testament* (London, 1918).

——, *The Golden Bough* (London, 1911).

Freud, Sigmund, "Dostoevsky and Parricide", *Dostoevsky*, ed. René Wellek (Englewood Cliffs, New Jersey, 1962), pp. 98-111.

——, *The Interpretation of Dreams*, trans. A. A. Brill (New York, 1950).

Gerhardt, Dietrich, *Gogol und Dostoievskij in ihrem künstlerischen Verhältnis* (Leipzig, 1941).

Gide, André, *Dostoevsky* (New York, 1961).

Gippius, V., *Gogol'* (= *Brown University Slavic Reprint Series*, 1). (Providence, Rhode Island, 1963).

Gode von Aesch, Alexander, *Science in German Romanticism* (Columbia, 1941).

Gogol, Nikolai, *The Collected Tales and Plays of Nikolai Gogol*, trans. C. Garnett, rev ed. Leonard J. Kent (New York, 1964).

——, *Dead Souls*, trans. B. G. Guerney (New York, 1961).

Goldsmith, Margaret, *Franz Anton Mesmer: A History of Mesmerism* (New York, 1934).

Gose, Edmund, "Richardson", *English Literature*, III (New York, 1935).

Gorky, Maxim, *Literary Portraits* (Moscow, 1959).

Gorlin, M. N. V., *Gogol und E. Th. A. Hoffmann* (Leipzig, 1935).

Gruener, Gustav, "Notes on the Influence of E. T. A. Hoffmann on Edgar Allan Poe", *Publications of the Modern Language Association*, XIX (1904), pp. 1-25.

Hare, Richard, *Russian Literature* (London, 1947).

Harkins, William, *Dictionary of Russian Literature* (New York, 1956).

Hawthorne, Nathaniel, *The Novels and Plays of Nathaniel Hawthorne* (New York, 1937).

Hewett-Thayer, Harvey W., *Hoffmann: Author of the Tales* (Princeton, 1948).

Hoffmann, E. T. A. *Poetische Werke*, 6 vols. (Berlin, 1958).

Hoffman, Frederick, *Freudianism and the Literary Mind* (New York, 1959).

Ivanov, Vyacheslav, *A Study in Dostoevsky*, trans. Norman Cameron (New York, 1960).

Jackson, Robert L., *Dostoevskij's Underground Man in Russian Literature* (The Hague, 1958).

Jean Paul (Richter), *Werke*, 3 vols. (München, 1939).

Kasack, Wolfgang, *Die Technik der Personendarstellung bei Nikolaj Vasilevič Gogol* (Wiesbaden, 1957).

Kaun, A., "Poe and Gogol: A Comparison", *Slavonic Review*, XV (1937), pp. 389-399.

Kayser, Wolfgang, *Das Groteske, seine Gestaltung in Malerei und Dichtung* (Oldenburg, 1957).

Kent, Leonard J., "Introduction", *The Collected Tales and Plays of Nikolai Gogol* (New York, 1964).

Killen, Alice M., *Le roman terrifiant ou roman "Noir"* (Paris, 1920).

Koziol. H. "E. T. A. Hoffmann's 'Elixiere des Teufels' und M. G. Lewis' 'The Monk'", *Germanisch-Romanische Monatschrift*, XXVI (1938), pp. 167-170.

Krieger, Murray, "Dostoevsky's 'Idiot': The Curse of Saintliness", *Dostoevsky*, ed. René Wellek (Englewood Cliffs, New Jersey, 1962), pp. 39-52.

Lavrin, Janko, *Dostoevsky* (New York, 1947).

——, *Gogol* (New York, 1926).

Lévy-Bruhl, Lucien, *The "Soul" of the Primitive*, trans. L. A. Clare (London, 1928).

Lewis, C. S., *The Discarded Image* (Cambridge, 1964).

Lincoln, Jackson, *The Dream in Primitive Cultures* (London, 1935).

Locke, John, *Essay Concerning Human Understanding* (New York, 1959).

Lucas, F. L., *Literature and Psychology* (Michigan, 1962).

Magarshack, David, *Dostoevsky* (London, 1956).

——, *Gogol* (London, 1950).

Mann, Thomas, "Dostoevsky — in Moderation", *The Short Novels of Dostoevsky* (New York, 1945), pp. vii-xx.

Margetts, E. L., "Concept of the Unconscious in the History of Medical Psychology", *Psychiatric Quarterly*, 27 (1953), pp. 106-114.

Matenko, Percy, "Tieck's Russian Friends", *Publications of the Modern Language Association*, LV, 4 (1940), pp. 1138-1143.

McIntyre, C. F., *Ann Radcliffe in Relation to Her Time* (New Haven, 1920).

McLean, H., "Gogol's Retreat from Love: Towards an Interpretation of *Mirgorod*", *Slavic Printings and Reprintings*, XXI (1958), pp. 225-243.

Mesmer, Franz Anton, *Mémoire de F. A. Mesmer*, trans. J. Eden (New York, 1957).

Mirsky, D. S., *A History of Russian Literature* (New York, 1959).

Molière, "Amphitryon", *The Plays of Molière*, ed. A. R. Waller (Edinburg, 1907).

Mortimer, Ruth, "Dostoevski and the Dream", *Crime and Punishment*, ed. George Gibian (New York, 1964), pp. 641-654.

Muchnic, Helen, *Introduction to Russian Literature* (New York, 1957).

Nabokov, Vladimir, *Gogol* (Norfolk, Connecticut, 1946).

Nilsson, Nils Åke, "Zur Entstehungsgeschichte des Gogolschen *Mantels*", *Scando-Slavica*, II (1956), pp. 116-133.

Passage, Charles, *Dostoevski the Adapter* (Chapel Hill, 1954).

——, *The Russian Hoffmannists* (The Hague, 1963).

Pereverzev, V. F., *Tvorchestvo Dostoevskogo* (Moskva, 1928).

Pochmann, H. A., "Irving's German Sources in the *Sketch Book*", *Studies in Philology*, XXVII (1930), pp. 477-507.

——, "Irving's German Tour and its Influence on His Tales", *Publications of the Modern Language Association*, XLV (1930), pp. 7150-7187.

Poe, Edgar Allan, *The Collected Tales and Poems of Edgar Allan Poe*, ed. Norman Holmes Pearson (New York, 1938).

Rank, Otto, *Der Doppelgänger* (Leipzig, 1925).

Ratcliffe, A. J. J., *A History of Dreams* (Boston, 1923).

Rose, H. J., *A Handbook of Mythology* (New York, 1959).

Rothmund, Toni, *Mesmer, Genie oder Scharlatan* (Berlin, 1940).

Ryle, G., *The Concept of Mind* (New York, 1949).

Schubert, G. H., *Die Symbolik des Traumes* (Leipzig, 1840).

Seduro, Vladimir, *Dostoyevski in Russian Criticism* (New York, 1957).

Shakhnovski, *A Short History of Russian Literature* (London, 1910).

Shelley, Mary, *Frankenstein* (London, 1951).

Simmons, E. J., *Dostoevsky: The Making of a Novelist* (New York, 1962).

——, "Gogol and English Literature", *Modern Language Review*, XXVI (1931), pp. 445-452.

Slavson, S. R., *Child Psychotherapy* (New York, 1952).

Slonimskij, A., *Texnika komičeskogo u Gogolja* (in *Brown University Slavic Reprint Series*, 2) (Providence, Rhode Island, 1963).

Spector, Ivar, *The Golden Age of Russian Literature* (Los Angeles, 1939).

Stender-Petersen, A., "Der Groteske Stil Gogols", *Welt und Wort*, XV (1960), pp. 71-73.

——, "Gogol und die deutsche Romantik", *Euphorion*, XXIV (1922), pp. 628-653.

Stephen, Leslie, "Introduction", *Pamela* (London, 1935).

Stevenson, Lionel, *The English Novel: A Panorama* (New York, 1960).

Stilman, Leon, "Gogol's 'Overcoat' — Thematic Pattern and Origins", *American Slavic and Eastern European Review*, XII, 3 (1953), pp. 138-148.

Tieck, Ludwig, *Werke*, 6 vols. (Leipzig, 1892).

Trahan, Elizabeth W., "The Golden Age — Dream of a Ridiculous Man?", *The Slavic and East European Journal*, XVII (1954), pp. 349-371.

Troyat, Henry, *Firebrand: The Life of Dostoevsky* (New York, 1946).

Turner, Charles, *Studies in Russian Literature* (London, 1882).

Tymms, Ralph, *Doubles in Literary Psychology* (Oxford, 1949).

——, *German Romantic Literature* (London, 1955).

Tynyanov, Yu, *Dostoevski i Gogol'* (Moskow, 1921).

Vinogradov, Viktor, "Sjuzhet i kompozicija povesti Gogolja 'Nos', *Načala* (1921), pp. 82-105.

Wellek, René, "German and English Romanticism: A Confrontation", *Studies in Romanticism*, IV, 1 (1964), pp. 35-56.

——, *A History of Modern Criticism: 1750-1950*, II (New Haven, 1955).

——, "Introduction", *Dead Souls*, trans. B. G. G. Guerney (New York, 1961).

——, A review of "Passage's *Dostoevski the Adapter*", *Journal of English and German Philology*, LV, 1 (1956), pp. 173-177.

Whyte, L. L., *The Unconscious before Freud* (New York, 1960).

Yarmolinsky, Avrahm, *Dostoevsky* (New York, 1936).

Zeydel, E H., "Washington Irving and Ludwig Tieck", *Publications of the Modern Language Association*, XXVIII (1931), pp. 946, 947.

INDEX*

* The numbers printed in italics refer
to the notes.

SLAVISTIC PRINTINGS AND REPRINTINGS

Edited by C. H. van Schooneveld

		f	$
59.	Dale L. Plank, *Pasternak's Lyric: a Study of Sound and Imagery*. 123 pp.	21,50	6.15
60.	Henry M. Nebel, Jr., N. M. *Karamzin: a Russian Sentimentalist*. 190 pp.	32,—	9.15
61.	Kazimierz Polánski/James A. Sehnert (ed.), *Polabian-English Dictionary*. 239 pp.	52,—	14.85
62.	Carl R. Proffer, *The Simile in Gogol's "Dead Souls"*. 208 pp. 28,— / 8.00		
63.	Julius M. Blum, *Konstantin Fedin: a Descriptive and Analytic Study*. 235 pp.	30,—	8.60
65.	David J. Welsh, *Russian Comedy, 1765—1823*. 133 pp.	21,50	6.15
66.	*Poètika: Sbornik statej* Leningrad, 1926	25,—	7.15
67.	P. A. Lavrov, *Materialy po istorii vozniknovenija drevnejšej slavanskoj pis' mennosti* Leningrad, 1930. 258 pp.	34,—	9.75
70.	Howard I. Aronson, *Bulgarian Inflectional Morphophonology*. 189 pp.	32,—	9.15
72.	Robert L. Belknap, *The Structure of "The Brothers Karamazov"*. 122 pp.	22,—	6.30
73.	Maria Zagórska Brooks, *Nasal Vowels in Contemporary Standard Polish: an Acoustic-Phonetic Analysis*. 55 pp., 8 plates	18,—	5.15
74.	Sigmund S. Birkenmayer, *Nikolaj Nekrasov: his Life and Poetic Art*. 205 pp.	35,—	10.05
80.	Henry Kučera (ed.), *American Contributions to the 6th International Congress of Slavists*, Prague, 1968, I: *Linguistic Contributions*. 427 pp.	94,—	26,90
81.	William E. Harkins (ed.), *American Contributions to the 6th International Congress of Slavists*, Prague, 1968, II: *Literary Contributions*. 381 pp.	94,—	26.90
82.	Krystyna Pomorska, *Russian Formalist Theory and its Poetic Ambiance*. 127 pp.	22,—	6.30
83.	Jacques Veyrenc, *La Forme poétique de Serge Esenin: Les rythmes*. 222 pp.	42,—	12.00
91.	M. Geršenzon, *P. Ja. Čaadaev: Žizn' i myšlenie* [St. Petersburg, 1908]. 329 pp.	38,—	10.90
92.	A. N. Pypin, *Istorija russkoj literatury*, I-IV [2nd edition, St. Petersburg, 1902]. 4 vols. 2,347 pp.	261,—	74.65
94.	Byloe: *Žurnal posvjaščennyj istorii osvoboditel'nago dviženija*, Volume I, 1-6 [St. Petersburg, 1906]. 3 vols. 2,054 pp.	470,—	131.50
99.	Alexandre Eck, *Le Moyen-Age russe* [2nd edition, Paris 1933]. 610 pp.	60,—	17.15
100.	A. Romanovič-Slavatinskij, *Dvorstjanstvo v Rossii ot načala XVIII veka do otmeny krpostnogo prava* [2nd edition, Kiev, 1912]. 596 pp. 72,— / 20.60		